British Society and the
French Wars, 1793–1815

British Society and the French Wars, 1793–1815

CLIVE EMSLEY

ROWMAN AND LITTLEFIELD
TOTOWA, NEW JERSEY

First published in the United Kingdom 1979 by
The Macmillan Press Ltd

First published in the United States 1979 by
ROWMAN AND LITTLEFIELD, Totowa, N.J.

Library of Congress Cataloging in Publication Data

Emsley, Clive.
  British society and the French wars, 1793–1815.

  Bibliography: p.
  Includes index.
  1. Great Britain—Social conditions. 2. France
—History—1789–1815. 3. Great Britain—History—
1789–1820. I. Title.
HN385.E45 1979   941′.073   78–10189 ✓
ISBN 0–8476–6115–6

Printed in Great Britain

Contents

This book is dedicated to my wife Jennifer; and to my children, Mark and Kathryn, hoping that their generation escapes the war experience of their grandfathers and great-grandfathers.

Preface

The idea for this book emerged from a course on War and Society which I helped to prepare for the Open University. Much has been written in recent years on the social effects of the World Wars of the twentieth century; it seemed logical to look in the same sort of way at the twenty-years struggle between Britain and Revolutionary and Napoleonic France – the conflict between the Whale and the Elephant, as my old tutor and friend Gwyn Williams once characterised it.

Acknowledgements are due to the Open University Research Committee for a grant which enabled me to complete the work for the book, and to the librarians and archivists of the various national, county and borough libraries and archives who coped with my enquiries. Crown-copyright material is reproduced by kind permission of the Controller of H.M. Stationery Office; quotations from the Wentworth Woodhouse and Spencer Stanhope MSS in the Sheffield City Library and from Samuel Whitbread's MSS in the Bedfordshire County Record Office are made by kind permission of Earl Fitzwilliam and his trustees, S. W. Fraser, and S. C. Whitbread respectively.

Many friends and colleagues have given me help and advice in preparing the book, in particular Professor Michael Drake of the Open University, Professor Norman McCord of the University of Newcastle-upon-Tyne, Dr Marianne Elliot of University College, Swansea and Dr Iorwerth Prothero of the University of Manchester Professor Arthur Marwick, Dr Christopher Harvie and Mr. John Golby, all of the Open University, kindly read the manuscript and sorted out some of my weaker generalisations and woolliest phrases – those that remain, together with any errors, are my own fault entirely. My thanks to Mrs Dorothy Packard for typing the many versions of the manuscript, and to my wife, Jenny, for putting up with the moods of my labour.

Acknowledgements

The author and publishers wish to thank the following for permission to use copyright material: the Trustees of the British Museum for Plates 1–6 and the cover illustration, the Mansell Collection for Plate 7, the Lincolnshire County Records Office and Mr P H Gibbons of Holton-le-Moor for Plate 8a, and the East Sussex Records Office and Mrs E M Fooks of Horsted Keynes for Plate 8b.

Introduction

During the nineteenth century and up to 1914, whenever a Briton spoke of the 'Great War' he meant the twenty-two years' struggle between Britain and revolutionary and Napoleonic France. Yet, surprisingly, as late as 1911 Sir John Fortescue noted that there was virtually no 'single history . . . of England during the years 1789–1815'.[1] Possibly the interruption of the second 'Great War' held up such a book, but it was not until the Second World War that this simple history was produced and at least one spur to its production was the possibility of comparing the struggle against Nazi Germany with the earlier struggle against revolutionary and Napoleonic France. In the preface to *The Years of Endurance 1793–1802* Arthur Bryant suggested that his reader would find in the book 'many of the familiar phenomena of our own troubled time'.

> He will see that proscription, imprisonment and murder of political opponents, the denial – in the name of liberty and patriotism – of all freedom of speech and, as the appetite for blood grew, an orgy of sadistic cruelty. . . . He will see mass hatred employed as a motive force and ideological ends held out as justifying every means, however base and destructive. He will see a 'great nation' denying all morality but unconscious allies or dupes in every decaying eighteenth-century state turned by war into 'fifth-columnists' and by defeat into 'quislings'.[2]

Bryant returned to this theme in his sequel *Years of Victory 1802–1812*. The heroic stance of a Britain alone was implicit in Carola Oman's *Britain against Napoleon* and explicit in Sir Charles Petrie's *When Britain Saved Europe: The Tale and the Moral*. C. Northcote Parkinson's editorial preface to *The Trade Winds: a Study of British Overseas Trade during the French Wars 1793–1815*, like Bryant, drew a direct comparison: 'the records of that former struggle against dictatorship read like a description of the years through which we have ourselves lived'.[3] The need for such comparisons has passed and the best books on British involvement in the revolutionary and Napoleonic wars published in recent years have each tended to concentrate on one single aspect of the wars. There have been specialised studies of military campaigns and commanders, of the blockade and of Britain's subsidies to foreign powers. Social historians, however, have generally referred to the war only in passing, preferring to concentrate on the effects of industrialisation, on the Old Poor Law, on popular radicalism and Luddism rather than on the effects of war. During the revolutionary and Napoleonic wars Britain was undergoing enormous changes as a result of the industrial revolution. The Hammonds believed 'that the war aggravated every problem that the Industrial Revolution presented to the age'.[4] But war itself can generate change, especially when it is total.

The eighteenth century was by no means pacific, but European powers did not fight each other with the kind of fury and venom to which we have become accustomed in the twentieth century. Vast areas of territory changed hands in the Anglo-French colonial struggles during the century, but there were few great changes in Europe as a result of war. The governing classes of the *ancien régime* had more in common with each other than with many of those whom they ruled, and in war they did not seek unconditional surrender or the total destruction of their enemies. Wars were not ideological, and aggressive nationalism was never a driving force. Armies were small; often their soldiers had little emotional attachment to the country or to the governments for whom they fought and there were contingents of foreign mercenaries in the armies of many states. Campaigns consisted largely of attempting to outmanoeuvre and wear down an opponent; pitched battles were costly even to a victor since the kind of tactics employed resulted in heavy casualties and consequently battles were often avoided. In general civilians were not involved in war, unless the area in which they lived became the scene of a campaign. There were exceptions and there were military men who sought ways of fighting battles which would destroy an opponent; but 'restrained' and 'limited' remain the key adjectives for describing eighteenth-century warfare.

The wars of the French Revolution and of Napoleon changed this. They were not 'total' in the sense that twentieth-century wars have been 'total' – obviously eighteenth-century technology would not permit the terror bombing of civilian populations and eighteenth-century government machinery, even that of Jacobin and Napoleonic France, would not allow the complete mobilisation of society for war – but given these limitations the wars of 1793–1815 were qualitatively and quantitatively different from their immediate predecessors. As Alexis de Tocqueville noted over a century ago, the French Revolution created the atmosphere for a crusade. The revolutionaries sought to bring the blessing of their revolution to the other peoples of Europe. At the end of 1791 Brissot called for 'a new crusade, a crusade of universal freedom!' A year later Danton spoke of France's 'great destinies': 'Let us conquer Holland, let us revive the republican party in England, let us set France on the march, and we will go gloriously to posterity.'[5] Apart from the obvious bombast there was a pride and a certainty among most of the revolutionary leaders that Liberty was fighting under the Tricolour. Counter-revolutionaries, both inside and outside France, fought back with the same kind of fervour. Their aim was to destroy the Revolution utterly. In July 1792 the Duke of Brunswick, the commander of the allied armies, threatened Paris and the Parisians with 'exemplary vengeance forever memorable' should any harm come to the French royal family. Brunswick commanded a traditional eighteenth-century army, but both the sentiments and the tone of his manifesto were alien to the traditions of eighteenth-century warfare.

The crusading ideals of the early years of the wars did not continue to Napoleon's final defeat at Waterloo, but the new intensity of warfare did. The commanders who sprang to the forefront in the revolutionary and Napoleonic Wars sought battles with the intention of annihilating their enemy. Nationalism became a motivating force behind the armies – students of nationalism tend to date its first modern manifestations from the French Revolution. Peoples, rather than the mercenary armies of absolutist monarchs, marched to fight each other. The French decree of the *levée en masse* in August 1793 required that:

> The young men shall go to battle; the married men shall make arms and transport provisions; the women shall make tents and uniforms, and shall serve in hospitals; the children shall make old clothes into bandages; the old men shall go out into the public squares to boost the soldiers' courage and to preach the unity of the republic and the hatred of kings.[6]

Not only the French nation went to war. The spontaneous uprising of the Spanish *pueblo* against Napoleon's armies in 1808 and, to a lesser extent, the organised uprisings in Russia and Germany in 1812 and 1813 offer other examples. The new forces released on the battlefield led to whole areas of Europe changing hands; old states and principalities disappeared. The mass armies now at the disposal of Napoleon enabled him to fulfil, albeit briefly, Louis XIV's dream of French hegemony in Europe: a key factor in maintaining British hostility.

Britain and France had fought each other throughout the eighteenth century. The incidence of war was such that it has been suggested that the peace treaties which concluded the different wars are best described as mere truces.[7] Britain and France were rivals in systems of government: France under Louis XIV had provided the model for eighteenth-century absolutism, while Britain prided herself on being the model for countries wishing for liberty and a balanced constitution. They were opposed in religion: even when the King of France and the Pope were at odds with each other, Englishmen continued to regard France as the embodiment of a popish state. Increasingly as the century progressed they were rivals in economic interest, especially in the promising colonial areas of the East Indies, the West Indies and North America.

Britain was not involved in the first stage of the revolutionary wars. France declared war on the Austrian Emperor in April 1792 – significantly naming a monarch as the enemy of 'a free people' and not considering the war as a conflict of nations. The Franco-British war began on 1 February 1793 and then, continuing the pattern of the preceding century, the two countries became each others' most consistent enemies in twenty-two years of fighting. William Pitt became the arch-enemy of the revolutionaries in France; his gold was seen financing counter-revolution everywhere; the manner in which the Parisian Section of William Tell singled him out was typical: 'Pitt, ah, what an odious name! He is the destroyer of all virtue, source of universal corruption, the enemy of liberty, the scourge of the human race; his memory will be more abhorred than Attila.'[8] Napoleon was one of many to characterise the Franco-British struggle as a repetition of the conflict between Rome and Carthage. Other countries joined British-financed coalitions and were knocked out of the wars or else sued for peace at different intervals, but the hostilities between Britain and France continued, with the exceptions of the respite of the Peace of Amiens and the brief first Restoration of Louis XVIII, until Napoleon's second abdication in July 1815.

Britain's participation in this struggle put enormous strains on her government, her economy, her finances and her manpower. The demands for men and especially money affected all ranks of society, albeit in varying degrees. Indeed, if there was a common experience shared by all Britons in the last decade of the eighteenth and the early years of the nineteenth centuries, it is to be found less in the changes resulting from the industrial revolution and more in the demands of war. It is the aim of this book first to describe British government and society during the revolutionary and Napoleonic wars, and how they coped with the demands and pressures of war, and second, to suggest how far changing attitudes may be attributed, at least partly, to the wars.

1. Britain in 1792

I Society and Government

In 1792 Britain was one of the major powers of Europe. She had been humbled by the loss of her thirteen American colonies ten years before, but she still possessed a vast overseas empire. There were the largely unpopulated and unexplored wastes of Canada and New South Wales, the more populous and far more commercially profitable possessions in the West and East Indies; closer to home, George III was also King of Ireland and Elector of Hanover – though this German possession, while it might be relied upon to support Britain in European squabbles, was not part of the British Empire and was not run by men responsible to the parliament at Westminster. Probably only a minority of the population of England, Scotland and Wales were aware of Britain's international position. The bulk of the population lived in a rural environment and really travelled great distances within the three countries. Agriculture employed the largest proportion of the working population; rather more than one third. The major manufacturing industry was wool production, a handcraft industry scattered across the South-west, Norfolk and the West Riding. But significant changes were under way in both the size and location of the population, and in the economy.

The pace of population growth in Britain, like other European countries, had quickened since the middle of the century. England, Scotland and Wales had a population of about ten million; there were about another four million in Ireland. The largest single concentration of the British population was in and around London; about 900,000 people made the metropolis the largest European city of the period and it experienced a constant flow of both immigrants and emigrants. But the most significant population change in the last quarter of the eighteenth century was the growth of the new urban concentrations in the area of the north-western coal deposits. People were drawn from neighbouring counties and from Ireland, especially to the district south of the river Ribble, attracted principally, it appears, by the prospect of higher wages and better employment opportunities. Much of the work in this area continued to be handloom weaving but there were forty cotton-spinning mills in south Lancashire by 1788 and some of the more adventurous manufacturers were installing steam engines, rather than continuing to rely on water-power to drive their mills. Vast capital investment was being made elsewhere also, in canals, bridges and roads, which made travel, communication and transportation quicker and easier.

There continued to be vast differences between the orders of society. The landed gentry had annual incomes running into hundreds, often thousands, of pounds, from their estates and their industrial concerns. Craftsmen, possibly aided by members of their family or by one or two journeymen, worked at their own pace to complete orders for sums ranging from a few shillings to a few pounds. Agricultural labourers worked from dawn till dusk, the intensity and type of work regulated by the seasons, and received a few pence for each day; in some districts they still received payment principally in kind rather than in coin. New groups were making their appearance within the gradations of society; men who had made their fortunes in overseas adventures purchased estates and became landed gentlemen, or at least enabled their sons to do so. Some of the new industrial élite were rivalling the gentry in size of fortune; at the other end of the scale a few factory hands, whose hours of work were dictated by a new time-work discipline, were appearing in the new urban sprawls. The relationship between the social orders was characterised by paternalism and deference, though the deference shown by the lower orders was much less marked in England than elsewhere in Europe. Foreign travellers to London were generally surprised by the way in which common men regarded themselves as good men as the King and the King's ministers, and the way in which workmen in working clothes freely mingled with their social superiors in public places. It is impossible to assess how widespread this rough equality was, but it probably spread to other large provincial centres. By the end of the century some gentlemen considered that the lack of deference was increasing, that crime also was increasing and that the whole structure of society was breaking down.

The social orders might confront each other on questions of enclosures, the ravages of a gentleman's deer or rabbits on his poorer neighbours' crops, but in labour disputes confrontations between the social orders were less common. Masters and journeymen often had the same kind of background. Workmen in dispute still sought redress in their work or wages by petitioning central or local authorities; but there were also strikes or 'combinations'. and what has been termed 'collective bargaining by riot', when workmen sought to coerce an employer by threats, or by actual violence to his person or premises.[1] The most common form of popular disturbance in eighteenth-century Britain, however, was the provision riot, again not a confrontation between orders. The most important single element in both the diet and budget of most families in Britain during the eighteenth century was bread. Consumption varied from region to region and between different income groups, but the average *per capita* consumption in the last decade of the century appears to have been about one pound a day.[2] Improvements had been made in agriculture during the century and, mainly by enclosure, farmland had been extended. Most of the new farmland was used for arable produce, but the increasing population and the decline in the number of bountiful harvests during the second half of the century led to Britain gradually ceasing to be an exporter of grain. On several occasions from the mid-sixties onwards large imports were made to offset shortages, for shortages, or the fear of shortage of bread or any other necessity of life, led to crowds fixing prices in markets, preventing the movement of particular foodstuffs out of their locality, and attacking the person or property of a suspected profiteer – usually a miller or a farmer. The Corn Law of 1791 attempted both to encourage and protect the farmer by offering bounties on wheat exports when the price in the home market was forty-four shillings a quarter or less, and by putting high tariffs on foreign imports until the price was fifty-four shillings or more.

Britain had been governed in much the same way for a century. It was a monarchy but unlike its Continental counterparts not an absolute one. The King appointed his ministers, but those ministers needed a parliamentary majority to be able to govern. Parliament was divided into two chambers, the Lords consisting of bishops and peers of the realm, and the Commons consisting of 558 elected members. These members were chosen by a limited electorate of some 250,000. The right to vote varied from constituency to constituency; for a variety of reasons glaring inadequacies had evolved, with the notorious grass mound of Old Sarum sending an MP to Westminster while the expanding manufacturing towns of the North and the Midlands sent none; and every county was allowed two representatives irrespective of size, its population or its wealth. Furthermore even if a man had the right to vote, he was not always given the opportunity of exercising this right; between 1754 and 1790 twelve counties were never contested in a general election and a further fifteen were contested only once. Many constituencies, both borough and county, were in the hands of patrons. There were no political parties, although Sir Lewis Namier has suggested that three broad divisions might be detected in Parliament: the Placemen, those who were ready to support any ministry of the King's choice and who sought employment or bounty in return; the Country Gentlemen, and their urban counterparts, whose boasted watchword was independence, and who refused honours and profits and any regular support for an administration or its opposition; and the Factions, made up of the men who sought power and position, and their relatives, friends or dependants who could be relied upon for unqualified support.[3] Electors voted for individuals while governments were formed by different groups coming together and breaking up as opportunity, interest, financial reward (the monarch and the ministry still possessed considerable patronage), ambition, and a variety of motives and incentives dictated.

England, Wales and Scotland were legislated for by the parliament at Westminster. Ireland, however, had its own parliament of 300 MPs in Dublin. The Irish Parliament contained a majority of members who were returned by rotten boroughs in the control of a few great Anglican Irish families. The bulk of the population, both the majority of Catholic peasantry and the Ulster Presbyterians, were consequently even more remote from this parliament than the lower order in England. The link between the London and Dublin parliaments was that they each recognised the King of England as their head. But Irish MPs had no say in the selection of the King's government in Ireland: the Viceroy and the Chief Secretary were selected in England. Friction was the inevitable result, with the Irish Parliament developing a kind of opposition mentality.

Since December 1783 George III's principal minister had been William Pitt the Younger. Pitt had successfully restored the country's finances to a sound and stable footing after the disasters of the American war. Following Lord Shelburne, who had given Pitt his first Cabinet post and who had handled the unhappy task of negotiating the peace of 1783, Pitt was ready to consult experts on governmental and administrative issues. Previously men who attempted systematic studies of economics or administration had been generally frowned upon by the rulers of eighteenth-century Britain. Pitt followed Shelburne in showing an interest in developing some kind of career structure for the Civil Service and an institutional framework for the business of government. But change was only gradual, and on the eve of the revolutionary war vast areas of national life remained quite outside the remit of the government. There was, for example, no Board of Agriculture; no eighteenth-century government had an agricultural policy. A board was established (by royal charter) in August 1793, but it remained inde-

pendent of government, and received only a small annual grant of
£3000. There was a Board of Trade which acted in an advisory capacity
rather like a standing committee of the Cabinet. It had about twenty
members, drawn largely from the Cabinet, but including, among others,
the Archbishop of Canterbury. Neither the President of the Board nor
the Deputy President were paid for acting in these capacities; but the
administrative duties of the board did require a salaried staff of a dozen
secretaries, clerks and messengers. Other government departments were
tiny. The permanent establishment of the Treasury was a mere seventeen
clerks. Both the Home Office and the Foreign Office in 1792 each had a
total establishment of only nineteen, including the Secretary of State, the
two permanent under-secretaries, a dozen or so clerks, and at the
bottom of the hierarchy the chamber keeper and the 'necessary woman'.

The bureaucracy of central government was small, that of local
government even smaller. At the head of the county administration was
the Lord Lieutenant, appointed by the Crown, who was, in general, the
head of the leading family in the county. The position could be purely
honorific, but in time of national emergency, as the wars were to show,
the Lord Lieutenant could play an important role in organising his
county's defences. He commanded the county militia, nominated the
clerk of the peace and suggested to the Crown possible appointments to
the position of county magistrate. Directly beneath the Lord Lieutenant
came the county sheriffs and the deputy lieutenants; neither of these
positions was paid or full-time. The bulk of the administration of the
county fell to the magistrates who met in quarter or petty sessions, where
they tried local offenders, appointed parish officers such as constables
and overseers of the poor, supervised the upkeep of bridges and roads,
directed the removal of vagrants to their parishes of origin and so forth.
Those cities and towns which had succeeded in obtaining charters relied
in general on their corporations for the administration of local
government; here mayors and aldermen held commissions of the peace
themselves and met in their own sessions. The City of London was the
corporate town *par excellence* with the Lord Mayor treated by the
central government in much the same way as a Lord Lieutenant. The
magistrates' administration depended on the notion of universal
obligation. Thus it was not the business of either central or local
government to have a policy for the construction of the repair of roads,
rather it was the duty of the parish through which a road ran to maintain
it. Should the road be in a bad state of repair, should a bridge collapse, it
was held to be the fault of the local parish, which would then be ordered
by the justices to make good the situation either through a rate or
through personal service. The parish itself had a role to place in local

administration with its vestry meetings. Some vestries were open to all local inhabitants, in which case the meetings were democratic but often rowdy and turbulent. A greater number of vestries were closed, with oligarchies coopting such men as they needed or wanted. Some took a lively interest in the activities of their local officials; others showed no interest and made no requests to see their official's accounts, as a result extravagance, waste and speculation were often rife. This was especially true in expanding urban parishes such as Manchester, where a series of investigations during the 1790s revealed a vast amount of corruption and negligence.

It was possible to make local reforms by Act of Parliament, but there was no general movement within society to inaugurate any overall reorganisation of the structure of local government. Nor were there constant and vociferous demands for the reform of Parliament. In the dark days of the American war the County Association Movement had demanded such reform and limits to government and Crown expenditure and patronage. The initial moderate demands of the Association Movement met with some satisfaction in the 'economical' reforms of the early 1780s, but the demands for parliamentary reform made no headway. In 1785 Pitt himself introduced a bill for reform, but Parliament rejected it and Pitt let the matter drop. The issue of parliamentary reform remained dormant for the rest of the decade. Significantly the Association Movement was a movement of electors, not of the unenfranchised. The lower classes of eighteenth-century England showed an interest in politics (an interest which, like their lack of deference, surprised most foreign visitors) and they could have an influence on politics either at the hustings or, more potently, when encouraged on the streets by a John Wilkes or the politicians of the City of London – after the Gordon Riots of 1780, however, the City Fathers never again called upon their street allies. But such political demonstrations by the lower orders were the exception rather than the rule. The new business and commercial élites, many of whom were centred in fast-growing urban sprawls in the provinces which sent no members to Parliament, undoubtedly recognised that decisions taken at Westminster could influence their enterprises. One or two of them grew adept at political lobbying, and in 1785, faced with Pitt's Fustian Tax and proposals for freer trade with Ireland, English businessmen had recourse to the traditional eighteenth-century remedy of extra-parliamentary association, the short-lived Chamber of Manufacturers. But there was no general movement among these men for a reform of Parliament. There appears rather to have been a widespread fear in the new manufacturing towns of the kind of turbulence which resulted in contested elections. A correspondent of the *Leeds Intelligencer* in 1792 went so far as to attribute the progress of industry in Leeds and Manchester to their freedom from parliamentary elections.

> It is notorious that elections promote profligacy, immorality and indolence; it is also equally notorious that those manufacturing towns (such as ours and Manchester) which delegate no members are in a more prosperous condition than those which elect their representatives.[4]

Fear of popular turbulence probably exceeded any fears which British gentlemen had about war. Armed conflict between states was a fact of life and, with the exception of the American War of Independence, Britain had done well out of eighteenth-century wars, seizing and holding on to overseas possessions at the expense of France. War could disrupt overseas and coastal trade, but with the exception of a few privateering raids and cannonades Britain had not suffered the ravages of war on her home territory since the Jacobite rising of 1745, and the impact on that occasion had been limited to a few northern counties of England and to Scotland. The experience of war was confined to the soldiers and sailors who fought it and to the area in which campaigns were fought. At the height of the Seven Years War Laurence Sterne could travel to France to recuperate from illness and overwork and be idolised by Parisian society. Even more surprising, during the American War of Independence Sir George Rodney was detained in France, not because he was an English admiral, but simply because he was a debtor. The French Maréchal de Biron generously paid Rodney's debts and he was permitted to return to take command of an English fleet which subsequently smashed its French rival off the Iles des Saintes.[5]

It was the policy of the British government to keep the armed services to the barest minimum in peacetime, rapidly augmenting them by bounties and using the press-gang in an emergency. In 1792 the British army consisted of under 45,000 men, some two-thirds of whom were manning foreign garrisons. The morale and the efficiency of the army were low after the ten years of neglect since the conclusion of the American war. Discontent among the privates and NCOs over pay and conditions was only partly appeased by an increase in infantry pay at the beginning of 1792. The officer corps had been weakened by the Secretary of War's abuse of army patronage; Sir George Yonge, the Secretary, had permitted the sale of commissions to wealthy young men with no experience, and even to babes-in-arms and young women – the pay provided a regular pension. The navy had 115 ships of the line (thirty-nine more than either the French or Spanish navies) but only a dozen were in commission and there were only 16,000 men serving. The navy was not in the same plight as the army. In 1790 Sir Charles Middleton had resigned as Comptroller of the Navy in protest over the difficulties he faced in trying to reform naval administration, but he left his successor a well-equipped fleet, good stocks of stores and plans which were to enable a smooth transfer to a war footing. Neither service was particularly popular. The army was regarded as the repository of scoundrels and outcasts. Some gentlemen suspected it as a body which might be used to increase the power of the executive and thus encroach upon the Englishman's boasted 'liberties'. The lower orders disliked it since, in the absence of national or even local police forces, troops, armed with their conventional weapons of war, might be used to maintain public order. The navy was not viewed with the same degree of antipathy, indeed 'Jolly Jack Tar' was a popular hero, but service in the navy was not popular because of the appalling conditions, the poor rates of pay, which had not changed since Charles II's reign, and the fact that the largest proportion of men recruited in wartime were pressed. In case of war or insurrection the government could embody the county militia regiments. Theoretically there were 30,840 militiamen in England and Wales in 1792; there was no Scottish Militia and the Irish Militia had been allowed to lapse. The size of each regiment had been set by the Militia Act of 1757 and did not reflect the shifts in population which had occurred in the intervening thirty-five years; enquiries made in 1796 revealed that in most counties the regimental quota represented between one in twelve and one in eighteen of the available men, but in Dorset the proportion was as high as one in eight, while in Lancashire it was one in forty-three.[6] The regiments were recruited by a ballot of the able-bodied men between eighteen and forty-five, with numerous exemptions: poor men under five feet four inches or with at least one legitimate child, peers, army and militia officers (including ex-militia officers who had served for four years), members of the English universities, Anglican and Dissenting clergy, articled clerks, seamen, apprentices, regular soldiers, Thames watermen, workmen in the royal arsenals and dockyards. A ballotted man could avoid service by paying a £10 fine or providing a substitute. Service in the militia was for five years, but a substitute who was embodied was required to serve until the regiment received orders to stand down. When embodied the militia regiments were on the same footing as the regular army, the only exception was that they could not be ordered overseas. The unembodied militia received only twenty-eight days training a year but for reasons of economy after 1786 only two-thirds of each regiment received annual training. In 1792 the militia was hardly a force to be reckoned with.

In 1790 Parliament had voted £1 million as a military credit and prepared for war with Spain over fishing rights in the northern Pacific. In March 1791 Parliament voted to augment the armed forces so as to coerce the Empress of Russia in her dealings with the Turks. On each occasion the emergency passed without conflict. In February 1792 Pitt advised a reduction in the estimates for the armed forces, confident that the internal difficulties of France meant that she would not present any serious military or economic threat to Britain for many years. Almost exactly one year later, however, the French National Convention's declaration of war commenced the twenty-two years' conflict.

II   The Road to War

In general the French Revolution was welcomed in Britain. A few welcomed it since the upheaval was bound to weaken Britain's old rival. Still more believed that France was experiencing something similar to Britain's Glorious Revolution of 1688 and took pride in the fact that the Revolution in France followed hard on the heels of the centenary celebrations in Britain. Many of the Revolution clubs in Britain formed for the centenary celebrations struck up a correspondence with political clubs in France. But this honeymoon period was short-lived; after the royal flight to Varennes in June 1791 there was a radical lurch in the Revolution and the British clubs allowed their correspondence to decline.[7] In the summer of 1792 the war against Austria and Prussia contributed to a further radicalisation of the Revolution; inflamed by, and in defiance of, the Duke of Brunswick's manifesto, on 10 August the Paris Sections, backed by military volunteers from the provinces, stormed the Tuileries Palace and the monarchy was suspended.

In Britain, where demands for reform had begun to revive under the impetus of the centenary of 1688 and the events in France, there was a polarisation of attitudes towards both reform and the Revolution. Many began to see any reform, even the abolition of the political bars against religious dissenters and the abolition of the slave trade, as the thin end of a wedge which would eventually open the door to the anarchy which they perceived in France. Edmund Burke's *Reflections on the Revolution in France*, published in November 1790, became the focus for such men. Others, sympathetic to the French, continued to advocate reform of Parliament. Among the reformers were men who had participated in the Association Movement; but as well as these there were new, more radical political societies organised by and for members of the lower orders – men who did not have the vote who now called for universal manhood suffrage and a variety of other radical reforms. Most notable among these new societies were the London Corresponding Society [hereafter LCS], whose prime mover and first secretary was Thomas Hardy, a forty-year-old Scottish shoemaker, and the Sheffield Constitutional Society, which had an enormous following among the masters and journeymen in the Sheffield cutlery trade. The popular radicals did not seek a violent revolution, but they failed to convince their opponents of this. Furthermore their principal text, Tom Paine's reply to Burke, *The Rights of Man*, contained, in its second part, a proposal for a complete reorganisation of British society. The French victories over the Prussians at Valmy and over the Austrians at Jemappes were greeted by these popular radicals with enthusiasm. In November 1792 fraternal delegates from Britain took congratulatory addresses to the new National Convention in France. 'Frenchmen', declared the London Corresponding Society, 'you are already free, but the Britons are preparing to be so.'[8] The encouragement given to the French was not merely verbal. The delegates of the Society for Constitutional Information [hereafter SCI] – a more genteel society than the LCS and one which had its origins in the radical wing of the Association Movement – were able to tell the Convention that a thousand pairs of shoes for the 'soldiers of Liberty', paid for by 'patriotic donation', were now at Calais, 'and the Society will continue sending a thousand pair a week for at least six weeks to come.'[9]

But while British radicals congratulated the Convention on its successes, these successes together with declarations issued by the Convention were causing considerable anxiety to Pitt's government since they appeared to threaten both Britain's internal and external security. The mouth of the river Scheldt was controlled by the Dutch though its course lay through the Austrian Netherlands. The Dutch intended to keep the Scheldt a closed river and prevent any serious commercial rivalry from Antwerp; in 1784 this determination had almost led to a war with the Austrian Emperor Joseph II. But when the French armies overran the Austrian Netherlands after Jemappes, the Convention decreed the opening of the Scheldt in accordance with 'the fundamental principles of natural law, which the French have sworn to maintain'.[10] The resulting confrontation between France and Holland threatened to involve Britain, since in 1788 she had signed a treaty guaranteeing Holland's internal and external security. Furthermore Pitt's government had no wish to see Antwerp developing into a more powerful commercial centre while the French occupation of the Austrian Netherlands looked suspiciously like another example of attempted French expansion in Europe. As the crisis developed negotiations were impeded by a lack of diplomatic machinery. Lord Gower had been recalled from the Paris embassy after the *Journée* of 10 August and not replaced, and Lord Grenville, the Foreign Secretary, on behalf of the government, refused to accept the credentials of Chauvelin, the new ambassador sent by France. Chauvelin himself, vain and inexperienced, made matters worse by mixing principally with members of the parliamentary opposition and allowing suspicions about his conduct and the intentions of the French to go unchecked.

Three days after the decree opening the Scheldt, the French issued their Decree of Fraternity promising 'fraternity and assistance to all people who wish to recover their liberty'.[11] There is no evidence that the Convention was deliberately seeking to foment disorder in Britain, but there were many in Britain who believed that this was precisely their intention. This decree, together with the exchanges between the English radicals and the Convention, confirmed such beliefs. As early as September the British government had received reports of French agents in the Country for 'wicked purposes', and of subsidies to opposition newspapers. In November and December rumours of French spies and saboteurs mingling with *emigrés* from France led to Bow Street police officers being sent to carry out investigations in towns on the main roads from the coast to London. The government did not take such reports or rumours lightly; many came from respectable sources. Lord Auckland, the ambassador at The Hague, for example, reported that he had received information of 'two hundred or three hundred emissaries from the *Propagande*, with allowances to live in taverns, coffee houses and ale houses to promote disorder'. He also described seeing bulletins prepared by the French and announcing an insurrection in London. At the beginning of December Pitt's government, fearful of some kind of insurrectionary disorder in London, ordered that the fortifications of the Tower of London be strengthened, brought troops into the metropolis, and called out a substantial part of the militia. This last action necessitated the recalling of Parliament within fourteen days. When Parliament met it sanctioned the government's measures. Significantly about one hundred opposition Whigs, nearly two-thirds of their number, followed the Duke of Portland's lead and voted with the government.[12] A bill was introduced, and rapidly passed, which authorised the ejection of undersirable aliens from the country; an augmentation was authorised for both the army and the navy; the export of grain to France was halted. (This move antagonised France further, but was probably designed to maintain internal tranquillity since there were fears of provision shortages. As early as October the Mayor and aldermen of Norwich had petitioned the King requesting that the export of grain be prohibited from Norfolk ports for a limited period so as to appease the apprehensive poor.)[13]

The government's measures coexisted with a loyalist upsurge in the country which followed the traditional pattern of extra-parliamentary association. At the end of November the Association for Preserving Liberty and Property against Republicans and Levellers was founded in the Crown and Anchor tavern in The Strand. The objects of the association were to support the laws, suppress seditious publications and defend persons and property against the threat of Jacobinism and 'French principles'. It hoped that its example would be followed throughout the country. Since few English gentlemen were unwilling to declare their hostility to republicans and riots, this happened, but by no means all of the associations founded up and down the country were as authoritarian or as conservative in their politics as the parent body. Charles James Fox, Pitt's arch-enemy in the Commons, sat on the committee of the association of St George's parish, Hanover Square. The association which met in the Merchant Taylor's Hall in London expressed sympathy for reform in its initial declaration. A recent historian of the Association Movement concluded 'that the declarations and resolutions which were passed by that great mass of loyalist meetings in late 1792 and early 1793 express sentiments which are capable of representing every type of contemporary ideological position short of revolutionary republicanism.'[14]

The more reactionary of these associations launched a furious counter-attack against the popular societies with tracts, pamphlets and broadsides. Some of the provincial associations organised the prosecution of local Jacobins – sometimes they also organised the jury to ensure a conviction; some organised and encouraged demonstrations, with Tom Paine being burnt in effigy. Such activities led to the popular societies seeing the entire movement as conservative and reactionary and in league with the government. For Pitt, however, these associations were marshalling loyal opinion in the fashion for which he had hoped at the end of November. In the middle of December Grenville wrote to Lord Auckland well assured by the spirit in the country: 'Nothing can exceed the good disposition of this country in the present moment.'[15]

Throughout December and January there was a growing expectancy of war against France. The opponents of reform and of the French Revolution in Britain looked forward to it; according to *The Times* it was to be a struggle for the preservation of the British Constitution against vagabonds, atheists, freebooters and Levellers; furthermore, because of the sorry internal state of France, it was bound to be a short war. The execution of Louis XVI increased the sense of outrage felt by this faction towards the revolutionaries in France. 'There surely never existed such fiends on the earth . . .', protested Lady Malmesbury, 'nothing but the humanity of John Bull makes it safe to be a Frenchman in London.' John Hawtrey, vicar of Ringwood, believed that all Europe would unite now against 'these sons of Hell' and 'that all the English will now wish for war that such wretches, through the blessings of Heaven, may be extirpated from the face of the Earth'.[16] The execution was the cue for would-be poets to describe drooping 'gallic lillies', and grinning 'triumphant ruffians' applauding. It added greater justice to the anti-French cause, becoming a symbol of the Revolution's atrocities.

> With Soldiers and Sailors and ships heart of oak,
> We will pay those French dogs for their barb'rous work.
> With spirits like fire we'll make them to dance,
> And we'll bafle [sic] the pride and the glory of France.[17]

Those sympathetic to reform, however, from the most extreme radicals within the popular societies to the young Whig aristocrats who had organised the liberal Association of the Friends of the People, and to veterans of the 1780 campaign like the Reverend Christopher Wyvill, were all opposed to the war. William Frend, fellow of Jesus College, Cambridge, a Unitarian, and a political reformer, rejected any idea that the execution of Louis XVI gave an Englishman the 'right . . . to cut a frenchman's throat'; furthermore, 'if all the kings on the continent were put to death by their subjects, it is not our business to punish their conduct. We should be indignant at their presuming to change our government. . . .' The opposition newspaper, the *Morning Chronicle*, believed that fighting for security, in support of allies, or to oppose aggrandisement might be permissible; but it could not accept that any of these justifications were present in January 1793. More serious, the war which loomed ahead threatened to be fought over 'principles' and there was a danger that 'we must go on killing as long as there are any Frenchmen left to kill, or leave their opinions, as all who ever made war upon opinions have hitherto left them, invigorated and exasperated by the conflict'. Division 12 of the London Corresponding Society believed that a majority shared their opinions and were 'utterly averse to a war with France and consider such an event as a calamity to the human race however it may gratify a Confederation of Foreign Kings'. The *Morning Chronicle* described each 'class' in the country as hostile to, or fearful of, war: thinking men rejected the idea of interfering with another country's internal politics; the manufacturing interest, now at the 'zenith of prosperity', feared that war would reduce its competitiveness by increasing the cost of raw materials and by leading to 'an augmentation of the extortionate rate of labour which their people have combined to exact'; the trading interest feared that its prosperity would be a prey to French privateers and adventurers, the more so because French commerce and her merchant marine had collapsed as a result of revolutionary upheaval; the landed interest was fearful that war's adverse effects on manufacturing and trade would in turn lead to higher taxation and more poor to be maintained at the expense of the parish; and finally 'the great mass of the people' opposed war, recognising that, in spite of the execution of Louis XVI, the French were trying to follow the lines of the British Constitution.[18] But public opinion or 'the mood' of the country is never easy to assess. Probably a majority of men of property – those who might be expected to feel threatened by 'French principles' – were behind the government and were prepared for war if necessary. Certainly the upsurge of loyalty which so satisfied Pitt and his ministers would suggest something of this sort. As for the great majority of the lower orders, they did not belong to popular societies and their attitudes were probably coloured on one side by traditional loyalty to their country and hostility to the old enemy, France, and on the other by fears of militia ballots, press-gangs and perhaps even increased taxes on their food and other necessities.

Even a loyalist like Hawtrey doubted his government's explanation of the war and considered that 'both parties appear to have acted in a strange haggling manner if they really meant *not* to go to war.' The military preparations of Pitt's government increased tension, as did the halting of grain exports. Chauvelin's passport was returned after Louis XVI's execution. In France, the activity of the ruling Girondin faction behind the scenes suggests that they would have much preferred to make concessions and come to some kind of agreement with Pitt. But many members of the French National Convention were misled by the acclaim which they had received from British radicals and believed that the British people were ready to rise against Pitt. Furthermore the factional fighting in the Convention landed the Girondins in a situation where, to maintain their position and their image as 'patriot', they made furious public speeches against Britain, refusing both to retract the decrees which caused offence and to guarantee the security of Holland. On 1 February 1793 the Convention declared war; given the growing expectation of war they probably pre-empted similar action by Britain.[19]

2. The Initial Impact: 1793–94

I Policies and Attitudes

The French declaration of war did not unite the opposing factions in Britain. Radicals and reformers continued to criticise the government for adopting a hostile attitude to France and for allying with a confederation of absolutist monarchs. William Fox, questioning whether ideas could ever be destroyed by war, maintained that the home of modern revolutionary ideas was England (citing Locke's *Treatise on Government* in particular) and warned that the 'despots' of Europe might turn on England should France be destroyed. The same point was made by an anonymous author, possibly Daniel Isaac Eaton of the LCS, who prophesied that 'when the combined Powers shall have established what they call *Order and Tranquillity* in France, they will probably discover that there is too much Jacobinism in the English Constitution and lend their *humane* interference to relieve us also from this dangerous evil'. On the other side, however, 'a Friend to Peace' considered that the war was both just and necessary since it was against a new kind of enemy, 'one who fights not merely to subdue states, but to dissolve society – not to extend empire, but to subvert government – not to introduce a particular religion, but to extirpate all religion'. John Bowles, a barrister and a regular author on the government's behalf, emphasised the same danger and expressed additional fears about the new principles by which France professed to wage war,

> [which] render her ambition and her conquests particularly alarming with regard to the security and the independence of the rest of Europe, for instead of admitting the necessity of any national difference, of any actual aggression of injury, as a motive for war, she assumes the hitherto unheard of right of invading and subduing other countries, for the avowed purpose of interfering in their government, and without existing cause of quarrel or dissention.[1]

The pro-government press made venomous attacks on the French. Early in February 1793 *The Oracle* commented:

> The French, as a Nation, we always knew to be insincere: the only thing which made communication with them agreeable, was the courtesy of their external manners. But as this is now effectually removed, and offensive coarseness and affected rudeness are substituted for civility, they can excite no emotions but those of disgust.

The Times maintained that British families should not be allowed to have French servants and urged the introduction of a bill putting a prohibitive tax on them. It suggested further that French milliners be repatriated as they were taking bread from the mouths of English women. Private individuals had similar ideas; several urged the government to enforce the new Alien Act more stringently, or proposed additional measures whereby dangerous foreigners might be silenced. At the end of 1793, for example, Thomas Parker, who was employed occasionally as an agent by the Home Office, informed Sir Evan Nepean, the Permanent Under-Secretary, that a French usher at a school near London had been endeavouring to disaffect the boys in his charge. Parker suggested that teachers, both foreign and native, should be required

> to make and subscribe a Declaration, acknowledging the Authority of Government as established by the Laws; and an engagement not to teach any thing contrary to them, and this as the condition of their receiving a certificate from a justice of the peace, or the Quarter sessions of the county, as a licence for keeping a school or academy, or assisting as a teacher.

This declaration, together with the certificate, he said, should be displayed in the schoolroom where the pupils could read it.[2]

Such extreme suggestions were not adopted; but, fearful of French spies and saboteurs in the weeks before the declaration of war, Pitt's government had taken wide powers over all foreign nationals in Britain by the Alien Act which had received royal assent on 8 January 1793. Ship's masters were required to provide lists of all foreigners on board their vessels to customs officers at the port of arrival. Foreigners landing after 10 January 1793 had to register at the customs office on disembarking, give up any arms in their possession and then wait to be granted a passport by the Home Secretary or by a local magistrate. If the passport was granted by a magistrate then a copy had to be forwarded to the Secretary of State. Any alien who had landed since 1 January 1792 had to obtain a passport before changing his place of residence. The

Home Secretary was given powers to deport undesirable aliens; magistrates could require foreigners to reside in specific areas, and could require householders to present accounts of any foreigners lodging with them. An Alien Office, a small addition to the Home Office bureaucracy, was created to see to the functioning of the act; it consisted of a superintendent, initially William Huskisson, who took up the appointment on 10 January, and one clerk, later two. The office printed special forms to enable customs officers and others to fill in desired information about foreigners; it also enquired into the background of people wishing to become naturalised, and issued licences and passports to anyone, British citizens included, who wished to travel abroad.

Further legislation for the war was introduced into the Commons by the Attorney General on 15 March. The Traitorous Correspondence Bill was designed to prevent British subjects from assisting the French war effort. First, the bill made it a treasonable offence to supply the French government with arms, bullion, military stores or supplies; second, since the French were seeking to finance the war by selling land, it became treasonable for any Briton to purchase land or funds in France, or to lend money for such a purchase; third, it became an offence (not treason) to travel to or from France without a licence or passport granted by the Crown. The bill had a stormy passage, with the whole House resolving itself into a committee and the opposition protesting furiously about infringements on liberty and commerce. Fox would not accept that the current war was any different from its predecessors, and since these had all been 'contests of revenue, rather than of arms' he questioned 'whether it would not be of advantage to this country to trade with its enemies, and perhaps to sell to them even articles of arms, whilst we have prompt payment, at our own price for them'. John Christian Curwen criticised the curtailment of the 'gainful' trade of insurance; there was no reason, he maintained, why the French should not continue to insure their shipping in Britain. Burke, on the other hand, supporting the bill, described it as a necessary measure of 'war police . . . the necessities of war calling for an increase of the prerogative of the Crown, in progressive proportion to the difficulties that occurred in it'. The bill finally passed its third reading in the Commons on 9 April by the margin of 154 votes to 153.[3]

In spite of this new legislation Pitt's government was not made up of men committed to a new kind of total war, but they recognised that France was fighting in a different fashion. The Solicitor General, defending the Traitorous Correspondence Bill against Fox, warned that 'the French were waging war with their whole substance' and if they contended 'on the ground of revenue, they would certainly have the advantage'. Pitt's speeches at the outset of the war suggest that he saw the French Revolution as a threat to social order in Europe; he described the Decree of Fraternity as 'not hostile to individuals, but to the human race; which was calculated every where [sic] to sow the seed of rebellion and civil contention, and to spread war from one end of Europe to the other, from one end of the globe to the other'.[4] But neither Pitt nor any of his ministers expressed their antipathy to France with the same crusading zeal and single-mindedness as Burke. Pitt and Henry Dundas, who, though Home Secretary, had responsibility within the Cabinet for the conduct of the war, both believed that revolutionary France could not long survive, given the powerful forces ranged against her and her own financial weakness and internal chaos. They planned for a short war, employing the same strategy by which Pitt's father had successfully fought the Seven Years War thirty years earlier: subsidising major European land powers to keep armies in the field against France, while British fleets swept French merchantmen from the seas and convoyed troops to seize profitable French colonies. Additionally Pitt may also have sanctioned speculation against the *assignat* and the bribery of French officials to hasten the collapse of the enemy, but the evidence for this, though usefully employed by the Committees of Public Safety and General Security against their internal enemies, is by no means conclusive.[5]

Unfortunately for Pitt and Dundas the war steadfastly refused to follow the pattern which they had anticipated. Substantial subsidies were paid to European powers – over £8000 in 1793, just over half of which went to Hanover, and over £2,550,000 in 1794, of which half went to Prussia and about a fifth to Hanover – but they failed to defeat the French decisively. Several French West Indian islands were seized by British forces, but at an enormous cost in lives – mainly the result of disease. Furthermore more and more of the troops intended for the West Indies had to be diverted to the European theatre, either to reinforce the Duke of York's army fighting alongside German allies in the Low Countries, or to assist the French royalists who had opened the port of Toulon to Lord Hood's fleet in August 1793. However, if the fighting in Europe was indecisive it did produce the *levée en masse* and the significance of this was not lost on British ruling circles. Just one month after the decree the young Lord Castlereagh wrote: 'The tranquillity of Europe is at stake and we contend with an opponent whose strength we have no means of measuring. It is the first time that all the population and all the wealth of a great kingdom has been concentrated in the field: what may be the result is beyond my perception.' At the beginning of the new year Lord Sheffield lamented tersely: 'All we have done as yet is to make all France soldiers.' Sheffield was preparing to meet an expected French invasion force in the Weald of Sussex, for even before the war was a year old the government's expectation of a rapid victory had given way to fears of a desperate French landing on the British coast. In October 1793 the Duke of Richmond, the Master General of the Ordnance, informed Dundas of the need for 14,000 infantry and 1500 cavalry in Kent, Sussex and Hampshire to meet the threat. The ministers appear to have been confident that any landing could be defeated; but Grenville warned that the effects would be 'unpleasant' and Auckland feared the possibility of British Jacobins aiding the French.[6]

Early in 1794 questions raised by Fox in the Commons exposed the government's confusion over its war aims. If the object of the war was to establish a new government in France then, Fox argued, Toulon (which had been evacuated by its meagre allied defence force) was more important than the West Indies; but if the object of the war was to seize French colonies then clearly the West Indies were more important than Toulon. Robert Banks Jenkinson of the India Board was entrusted with the reply. The principal aim of the war, he stated, was the destruction of the existing government in France, but the capture of French colonies was not to be sacrificed to the importance of Toulon. Pitt reinforced the reply, arguing that the loss of the West Indian islands must surely have a 'collateral influence' on the main aim of overturning the Jacobin government. 'It is of little consequence to us in the prosecution of a war for which we do not ourselves possess sufficient military force, and in aid of which we must have recourse to our pecuniary resources, thus to procure the means of increasing these resources, by extending our commerce, and opening new sources of industry.'[7]

But if the government was confused about its war policy, the opposition was in serious disarray over the war itself. The old Whig faction, which had constituted a solid opposition to Pitt since 1783, was divided between the followers of Fox, who urged immediate peace negotiations, and the followers of the Duke of Portland, who, while critical of the government's conduct of the war, believed that revolutionary France had to be defeated. The split had become apparent in the closing months of 1792 when, in consultation with Pitt himself, the conservative Whigs Burke and Windham began urging their colleagues to support the government against what they saw as a growing threat from French Jacobinism. At the same time Pitt offered the Whig Lord Loughborough the position of Lord Chancellor. Loughborough accepted the seals in January 1793, and in the following month a group of Whigs under the hesitant leadership of Windham declared their separation from Fox and constituted themselves as a 'Third Party', hoping that Portland would follow their lead. During 1793 Portland and his supporters edged towards the 'Third Party', and by January 1794 the Whigs were completely divided though the Portland group continued to sit on the opposition benches. In April, tentatively at first, conversations began about coalition. Two months later Portland and his friends resolved that coalition was desirable, not the least because 'if We decline taking our share of responsibility in the present moments the danger with which this Country and all the Civilised World are threatened must be unavoidable and greatly increased'.[8] But any coalition was to be an equal partnership. Encouraged by Lord Fitzwilliam, who saw himself as the guardian of the traditions of the old Whig party, Portland demanded, and got, a significant Whig influence in the Cabinet and a generous distribution of honours. On 11 July 1794 five Portland Whigs entered Pitt's Cabinet: Fitzwilliam as Lord President of the Council, Lord Spencer as Lord Privy Seal, Windham as Secretary-at-War, Lord Mansfield as Minister without Portfolio and Portland himself as Home Secretary.

The distribution of posts and honours to the Portland Whigs is in itself an indication of how important Pitt considered the coalition to be. Dundas came close to wrecking the whole arrangement; he was aggrieved at losing the Home Office, in spite of the fact that Pitt created a third Secretaryship of State for him. Although as Secretary for War he would continue to direct military operations, it took agitated pleas from Pitt and a tactfully phrased letter from George III to persuade him to agree to the coalition. Others among Pitt's old supporters were not appeased, and grumbles continued for some months. But the coalition gave fresh blood and a broader basis to the government. It could now more easily combat the menace from Jacobinism, openly apparent abroad and constantly feared at home.

From the beginning the popular societies had opposed the war and demonstrated their sympathy for France. At the end of 1793, although their numbers had fallen from the peak of the previous November, delegates from the English societies met delegates from Scotland in a convention held at Edinburgh. Given that the French legislative body at the time was the National Convention, the choice of title for the Edinburgh meeting was provocative, and the more so since the delegates deliberately followed French procedure and employed French terminology. The convention was closed by the Edinburgh authorities and several of its leaders, including the two delegates from the London Corresponding Society, were given savage sentences of transportation. At the beginning of 1794 the LCS and SCI began discussing the possibility of calling a new convention in London. The government consulted the Crown law officers about the societies' legal standing; it also introduced into them more spies, who reported seditious expressions and stories of arming and drilling, though they were not able to produce much evidence of the latter. The law officers concluded that charges might be brought; in May 1794 the government began arresting the societies' leaders, and Parliament authorised the suspension of the Habeas Corpus Act. The arrests led to a further decline in the societies; only their most determined members, and a sprinkling of spies, remained.

There is little doubt that the government overestimated the danger from the popular societies in 1794. Where a genuine, if pathetic and hopeless, conspiracy was unearthed in Scotland, it appears to have been principally the work of a former government spy whose motives are unclear. He may well have simply been trying to get back his former employment, though he finished up on the gallows. A few pikes were discovered in Sheffield; there was evidence of an armed body within the LCS, but its numbers were tiny and its attempts to drill appear to have been shambolic. The Crown failed to convince three separate Old Bailey juries that the individuals brought before them – Thomas Hardy, the Reverend John Horne Tooke and John Thelwall – were guilty of high treason; on Thelwall's acquittal the government released the score of radicals still in custody, but the Habeas Corpus Act remained suspended for another five months, until 1 July 1795. Yet if the government did overestimate the danger, its fears are, perhaps, understandable. However imprecise Pitt's war aims were, there was an ideological element to the conflict and the popular societies professed to subscribe to the ideology of the enemy. The fervour expressed for France by Fox and his genteel allies could be tolerated since this group came from the social class of the ruling élite; but the popular societies consisted of men who, traditionally, had no voice in the government of the country and who came from the same kind of social milieu as the terrifying *sans-culottes* of the Paris Sections. Probably only a few hotheads in the societies hoped for armed insurrection and bloody revolution, but in spite of this, and in spite of the continual protestations by the societies of their abhorrence of violence and civil disorder, many members made declarations which, at the time, seemed inflammatory and threatening to both the government and a majority in Parliament. The *Reports* of the Committees of Secrecy, which ploughed through the publications and the seized correspondence of the societies in May and June 1794, are full of quotations to support their beliefs that the societies' intentions were treasonable and posed a threat to the Constitution. Consequently, for the first time in British history an ordinary working man stood trial for his life in a secular court for supporting what was seen as the ideology of an enemy state.

It is difficult to say whether the popular societies or Pittites and Portland Whigs reflected the attitude of the majority of the population to the war in 1793 and 1794. There was no mass media to shape and reflect popular opinion, and probably most people were only concerned, or even aware of the war, in so far as it affected their own lives. In general the propertied classes probably had their attitudes coloured by reports of what was happening in France. The Girondins, whose activities had appeared bad enough, were removed in the middle of 1793 by a more radical faction. Executions in Paris, mass killings in Lyon, Nantes and Toulon confirmed the worst fears of the Revolution. Then on 26 May 1794 the Convention introduced 'terror' on to the battlefronts by prohibiting quarter for British and Hanoverian troops. In the event this decree was hardly ever acted upon and was soon repealed but, as Fox noted, 'its having existed even on paper . . . must have the worst effect in hardening the hearts of mankind'. Some French prisoners of war played on the fears of their British captors; at Bodmin they frightened ladies by scratching a line across the king's head on English coins. The fervour which many prisoners showed for the Revolution prompted considerable apprehension, especially in coastal areas fearful of invasion. A Catholic priest in Kent answered those who scoffed at the idea of invasion by asking what would the French not do, 'who fear neither God, man nor Devil?' Popular credulity allowed the most bizarre views of the ranks and capabilities of the new French armies to circulate. William Rowbottom, the Oldham diarist who left a valuable record of his district for the war period and after (though, sadly, leaving little information about himself), recorded: 'It is true as it is extraordinary that the French armys have a great deal of women in [them] who act both as offecers and privates and at the late battle at Hocheim two women in offecers uniform where taken one had received 3 wounds and the other that evening was delivered of a fine boy.'[9]

Frenchmen, and other foreigners, who had lived in Britain for years now found themselves objects of suspicion. A Flanders staymaker named Lambert was partly to blame for his difficulties. He became involved with the popular radicals in Halifax and addressed their open-air meeting on Easter Monday 1794; as a result his employer was forced to dismiss him since no one patronised her shop while he remained working there.[10] Peter Le Gras, however, appears to have been innocent of any political disaffection. He had lived in Falmouth since 1779, acting as an interpreter. He seems to have been involved with smugglers and probably fell foul of Samuel Pellew, the local collector of customs, for this reason. Pellew informed the authorities that Le Gras was dangerous and should be ordered away from the port. The Mayor of Falmouth, on the other hand, was convinced that Le Gras was a royalist. Dundas was bewildered. 'It is strange,' he wrote, 'that the servants of the Publick in their different capacities should have such different conceptions on the subject.' He suggested that Pellew come to London to outline any specific charges against Le Gras, otherwise, he believed, 'there will be no end of writing on the subject'.[11] Not every Frenchman would have been as lucky as Le Gras in having a local official to stand up for him, and, of course, it was not only Frenchmen who were victimised by zealous local patriots. British Jacobins were also a target.

Victories such as the capture of the fortress of Valenciennes in July 1793 and the naval success of the Glorious First of June 1794 were cues for widespread celebrations, but this in itself is not evidence of mass popular support for the war. Probably there were feelings of national pride and xenophobia present among the crowds, but it would be difficult to say how much more crucial these were than, possibly, a general desire for jollity and conviviality for which the celebrations offered opportunity. The celebrations for the Glorious First of June were particularly rowdy in London; crowds roamed the streets for several nights in succession demanding that householders illuminate their windows, and smashing the windows of those who refused. The Lord Mayor lamented that the news of this victory reached the capital during the week of the Whitsun holiday and Bow Fair, 'which always causes a great assemblage of loose, idle, disorderly fellows'.[12] Perhaps elements of the crowd were seizing the opportunity of the victory celebrations to extend the fair-ground festivities on to the night-time streets of the city. Perhaps yet more believed that the victory heralded the end of the war.

Two months after these victory celebrations crowds were again on the streets of London, but on this occasion to tear down the houses of 'crimps', civilians who forcibly recruited men for the army. The reorganisation of the City of London Militia may have given added impetus to these riots, but they were not an isolated protest against forcible recruiting. Though crowds might rejoice at the success of British arms, the traditional antipathy towards military service and the press gang remained evident. In February 1793 the inhabitants of Whitby drove a press-gang from their town; in October, after the death of a merchant seaman resisting a frigate's gang, the Naval Recruiting Office in Liverpool was totally destroyed.[13] Resentment about the manner of recruiting and the demands of the armed forces can be found in legal records. In April 1793 James Raith entered a plea of guilty at the

Durham Quarter-Sessions for calling the press-gang 'a set of op-
pressors'. He was fined sixpence. At the Surrey Lent Assizes in 1794
John Wilkinson, a private in the Surrey Militia, was sentenced to three
months' imprisonment for a mouthful of invective, including: 'Damn
the regiment! They have no business with me, my time is out.' In April
1794 the Treasury solicitor advised against the prosecution of Thomas
Elston, a London weaver, in circumstances which reflect the authorities'
awareness of popular attitudes towards the services. Elston had written
to a cavalry recruit lamenting that he had joined the 'arm'd Banditry' of
the King, adding that if ever he was to enlist himself it would be 'to ride
[sic] the world of Tyrants and to banish those mo[n]sters call'd Kings
from the face of the Earth'. The Treasury solicitor advised that, even if it
could be proved conclusively that Elston had written the letter, it was
'evidently written with the approbation of Ives's [the recruit] Father and
Mother who appear much distress'd at their son having inlisted [sic] for
a soldier. This perhaps might induce a Jury to acquit.'[14]

II   Industry and Labour

People's lives, and their attitudes to the war, were also affected by the
economic disruption caused by the conflict. In spite of the British navy's
supremacy, French privateers and cruisers successfully preyed on
British merchant shipping throughout the war. On 12 February 1793
The Times reported that the price of coal in London had risen after a
report that several colliers had been captured. The colliers from the Tyne
and the Wear began travelling in convoy, but this led to hold-ups and
queues in the Thames, where the unloading system was not geared to
dealing with large numbers at the same time. Shipping which sailed out
of sight of the British coasts was, of course, even more vulnerable. In
October 1793 a deputation of merchants from London, Birmingham,
Halifax and Manchester waited on the Lords Commissioners of the
Admiralty to request a system of regular convoys. Arrangements were
agreed for convoys to Spanish and Italian ports, though the system did
not always work well in practice; bad weather or naval operations might
delay a sailing, and often the merchants themselves tried to delay
departures when their own goods were not ready.[15] But most of the
economic disruption attributable to the war was less the result of direct,
or the threat of direct, enemy action, and more the result of the closure of
markets and financial uncertainty.

    Not every economic fluctuation in the first two years of war (or during the subsequent twenty years of fighting) was the direct result of war, but the war did have an important influence. Indeed the disruptive effects of upheaval in Europe (the partition of Poland as well as the revolutionary Wars) began taking their toll even before France commenced hostilities against Britain. As a whole the year 1792 showed much evidence of an economic boom in Britain: market securities were up and, in some areas, there was shortage of labour. British industry continued to profit from the commercial treaty concluded with France six years before. But as early as April financial circles were feeling the effects of disorder in Europe, and in November matters grew serious when numbers of nervous clients began exchanging the promissory notes of the two hundred and fifty or so country banks for cash. These banks had increased as much as twentyfold in the preceding forty years; they acted chiefly as banks of deposit, though in industrial areas their main function was making advances to their clients; but they held very small reserves of cash and relied on correspondent banks in London to provide them with coin. Their clients' demands led to the country banks applying to their correspondents who, in turn, withdrew gold from the Bank of England. The outbreak of war aggravated the crisis; there was a run on the banks in all parts of the country and several failed. A committee of the House of Commons was established and, in response to its report, on 30 April Pitt moved a resolution authorising £5 million to be set aside in exchequer bills for merchants in difficulty. Only just under half the amount was issued. Credit improved, but a reluctance to take bills and bankers' drafts led to many well-conducted businesses collapsing, unable to satisfy their creditors. The number of bankruptcies in 1793 was twice that of the preceding year.[16]

The French declaration of war pointedly referred to the economic measures taken against France by Pitt's government at the end of 1792. The trade treaty of 1786 came under increasing attack within the Convention; the Traitorous Correspondence Act inhibited the treaty, but it was not finally and formally revoked until October 1793 when the Convention forbade the admission of all British manufactures into France. The figures of the official values of British exports to France in the first half of the 1790s speak for themselves:[17]

1790	£535,284
1791	£576,632
1792	£743,280
1793	£66,677
1794	£2680
1795	£0

Not every sector of the economy which exported to France was hit by the war. More than a quarter of Cornwall's tin exports had gone to France in 1788, but an overall decline in production at the end of the century, coinciding with an expansion in the home market, averted any serious effects even during the war's initial impact. But elsewhere the effects of war and depression were catastrophic. Early in March 1793 a committee of calico printers from Manchester visited Pitt to discuss the serious situation in which they found themselves as a result of disruption in Europe and the collapsing trade treaty with France. Before the war was three months old 7000 were reported to be out of work in and around Manchester.[18] Birmingham was also badly hit. Samuel Garbett, a prominent businessman and ironmaster, stated that 6000 paupers were on the parish in October. The following month the Corresponding Society in the town informed the SCI that 'Mr Pitt's "War of Humanity"' had 'almost utterly annihilated our Trade in the Town and driven a great number of our best members and Mechanics across the Atlantic. And those that remain are but little better situated than the wretched inhabitants of Flanders'. According to Garbett the general opinion of the town's merchants was that more than one quarter of the town's manufactures used to go to France. No precise figures are available, yet historians have been prepared to accept that something approaching one quarter of Birmingham's hardware, plated goods and glass was exported to Europe in 1790, with France a preferred market because of punctual payments. The situation may have been worsened by a move in British fashion away from Birmingham metal buttons and buckles.[19]

Wool production, prospering before 1793, declined as European markets contracted and financial uncertainty discouraged the purchase of raw wool at the county fairs. In Huntingdonshire the price paid to weavers for their labour was reduced by one quarter; William Frend met a group of poor women in St Ives who protested: 'We are scotched three pence in the shilling, the fourth part of our labour – for what?' A gentleman in Norwich informed the Home Office of the serious effects of 'this just and inevitable war' on wool manufacture there: 'languid trade has doubled our poor rate, and a voluntary suscription of about £2,000 is found inadequate to the exigencies of the poor'. The poor of Norwich vented their anger and frustration on a recruiting party; as thirty recruits were marched out of the city they were first urged to desert and then stones were thrown.[20] But there were sections of the wool industry which recovered rapidly from these setbacks, and recovered principally because of the demands of war; the expansion of the army meant that more woollen cloth was required for uniforms.

A third area of textile manufacture was also depressed in 1793. At the end of the year the appalling plight of the Spitalfields silk weavers prompted subscriptions for their relief and resolutions from ladies of fashion to purchase silk dresses. The committee established to coordinate relief attributed the distress to 'the gradual, and (of late) general decrease in the wear of coloured and flowered silks'. Yet this did not prevent the anti-government *Morning Chronicle* attributing the distress to the stagnation of trade caused by the war.[21] Indeed there were those who argued that the war was the sole cause of the depression in the economy and who feared that it would only serve to boost the manufactures of Britain's rivals. As one pamphleteer put it: 'Every impoverishment to them [the enemy] is the loss of a customer to us; for the world is our market, supplying those things necessary to us, taking in return the fruits of our industry, and balancing the difference with their silver and gold.'[22] In Nottingham the anti-war partly took its stand almost entirely on economic grounds, making practically no comment on the Revolution in France. In the summer of 1793 leading merchants, manufacturers and inhabitants of both Glasgow and Paisley established Committees to petition George III for peace, which they believed would end unemployment and restore economic prosperity. Probably the seditious words, damning the King or wishing success to the French, for which several members of the lower orders of society were prosecuted in 1793 and 1794, were as much the result of economic distress as the proselytising of popular radicals. David Masters, a labourer of Warehome in Kent, for example, who attempted to organise a combination of his fellow labourers for an increase in agricultural wages and a limit to farmers' and traders' property, protested that a French invasion meant 'no harm to . . . any of the middling sort of people. We are as much imposed upon as they were in France.'[23]

Some industries, of course, profited as a direct result of war. Wool for uniforms was not the only military demand to be met. In Northampton the production of boots and shoes increased by about one-third, partly as a result of increased military needs. Copper had a variety of military uses, from sheathing the hulls of warships to the brass ornamentation on uniforms and equipment. Copper mining was a risky business; local rivalries, friction over steam-engine patents between Cornish engineers and Boulton and Watt, together with the exploitation of small but rich copper deposits in Anglesey, had thrown the Cornish copper industry into a period of strain and fluctuating fortunes in the two decades before the war. Fluctuations continued throughout the war but, as with other metallurgical industries whose product had a military value, copper mining in Cornwall gained a new impetus from the war. Naval demands put more work in the way of shipyards, both those owned by the Crown and those of private firms who accepted Admiralty contracts. In 1792 there were sufficient stocks of muskets to permit a doubling of the army, but the estimates of 1794 quintupled it. The Board of Ordnance did not have its own weapon-making establishments and therefore had to contract private gunmakers. The gunmakers themselves often preferred to finish other orders before turning to Ordnance requests since army weapons required a highly skilled job and the Treasury could be very lax in paying bills for Ordnance work. Nevertheless the war meant that there was no shortage of work for gunmaking concerns. The ordnance did have its own powder-making factory at Waltham; the demand for powder led the board to authorise Sunday working in January 1794, though the work boom here declined during the summer as the stocks of saltpetre ran out and the next consignment from the East Indies was awaited nervously.[24]

Additional demands on the work-force because of the war emergency gave workers new strength in any conflict with their employers. A powerful organisation developed among dockyard workers and towards the end of 1793 the ropemakers of Plymouth dockyard demonstrated their strength. A ropemaker was pressed for the navy, but was released when he managed to prove that he worked in the dockyard (such workers were exempt from pressing). However on his release the ropemaker insulted the captain responsible for pressing him and when this was reported to the commissioner of the dockyard he instantly dismissed the man. Promptly the 300 ropemakers in the dockyard walked out, demanding their workmate be reinstated. Work in the yard came to halt; a warship was unable to put to sea as its cables were left unfinished. *The Times* commented that if there was not a rapid return to work 'the public cause must suffer very materially'. After three days the commissioner capitulated; the offending ropemaker was reinstated and work recommenced.[25] As the Navy's press-gangs swept through dock areas merchant seamen were more and more at a premium. On 7 January 1794 *The Times* reported that upwards of sixty merchant ships were stranded in the Thames for want of crews; another seven East Indiamen were similarly stranded at Gravesend. Seamen of the northeast colliers also ran the risk of being pressed or being captured by privateers in the North Sea. But they were well organised before the war and those who avoided both press and privateers were able to negotiate favourable rates of pay because of the new danger and the high premium on seamen. The collier crews were paid for the round trip from the North-east to the Thames and back; in 1792, a good year for the trade, Newcastle seamen received about £2 10s. for the voyage. In February

1793 it rose to £3 18*s*., in April to £7. 17*s*. 6*d*., and at the end of the year it stood at £8. 1*s*. 6*d*. The rate was to fluctuate – summer rates were generally lower than winter – but in general the trend during the war years continued to be upwards.[26]

Towards the end of 1793, in spite of the war, those areas of the economy which were not geared to the war effort began to pick up and confidence began to be restored. Merchants looked around for new markets to exploit outside the war zones, a practice which they were to pursue with varying degrees of success throughout the war years. French successes and the virtual closure of Amsterdam in 1794, for example, had little effect on the cotton trade; by then British cottons were mainly entering Europe through German ports, and the United States was coming to prove an increasingly valuable market. Yet, as the accounts of Garbett in Birmingham and Rowbottom in Oldham show, improvements in the economy did not reach many workmen. The recruiting bounty continued to attract many impoverished and unemployed Birmingham artisans and Lancashire weavers, as well as men from other districts and other walks of life. In spite of the unpopularity of the army it became a refuge for many of the unemployed; and the demand for men was enormous. The estimates presented in February 1794 made provision for 175,000 regular soldiers, 52,000 embodied militiamen, and 85,000 sailors. Assuming 'military age' to be between eighteen and forty-five (the age of liability for the militia) the government was, whether it knew it or not, making provision for having about one in every ten men of military age in the United Kingdom under arms.[27]

III   Manpower and Administration

The armed forces are the institutions of a state most obviously tested by war, but Pitt's government had very little in the way of armed forces at the end of 1792. The problem of finding and maintaining sufficient sailors and soldiers to fight Revolutionary France was to vex the government throughout the war. The problem also put strains on overseas trade and sections of both central and local government not directly concerned with waging war.

Within a matter of weeks, thanks to Middleton's reforms and preparations, the navy had fifty-four battleships in commission and another thirty-nine ready. Middleton had foreseen also the problem of finding crews and had reorganised the recruiting service; recruiting offices were to be established in major ports and press-warrants were prepared ready for issue. There were hopes, however, that the first battle fleet sent out into the Channel would be manned entirely by volunteers, and the press-gangs were not turned loose during the mobilisation which preceded the declaraion of war.[28] On 1 December 1792 a royal proclamation offered bounties to volunteers: £3 to an able seaman and £2 to an ordinary seaman between the ages of twenty and fifty, and £1 to a landsman between twenty and thirty-five. Several towns offered money in addition to the royal bounty. Some men accepted; many of these probably reasoned that it was better to volunteer and collect the bounty than run the risk of probable impressment later, possibly receiving no bounty. But many more men were reluctant to volunteer. Some claimed that they had still not received all of their entitlements from the American War. Dundas was sent:

> The Humble Petition of a Body of Seamen Residing in London. Your Humble Petitioners Formaley Belong to Lood Hood Fleet in the West Indies Captured two-hundred Vesels likewise three Million of Money at the Iland of Saint Eustatica and Never received one Farthing your Humble Petitioners Haveing wifes and Fameleys and not willing to leave them in Distress Prays to have one Paymentes as soon as Possable as we are all willing to Enter into his Majestys Royal Navey.

In Newcastle seamen drew up a petition to Parliament requesting an increase in Royal Navy pay; the town's mayor reported that volunteering was slow, this in spite of an additional bounty of three guineas for the first hundred able seamen and one and half guineas for the first hundred ordinary seamen. In Lewes additional bounties were organised by a committee of the local Loyalist Association; they hoped that their bounties would reduce, if not completely obviate, the need for impressment 'which, though sanctioned by Law, and warranted by necessity, is too often productive of distress and ruin to many innocent and valuable members of the community'.[29]

In February 1793 the press-warrants were issued and the gangs began sweeping the ports of seamen. Two kinds of gang operated on shore: those run by land-based recruiting officers, and those sent ashore from warships for a quick raid to make up numbers. Probably some of the 'yellow admirals' who ran the regulating offices, or 'rendezvous' houses, in seaports were bitter, regarding themselves as passed over and looking upon the post of regulating captain as the end of their career. Some were corrupt and disreputable; but by no means all. Captain Peter Rothe, who opened the recruiting service on the Tyne and the Wear in December 1792, abided by the rules. After a 'hot press' in North Shields in March 1793 he released twenty-two of the sixty men seized, acknowledging that they were mates, ship's carpenters, or apprentices and therefore exempt. After a similar press in the following months he released all but 40 of the 250 men seized. The *Newcastle Courant* went so far as to describe Rothe as the seaman's 'favourite' after his involvement in a seaman's strike and his sympathy for their case.[30] Captain Smith Child, who ran the regulating office in Liverpool, appears to have been an officer of a similar stamp. During the first twelve months of war Smith Child reported that his office had received 976 volunteer landsmen, 688 volunteer seamen, 136 'presst' men, and 18 seamen sent by the magistrates. Probably the small number of 'presst' men, about one in fourteen, can be accounted for by Smith Child offering men seized by the press-gang the option of volunteering and taking the current bounty; this was a procedure followed by several officers of the Impress Service. Of course the regulating officer had to live in a partiuclar district and it was in his own interest to establish a rapport with the local population. The gangs sent ashore from men-of-war had no need of such considerations and could give the local regulating officer himself difficulties. In October 1793 a frigate Captain ignored Smith Child's advice and landed a press-gang in Liverpool. During the ensuing fracas one of the frigate's midshipmen killed the master of a merchant ship. The coroner brought in a verdict of wilful murder and the midshipman was committed to gaol in Manchester, but this did not appease the population of Liverpool, which turned on Smith Child and his men. Between 400 and 500 carpenters and seamen destroyed two recruiting houses; they were active for about seven hours and the local authorities made no move against them.[31]

Generally, at least in the early stages of the war, it was only seamen who were likely to be seized by a press-gang. A reluctant landsman was likely to be a liability in a storm at sea, or even performing day-to-day ship's tasks; it would take time to train such a man. Seamen were easy for the gangs to spot; they dressed in a distinctive way and, having grown accustomed to keeping their balance on a sailing-ship, they also walked in a distinctive way. But the removal of thousands of men from the pool of merchant seamen for service on warships created problems for merchant shipping. Parliament took action to ease the situation in April 1793 with an act authorising any British merchant ship to have foreign nationals comprising three-quarters of its crew for the duration of the war. An act of the following year set out to ensure that British merchant seamen serving in the Royal Navy would get their peacetime jobs back at the end of the war; it stated that on the return of peace any vessel registered as British must have a British master and three-quarters of its crew made up of British subjects, while British coastal vessels must have wholly British crews. This latter was probably little consolation to seamen forced to serve on warships, and the former could not guarantee crews for merchant ships. Nor were merchant ships safe when at sea. Returning from a voyage to the East Indies in the summer of 1794 John Nicol recalled having 'allowed my beard to grow long, and myself to be very dirty, to be as unlikely as possible, when the man-of-war boats came on board to press the crew'. It was to no avail; Nicol and sixty men found themselves on HMS *Edgar* and their ship, the *Nottingham*, 'was forced to be brought up the river [Thames] by ticket-porters and old Greenwich men'.[32]

Recruitment for the army was chaotic. There was no inspector-general for recruiting when war commenced, nor for some years after. There was no satisfactory method of examining the fitness of the recruits. Recruiting parties vied with each other for men, and not only parties from established regular regiments. Within two months of the outbreak of war the government authorised the formation of fencible regiments, regulars to be raised for home defence for the duration of the war only. Among the first recruiting parties in Oldham was one from the Derbyshire Militia[33] – the militia regiments had to find recruits to serve in place of those men who had paid the fine rather than procured a substitute, furthermore a recruiting party avoided the administrative problems of a ballot. But the multitude of recruiting parities could not get enough men for the government's needs, and consequently the formation of 100 independent companies of 100 men each was authorised; the men raised in this way were to be drafted into existing battalions. The cost of recruiting fell to the individual who raised the company, but it guaranteed him a commissioned rank. This practice favoured men with money rather than poor but experienced subalterns. In 1794 it was authorised that an unlimited number of men could be raised under an extension of this system. Again men who had no military experience, but who had sufficient wealth to raise a quota of men – often by resort to crimps – were given commissions relative to the numbers they raised. Officers who could not be absorbed when their quotas were drafted went on half pay; consequently a man might get a pension for life by raising a quota of recruits, and the historian of the British Army, Sir John Fortescue, gives the example of one lieutenant drawing half pay for eighty years after his men were drafted.[34] Those officers who went with their recruits were often totally unsuitable, having achieved responsible rank with no experience. The employment of crimps by the men recruiting for rank aggravated popular antipathy towards the army. In the popular mind crimp was synonymous with kidnapper and some months before the outburst of anti-crimp rioting in London during the summer of 1794, magistrates were warning that crimps might provoke disorder. Finally, the shambles of the recruiting system gave opportunities for the small-time blackmailer. A few men were brought before quarter sessions for extorting money out of others by threatening to have their victim arrested as a deserter unless an appropriate sum was paid.[35]

Many of the recruits came from the ranks of the unemployed. But there were other reasons for enlisting. Some men probably sought adventure; soldiering promised more excitement than the drudgery of an apprenticeship. Several young men were brought before different quarter sessions for enlisting while apprenticed and not legally free to leave their masters. Rowbottom noted a 'universall pant for glory', as well as economic distress, among enlisting weavers.[36] Others undoubtedly were tricked by crimps or recruiting sergeants and many literally woke up in the army with a sore head – the result of the crimp's cudgel or the sergeant's liberality with drink. Those recruited into the regular army in the early stages of the war had their lives squandered pitifully. Naval recruits were often bred to the seaman's life, but not so army recruits. The men who were sent to Flanders or the West Indies in the first years of war had the minimum of training, were ill-equipped and poorly clothed. There was no clothing department in the War Office; the clothing of a regiment was arranged by the colonel, who was expected to make a profit out of the funds allowed for the purpose – this was one perquisite of a colonelcy. The colonel received a sum of money for clothing his regiment each year and negotiated either personally, or through his agent, with a wool merchant. The sum he received was based on the estimate of the regiment's full complement, irrespective of whether or not it was up to strength. The colonel's profit was therefore something of a gamble depending upon how far the regiment was recruited, and how far it had suffered casualties. On occasions newly recruited replacements arrived in Flanders in linen slop-clothing, quite unsuitable for campaigning, and there was not time to make up their uniforms before they were in the front line. In an attempt to prevent regiments having to spend time making up and fitting their own uniforms in a war situation, a General Order was issued by the War Office on 12 October 1794 stating that in future colonels and their regimental agents were to send clothing to the regiments already made up. But for the public donations of money and clothing in the winter of 1793–4 (estimated at near £32,000 by John Lodge, who superintended the reception of the donations), sickness among the Duke of York's army would have reached alarming proportions. Shoes were also in short supply; this was serious enough in Flanders, but it led to men being disabled by crippling diseases in the West Indies. In November 1793 Sir

George Yonge suggested that the public donations might best be spent on shoes since the army's consumption of them 'often exceeds the present funds for providing them'. At no time during the first years of the war does the government appear to have considered increasing these funds instead of relying on public generosity. During the terrible winter of 1794–5 the only troops with greatcoats in Flanders were those regiments lucky enough to have been issued with them out of the public donations of the previous year; the rest of the army had to try to keep warm in flannel waistcoats supplied by the officers, who had subscribed over £1000 for this purpose. If the army was found wanting, government parsimony must take some of the blame.[37]

Besides the men of the regular army and of the embodied militia, a third type of soldier also appeared in the first weeks of the war, the volunteer. Three weeks after the opening of hostilities the *London Chronicle* reported: 'In all the counties fronting the French coast, the Gentlemen are now mounting themselves on horseback, and are determined to act as a patrole [sic], to establish a chain of communication, and to defend their property against all attack'. On 25 February Dundas informed the Commander-in-Chief:

> Since the Declaration of War . . . a great number of Letters have been received from different Persons residing chiefly upon the coast opposite to France, wherein they have signified their Readiness of embodying themselves in order to resist any incursions which may be attempted to be made by the Enemy and have requested that Government will order them to be supplied with Arms and Accoutrements for their use during the continuance of hostility.

Dundas approved of these requests and believed that some rules should be set down with reference to the precedents of the American war.[38] But it was over a year before an act of Parliament was passed for encouraging and disciplining corps of volunteers. It has been argued that the volunteers were the outward expression of the marshalling of public opinion behind King and Constitution in defiance of any kind of reform.[39] While there is some truth in this it remains significant that the first volunteers were organised in coastal areas; there is no doubt that men feared French raids on the coast from the outset of the war and that a genuine fear of invasion developed from the beginning of 1794.

It was not only the military institutions of Britain which were subjected to new pressures by the war. The militia regiments had to be brought up to strength and, even though some recruiting parties were out, the bulk of this work fell to local authorities, who had to organise ballots. The clerks appointed by the Lords Lieutenant to see to militia organisation were often poorly remunerated; pluralism and bad clerical work were a common fault. In 1795, two years after his regiment had been embodied, the adjutant of the Cambridgeshires complained that he had still not received a roll showing which men should be with the regiment and consequently he did not know which parishes were deficient in their quotas.[40]

The task of swearing in militiamen and other recruits fell to the magistrates, who, together with mayors or constables, also had to organise transport and allocate billets for any troops marching through their locality. The billets were in local inns, and the policy was burdensome to innkeepers, who might find themselves with no room for their ordinary guests when a regiment descended on their district. Furthermore, although they received reimbursements for the expense of quartering men and horses, these were often insufficient and could be some time in coming. From the beginning of the war the government received petitions from innkeepers, often backed by local magistrates and principal inhabitants, requesting that troops be diverted from their district, or that barracks be built in the vicinity. Bedford was so overcrowded in November 1793, with 600 troops in the town and more and more recruits arriving every day for a regiment being raised there, that an officer in the Derbyshire Militia added his voice to the local inhabitants' petition protesting that his own men were 'put to great inconveniences from the great number of recruits that are constantly arriving'. In replying to a petition from Chichester that same month Dundas commented: 'So many applications of a similar nature have of late come before me, that I am sensible the subject must soon undergo the consideration of government in a general point of view.'[41] In fact the government had already started doing something about the problem by appointing a barrackmaster-general and authorising the construction or renting of barracks out of the extraordinaries of the army (which neatly side-stepped the need for initial parliamentary approval) in June 1792. The largest barracks built under this policy during the war years were on or near those coasts threatened by invasion; several small cavalry barracks were built in, or close to, the expanding manufacturing areas and were designed principally as a police measure. But in spite of the building of barracks, innkeepers had to bear the burden of quartering military personnel throughout the war years.

Following the precedent of the American war Parliament authorised a weekly allowance of one day's labour at the local rate for the wife, and each lawful child under ten years of age, of a militiaman, if they did not follow the regiment. This allowance came out of the rates, and the resentment which it provoked among ratepayers was noted from the outset.[42] The departure of married men for the regular army or the navy could also put additional burdens on the poor rate; when the principal breadwinner was gone and once any bounty money left them (and a substantial part of the bounty was often required for necessaries in the army) had been spent, many families had no other recourse but the parish. In September 1793 the overseers of the poor of Sunderland estimated that their poor rate would increase from the usual £1000 a year to about £3000 and 'the difference in the expence . . . arises totally from the families of impressed men'. In the parish of All Saints, Newcastle, where most of the town's seafaring population lived, the parish rate doubled to sixpence in the pound during the first year of war as a result of the wives and families of impressed or volunteer seamen turning to the parish for assistance.[43] Unlike the specified allowance for militia families, the rate and nature of relief granted to the impoverished families of other servicemen was the same as that granted to ordinary parish paupers. The question which remains unanswerable is: how great would the burden have been on the rates if so many men had not enlisted as a refuge from unemployment?

The war hit people's pockets in other ways. The armed forces, their equipment, the subsidies for foreign powers all had to be found by the Treasury. To meet these Pitt believed it would be sufficient to augment existing revenue with negotiated loans and new taxes. In his first major war budget, that of February 1794, he announced negotiations for a loan of £11 million and a series of new taxes on attorneys, as well as on spirits, bricks and tiles, crown and plate glass, and paper. He recognised that these taxes would affect people in all walks of life but, he urged, 'when the contest, in which we were engaged, was for the whole that we possess, surely no man could hesitate to contribute a part'. Pitt was optimistic about a speedy end to the war; he did not expect to have to ask for so much money again and there was, he believed, some limited satisfaction to be had from the fact that the budget of the previous year had been exceeded principally because of the speed with which the armed forces, especially the navy, had been augmented.[44] But his demands for money, and for men, were to grow, and a series of crises and disasters led Britain, not France, to initiate overtures for peace.

3. Crisis upon Crisis: 1795-7

I 'Bread! No War! No King!' 1795-6

In the last week of January 1795 motions calling for peace were introduced into the House of Commons by Charles Grey, and into the House of Lords by the Duke of Bedford. Both were defeated. But if Pitt could still muster large majorities in Parliament to support his conduct of the war, the kind of unanimity in favour of combatting 'French principles' abroad, as well as at home, which he and his colleagues had detected two years before, was fast disintegrating. Even before the news of the disastrous conclusion to the Flanders campaign had reached Britain, petitions were being drawn up calling for peace. Several of these condemned Britain's allies, who had achieved nothing in spite of the enormous subsidies paid to them. But the principal complaints were about the cost of the war and the increase in the National Debt. The freemen of Carlisle saw no chance of achieving any of the 'avowed purposes' for which the war was being fought and were 'alarmed at the immense expenditure of public money'. The City of London deplored 'the calamitous effects of the present war on the trade, manufactures and commerce of the British Empire'. Similar sentiments were subscribed to in Durham, Liverpool, Manchester, Norwich, Southampton and York. Intense passions were aroused and counter-petitions from some of the same centres challenged the requests for immediate peace, expressed the hope that peace would only be signed with honour, and the belief that the termination of the war was best left to the discretion of the ministers and Parliament.[1]

Some of those who signed the peace petitions may moreover have been prompted by fears of popular disorder. The harvest of 1794 had been appalling, and a poor harvest was the herald of market disturbances. The corn shortage of 1795 would have been bad enough in peacetime, but war aggravated the situation. At the beginning of April a gentleman living near Plymouth informed Portland of an additional cause of scarcity and high prices which may not immediately occur to Your Grace, by which this district is particularly effected – I mean the long continuance of the outward bound Fleets on the coasts near Plymouth, from which market and that of the Dock Twenty-five thousand inhabitants more than usual were fed for several months; a number nearly equal to all the stationary inhabitants of both those places. During their continuance here, after the vicinity had been much drain'd of oxen, sheep, corn and potatoes, supplies were drawn from the several counties of Somerset, Dorset, Gloucester and Worcester.

Three months later the Mayor of Plymouth made the same point, noting 'an extraordinary influx of occasional inhabitants now serving in the Navy and Army, as well as . . . a very large number of prisoners of War'. Such complaints were not confined to Devon.[2]

Troops quartered at home were expected to provide for themselves out of their weekly pay: consequently the rise in provisions affected them as much as everyone else, especially along those areas of the south coast where their presence in vast numbers worsened the shortages. For the authorities the most alarming aspect of the provision disturbances of 1795 was the participation of soldiers. Some regular troops were involved; usually they were new recruits. Rioters in Plymouth were joined by recruits of the 67th Foot. Men from the newly raised 122nd Foot fixed prices at bayonet-point in the market at Wells in Somerset; men of the new 114th Foot quartered at Wantage and Faringdon threatened to destroy bakers' ovens and sell bread and meal at their own price. But more often it was militiamen – like new recruits, less well disciplined than regulars of long-standing – who were involved. In March the South Hampshires rioted at Canterbury; in April it was the Gloucestershires in Portsmouth, the Herefordshires in Chichester, the Northamptonshires in Plymouth. Most serious of all was the two-day rampage of the Oxfordshires at Seaford and Newhaven. This began as a provision riot but the claims sent to the Home Office by local shopkeepers and publicans suggest that it finished as a drinking bout. Thirteen of the regiment were subsequently court-martialled, two of these were shot.[3] The Duke of Richmond, then the general commanding the southern district, explained to Windham that a principal complaint among the soldiers under his command was 'that while the country people are relieved by their parishes and subscriptions, the soldiers receive no such benefit, and are unable to live at the present high price of corn and meat'. He suggested that instead of the allowance for bread in their pay, which, he suspected, was often spent on other things, the troops might be issued with bread. Pitt approved of this idea, fearing that unless something was done more serious disturbances would occur in May. Eventually, by diverting emergency supplies and authorising army victuallers to draw on supplies earmarked for London, the authorities ensured that the soldiers received bread.[4]

The disturbance among the Northamptonshire Militia prompted a gentleman of Falmouth to write to Portland requesting that the Northamptonshires, then ordered to Falmouth and its neighbourhood, be sent elsewhere. Given the tense situation with the unruly Cornish tin-miners, the local magistrates wished 'to have such of the Military in, and near the place, as will . . . resist any illegal proceedings'.[5] But on no occasion during the disturbances of 1795 and 1796 did troops, either regulars or militiamen, refuse to act against rioters when so ordered by a magistrate. Furthermore, probably as a result of the authorities ensuring that troops received their daily bread, and possibly also because of a general tightening-up of discipline over the next few years, the involvement of recruits and embodied militiamen in provision riots was hardly seen again during the years of dearth and high prices which were to recur throughout the war. But if soldiers were reliable in dealing with provision rioters, their presence could disrupt localities in other ways. They were boisterous and often unruly and violent. When newly formed regiments were ordered to be broken up and drafted into older, existing corps (often because they lacked both good discipline and capable officers) these regiments, in their turn, could become particularly turbulent. Troops in the large camps on the south coast became restless and bored. In their civilian lives many of the militiamen and the new recruits had worked twelve or even more hours a day. They could not be drilled and trained with the same incessant regularity; and the French invasion did not come. Many troops took to rambling over the countryside near their camps during their spare time; they trampled corn fields and left gates open. They cut down wood for fires, they poached, they stole vegetables.

The coincidence of war and serious provision shortages put new pressures on central government and led to it taking new powers and accepting new responsibilities. Legislation was introduced forbidding the use of wheat in distilling and in the making of starch. Early in 1795 wheat had already priced itself out of the market in both these areas, but the law reinforced the prohibition. An excise was introduced on hair powder, much of which was made from wheat. At the end of the year an act of Parliament sought to ensure the free circulation of grain by making the whole hundred liable to fine and imprisonment should either rioters or, as was implied in the act, local authorities attempt to prevent such circulation. Between 31 January and 6 August 1795 the Board of

Trade devoted thirteen meetings to the corn shortage; between 27 April and 25 November the Privy Council devoted forty-three meetings to the question. At senior government level the burden weighed most heavily on Lord Hawkesbury as President of the Board of Trade and Portland as Home Secretary. On four of the above occasions Hawkesbury alone constituted the Board of Trade, and he was present at the Privy Council at forty of its meetings on the shortage, just one more than Portland. The government took the novel step of trading in corn itself; as one contemporary London corn factor noted, 'government imports to secure supplies; merchants import to make profit'. Whether supplies would have been maintained had foreign imports been left in the hands of private merchants remains a moot point. The government had doubts and consequently scoured foreign markets and chartered merchant ships; fifty-six ships were despatched to Canada to purchase and carry back wheat originally destined for Portugal and Spain. All of the wheat imported up to the end of 1795 was purchased by the government and carried in government or government-chartered ships. The wheat was released on to the London corn market by Claude Scott, a London corn factor, who advised the Board of Trade and the Privy Council throughout the crisis. He released the wheat cautiously at, or just below, the market price so as to keep the price steady or reduce it marginally. The London market was a barometer for the rest of the country. The government's control here kept prices down when they could have reached new and alarming peaks in February and March 1796 – the harvest of 1795 being as deficient as that of the preceding year. This action, coinciding with the arrival of private imports, severely hit many merchants who were endeavouring to resume responsibility for the country's grain supply, but not until May 1796 did the government finally surrender its command of the market to the traditional suppliers. The government ordered grain ships to regional ports; this, together with local publicity of the event, often prompted farmers to market stocks which they had been holding back for yet higher prices. The government also arranged sales in inland markets, yet in spite of the pleas from many local authorities it steadfastly refused to interfere with the traditional movement of home-produced grain.[6]

Other moves taken by the government during the emergency were less successful. A proposal to construct state-controlled granaries was dropped after a savage rebuke from, among others, Edmund Burke.

> The construction of such granaries throughout the Kingdom would be an expense beyond all calculation . . . the rick yard of the farmer . . . and the barn . . . have been the sole granaries of England

from the foundation of its agriculture to this day. . . . The moment that government appears at market, all the principles of market will be subverted.[7]

The collection and publication of accurate statistical information about agricultural matters had always been the preserve of private individuals and societies, but in October 1795 Portland requested the Lords Lieutenant 'to procure an account of the produce of the several articles of grain . . . comparing the same with the produce of a fair crop of every such article of grain in common years and with the produce of the crop of 1794 of every such article of grain . . . and to report such account as early as possible'. The collection of information fell to local magistrates and high constables; it was made fairly rapidly even though it was not universally welcomed. The returns varied greatly in format and content and consequently little but the most general conclusions and comparisons could be drawn from them. The government learned from its mistakes and later in the war more successful attempts were made to collect statistical information using local authorities. In 1798 information was assembled of livestock and crops, especially in those parishes within twelve miles of the sea, so that the government might plan a scorched-earth withdrawal in the event of invasion. In 1800 the Home Office, the Board of Trade and the Board of Taxes all initiated statistical investigations into the state of agriculture when the country was again suffering serious provision shortages. On this occasion the Home Office used the Church rather than the hard-pressed local authorities; the bishops were requested to secure answers from their subordinate clergy to a series of questions. In 1801 the circulation of printed forms to the clergy ensured that the evidence amassed was comparable between counties.[8]

It is unlikely that anyone starved to death during the shortages, but, of course, they had a debilitating effect on the poor and probably weakened their resistance to disease. The shortages highlighted the situation of the poor. Many of the better-off followed the lead of the royal family, Parliament and the different quarter sessions by publicly resolving to reduce their consumption of bread and to eat more brown than white bread. They opened subscriptions and sent agents far and wide to find bread for the poor. Alternatives to wheaten bread were advocated in the correspondence columns of the press. The problem was that the poor, especially in the metropolis, were prejudiced against both brown bread and substitutes; fine quality was equated with whiteness. But subscriptions, and a reduction in the consumption by those who were never dependent on bread, were temporary expedients; some gentlemen applied themselves to the long-term question. Sir Frederick Eden embarked upon his monumental study of the condition of the poor, while the Reverend Thomas Malthus began to construct his phoney but potent ratio of population growth to food growth. Samuel Whitbread introduced a bill into Parliament proposing a minimum wage; initially, at the end of 1795, it was well received, but it did not survive an assault by Pitt during the second reading. Pitt then introduced his own proposals for a reform of the Poor Law; they were dropped after a discussion during which strangers were excluded from the Commons' gallery. At the local level the system adopted by the Berkshire magistrates at Speenhamland in May 1795, which fixed the rate of poor relief in relation to the price of bread, was taken up by other county benches. Where they were in operation, Speenhamland and similar systems probably served to cushion the rural poor from the major price rises of the war years.

It was a common occurrence during provision shortages for middle-men, farmers and millers to be accused of profiteering or creating artificial shortages. Such charges were made during 1795 and 1796. There were also rumours of exports to France. Lord Muncaster informed Dundas of ships which 'under pretence of carrying the grain coastwise . . . clear out for Portsmouth, Plymouth, etc. and run away to France, where they carry it in as smuggled, or in secret understanding suffer themselves to be captured by the enemy'. It is possible that this did happen, though there is no positive evidence. However supplies were surreptitiously sent to the forces of counter-revolution in Brittany. The Duke of Northumberland knew of 'flour for 10,000 men for three weeks' being sent to the Bretons in July 1795. He was outraged.

> According to what Rules of Justice Mr. Pitt has the assurance to require the poor Royalists of England to be curtailed of their usual pitifull allowance of Bread in order to feed the Royalists of France I know not. He may settle this matter with the public if he can. I know he is in a most horrid fright lest this transaction should be publickly known. I think it ought and the more publickly it is known the better. He possibley deserves to lose his head for it.[9]

For several 'royalist' gentlemen in England, probably unaware of the shipments to the Bretons, the scapegoats for the corn shortages were not middlemen, farmers, millers or merchants exporting to France. They suspected British Jacobins of hoarding grain in order to provoke a crisis which they could use to their own ends.[10]

Jacobin hoarders of grain were figments of alarmist mentality. But some popular radicals did seek to make political capital out of the shortages. *The Rights of Swine* explained that there was famine 'because in the time of national prosperity, house and land rent (consequently provisions) are always raised by the wealthy and voluptuous, till they are, at least, at par with high wages: but when WAR, or any other cause, has ruined or impeded commerce, and reduced wages, *rents* and provisions remain unabated'. There was no remedy to be found in charities or subscriptions for relief – 'nothing more than the appendages of Corruption, Extortion and Oppression!' *A Picture of the Times* listed:

> Meat seven-pence a pound; Bread nine-pence the quarter loaf; Coals two-shillings, half-a-crown, and three-shillings a bushel; all in consequence of this war. . . .
>
> My advice to you therefore is, pay no subsidies to allies . . . turn out all your present ministers, make peace with the French, insist upon an universal suffrage of the people and annual parliaments, abolish all sinecure places and unmerited pensions, cultivate your commerce, cherish your manufactories, love all men as your brothers, and never go to war but when you are obliged to do it in self-defence.[11]

One James Besey was reported to be travelling through Norfolk addressing meetings and distributing handbills which related the high cost of provisions to the war and urged the need for reform. Thelwall does not appear to have directly related the war to the famine, but his lectures at the close of 1795 contained severe strictures on the war and upon recruiting methods.[12]

The radicals' criticism of the war may have encouraged men to join or rejoin the popular societies, or to support mass meetings in 1795. But the acquittals in the treason trials probably gave the greatest boost to membership. The LCS assumed the leadership of the popular movement and pursued its twin aims of parliamentary reform and peace with renewed vigour; its correspondence with other societies during 1795 abounded with confidence.[13] The society demonstrated its new enthusiasm and strength with open-air meetings in the metropolis. At the first of these meetings, held in St George's Fields on 29 June, the society addressed George III, requesting that he dismiss Pitt's ministry, that the electoral system be reformed, and that peace be speedily restored. A second meeting was held on 26 October in the fields surrounding a tavern, Copenhagen House, in Islington. From three separate 'tribunes' radical orators harangued the enormous crowd present; an address was issued to the nation on the critical state of the country, and the King was sent a remonstrance. Three days after this meeting, as George III rode in state to open Parliament, his carriage was mobbed by crowds demanding bread and an end to the war. A missile, probably a small stone though at the time some believed a bullet, broke the carriage window. On his return the King was again pursued, and in St James's Park the door of his carriage was pulled open, possibly by accident. Many loyalists believed that an attempt had been made on the King's life, and the proximity of the Copenhagen House meeting to the attack led many to conclude that the LCS was responsible for the latter as well as the former.

Pitt's government reacted to the attack on the King first with a proclamation against seditious assemblies, and then with two bills hastily introduced into Parliament. The first bill made it a treasonable offence to incite people to hatred of the King, of his government or of the constitution by either speech or writing. The second restricted public meetings to less than fifty persons, unless a magistrate was notified well in advance, and it gave magistrates wide powers over such meetings; it also dealt with radical lecturers like Thelwall, whose lecture-rooms could now be closed as 'disorderly houses'. A diary entry made by William Wilberforce on 16 November after a meeting with Pitt suggests genuine fear, if not panic, on the Prime Minister's part. 'Pitt's language. "My head would be off in six months were I to resign." I see that he expects a civil broil. Never was a time when so loudly called on to prepare for the worst.'[14] Wilberforce, like others among the government's supporters, had doubts about the proposed legislation but regarded it as a temporary sacrifice brought about by necessity. The Foxites and the popular radicals were bitterly opposed to the bills and joined forces to campaign against them. Petitions poured into Parliament both for and against the bills. The majority were against.[15] But the kind of language employed by many of the popular opponents of the bills, further hostility shown towards the King and the mobbing of Pitt and Addington only served to maintain tension. George III felt it necessary to warn both Pitt and Portland that a meeting of Westminister electors to be held in Palace Yard might develop into a repetition of the Gordon Riots.[16] After a speedy passage through both houses, the bills received royal assent on 18 December.

It appears to be generally, if reluctantly, acknowledged that in a modern total war some restrictions will be put on the liberties of the individual by a government. In 1914 the British government introduced the Defence of the Realm Act for the duration of the war; in 1939 it introduced the Emergency Powers (Defence) Act. Both of these acts were far more draconian than anything contemplated by Pitt's administration, yet Pitt's anti-radical legislation during the 1790s covered some of the ground of these acts: measures against aliens, against correspondence with the enemy, against the subversion of the armed forces, and for the preservation of public order. Curiously, however, analyses of Pitt's anti-radical legislation have followed the track of his contemporary critics and generally ignored the wartime situation. Politicians, unfortunately perhaps, do not have the same opportunity and facility for compartmentalising problems as historians. The Cabinet which, alarmed by the assault on the King, introduced the two acts of 1795 was also faced with the threat of invasion, and with the other problems resulting from a major war – the problem of maintaining food supplies, the problems of manpower and war finance. When the Quartermaster General submitted a report on the danger of invasion in 1796 he believed the danger to be especially serious since the new rulers of France might consider taking risks undreamed of under the old regime and he emphasised the possibility of support for the French among sections of the British population.[17] The war against revolutionary France had an ideological aspect new to the eighteenth century; the popular radicals in Britain openly subscribed to the enemy's ideology and condemned the continuance of a war 'for the manifest purpose of destroying the Liberties of France, and insulting those of the British'.[18] The majority, of popular radicals up to 1795 at least were not disciplined cadres planning or even contemplating revolution, yet in the context of the time it was precisely in these roles that many men saw them, and the attack on the King served only to confirm such a view. The French 'terror' has been explained as an instrument of wartime government; the less dramatic, less bloody British 'terror', which affected the lives of far fewer individuals, was conducted also in an unprecedented war situation. This war situation probably contributed to the degree and severity of the British 'terror'. However, after the initial outcry against the repressive legislation of 1795 the majority in the country appear to have accepted it with no complaint.[19]

If relatively few felt the hand of government repression, most of the population felt to some degree the effects of the financial measures introduced by the government to meet the ever-increasing cost of the war. In his budget for 1795 Pitt proposed a new loan of £18 million and a series of new levies on wines and spirits, tea, certain wood imports, life insurance, the insurance of ships' cargoes, and on hair powder. The better-off felt the brunt of these taxes but Fox warned that the tea duty might lead to the poor having to give up the beverage. Pitt described the practice of powdering hair as a luxury, but a correspondent of *The Times*, commenting on the 'immense' and 'hardly credible' amount of wheat used (the corn shortage was an additional reason for discouraging the practice), noted how far down the social scale the practice went.

'Even the beardless apprentice willingly pays his sixpence on a Sunday, and issues forth from the polite regions of Shoreditch and Whitechapel, with his head decorated as fine as a peer on a birth night.'[20] Few apprentices could afford the annual fee of one guinea for a licence to wear hair powder; by the end of the century a high proportion of the wealthier, more genteel classes had also given up the habit.

In his budget for 1796 Pitt raised money on other items; again the impact was general. Assessed taxes were raised ten per cent; there was a new levy on the 'luxury' of tobacco; the tax on horses kept for pleasure was doubled to reach one pound, and a new tax of two shillings was put on horses kept for industry; the levy on printed calicoes was increased from threepence-halfpenny a yard to sixpence; the bounty on sugar exports was cut; discounts and allowances in the salt trade were reduced. Few escaped the new levy on calico since, as Pitt acknowledged, this cloth was an article of 'universal consumption'. How far traders lost by the altered regulations on sugar and salt it is impossible to say. In Cornwall in 1796 when the fishermen of St Ives landed a bumper catch of pilchards they chose to get their salt for preserving the fish by sending a smuggling vessel to France rather than making purchases in their home markets. But poor fishermen who did not share the Cornishmen's geographical advantages either had to pay the increase or else throw way fish which they could not afford to cure.[21]

Pitt's most significant new tax of 1796 was directed at property owners, for, as he stated to the Commons, 'in a war for the protection of property it was just and equitable that property should bear the burthen'. The new tax was to be levied on legacies on a sliding scale depending upon how distant a relative the inheritor was of the deceased; thus a son would pay only two per cent and a stranger six per cent. The measure was accepted when presented in the form of a bill, but a linked tax which would have granted a duty on succession to real estate to be paid over a period of four years after inheritance was withdrawn by Pitt in May 1796 because of the hostility which it aroused. The objections were twofold: first that the bill exposed a man's private finances to official snoopers and then to public gaze, and second because the bill imposed a tax on either capital or income – no one seemed quite sure which. Fox asked: 'why not fairly lay it upon income?' if it was indeed an income tax;[22] an ominous and prophetic question.

In the budget for 1797 Pitt returned to the old standby of chancellors of the Exchequer; he increased the duty of spirits: 'the consumption is so pernicious, that with respect to this article no man could wish that there should be any limits to the duty, so far as are consistent with the means of safely collecting it'. He also increased the duty on tea, but specifically exempted the coarser variety, which he understood 'to be the common beverage of the poorer classes'. A new tax on sugar however, was introduced 'with regret, but because it will fall in some degree on the lower classes of the people'. This went together with a variety of new customs and excise duties, and new taxes on the postal service, on stage-coaches and canal navigation. Finally a new house tax, levied 'in proportion to the other assessed taxes, as these might be supposed to bear a more certain proportion to the fortunes of the individuals', pointed tentatively backwards to Fox's question of May 1796 and forwards to the major innovation of 1799, the tax on incomes. Yet these proposals were reckoned insufficient for the expenses of the coming year and a 'Loyalty Loan' was commenced on 1 December 1796 to raise £18 million. The terms of the loan were generous, but the speed with which wealthy gentlemen subscribed was remarkable; the whole sum was subscribed in less than fifteen and a half hours, possibly the result of a fear that a compulsory contribution would be demanded if the loan were not raised.[23]

The taxation increases, of course, needed administering at the top and the Treasury staff found themselves swamped with the mass of new paperwork. Between 1792 and 1796 the number of registered papers received by the Treasury exactly doubled. Pitt tried to control the increase in paperwork in the same way that he tried to control the increase in expenditure, simply by additions to the old system. By 1797 ten new clerks had been added to the existing seventeen, but this could not solve the problem for the Treasury was feeling the strain at all levels. The Treasury Board seldom met; Pitt transacted the most important business at his own house while the less important decisions were left, of necessity, to the permanent secretaries.[24] The extraordinary cost of the war was to lead to a new tax departure in 1799; six years later it was also to lead to a total reorganisation and professionalisation of the Treasury.

While financing the war remained a difficulty, so too did finding the men to fight it. Military losses in the first years of the war were enormous. Sir John Fortescue estimated that between 1793 and 1796 40,000 soldiers were discharged as unfit and another 40,000 died as a result of enemy action and, principally, disease. The bulk of the fatalities – about 25,000 soldiers and 10,000 seamen – died in the West Indies; the raw recruits sent to this theatre as reinforcements did little more than 'fill the *hospitals and die*'. Several suggestions were made as to how the losses might be made up. *The Times* urged ladies to refuse to patronise shops which had men employed in work that women could do; this would have a twofold advantage in that employment would be provided for distressed women and the navy would be furnished with a number of stout hands which would be much more serviceable hauling a rope or working a gun than in measuring a yard of tape or carrying an ounce of pins to a Lady. It is really a disgrace to manhood, to see a great athletic fellow, bending as it were under the enormous burthen of a chip-hat or a muslin cap to the coach door of a customer, and there displaying the elegance and beauty of these female commodities.[25]

The effect of this exhortation is impossible to assess, but certainly the women of Britain did not say 'Go' with the same strident intensity employed by many 120 years later. Other advice on recruiting was sent straight to the authorities. Patrick Colquhoun, a London police magistrate and a future social commentator on the metropolis, suggested to Dundas that legislation from the American War of Independence be revived to enlarge the services.

By this Act, Justices of the Peace acting in conjunction with the Commissioners of the Land Tax are empowered to *raise* and *levy* able-bodied *idle, disorderly persons* (who cannot upon examination prove themselves to exercise and *industriously to pursue* some lawful trade or employment, or to have some assistance sufficient for their support and maintenance) to serve his Majesty as Soldiers.

The revival of such an Act while it gave amazing facility to the recruiting of the new levies would be the means of ridding society of a vast number of idle, desolute and abandoned characters which the law cannot reach at present although they live chiefly by the commission of crimes; and from the natural reluctance constantly manifested by this class of people it is evident that nothing will either reclaim them or prevent them remaining as nuisances and pests in society but that species of coercion which the Act above-mentioned authorised. . . .[26]

In April 1795 an act was passed (35 Geo. III. 34) enabling magistrates to ferret out any able-bodied, idle and disorderly men and hand them over to the navy. However few men appear to have been recruited in this way.

The trickle of 'idle and disorderly' men, the few men convicted at quarter sessions or assizes who were permitted, or directed, to enlist rather than serve prison terms, was not sufficient to meet the increasing demands for men, and 1795 and 1796 saw new legislation to fill the gaps and swell the ranks of both the regular and the auxiliary forces. Initially this legislation was directed towards increasing the navy, which the government considered its main priority – so much so that seamen were invited to leave the militia for the navy and Windham ordered that any seaman found enlisting in the army should forfeit his bounty money and be handed over to the navy.[27] In February 1795 an Order in Council had put an embargo on recruiting for British merchant ships in home ports until the navy was up to strength, and the government followed this up with novel recruiting legislation. The first Quota Act was passed on 5 March; each county in England and Wales was given a specific number of men to raise, ranging from 23 for Rutland to 609 for the West Riding, and making a total of 9769 men in all. Eleven days later a second act demanded quotas from the different seaports of England, Wales and Scotland amounting to 19,867 men. A third act required that the counties and burghs of Scotland find 1814 men. The burden of executing these acts fell chiefly on the existing local authorities. The quarter sessions had to break down the county quotas between the different parishes; it then became the duty of the overseers of the poor and the churchwardens to find the men and the bounties to pay them. Following the traditional eighteenth-century pattern there were fines for failure or for neglect of duty. In seaports the responsibility fell to commissioners who were specially appointed. The commissioners included the mayor, magistrates and the principal customs officers of the respective ports, together with men elected by and from the owners and masters of vessels and the merchants of the ports. London, which was expected to supply the largest seaport quota, 5704 men, was, as ever, exceptional and her forty-two commissioners were named in the act. Few trained seamen were enlisted under the Quota Acts, but the navy does appear to have got a high percentage of young men who could be trained to their new life. The government was sufficiently satisfied with the number of men raised to employ the system again. In November 1796 the coastal counties of England were directed to find 6124 men for the navy, while the inland counties together with those of Wales were to supply 6525 men for the army. Scotland was to supply another 2108 men. But at the end of 1796 men for the quotas were far more difficult to come by.[28]

At the end of 1796 the government also proposed augmenting the auxiliary forces for home defence. There was to be a Supplementary Militia of 60,000 men raised by ballot, trained for brief periods like the ordinary militia in peacetime, but not to be immediately embodied. A horse militia of 20,000 men, the Provisional Cavalry, was to be raised by a levy of one horse and one trooper for every ten horses in a county subject to the new horse tax. Seven thousand 'Sharpshooters' were to be raised by requiring all employers of gamekeepers to provide one man. The Supplementary Militia bill passed through Parliament without a division; there was more forceful opposition to the Provisional Cavalry, but the hostility to the 'Sharpshooter' proposal was such that the government withdrew it. In the event the Provisional Cavalry proved difficult to raise and virtually impossible to train; it was soon wound up. The prospect of demanding more manpower levies from their neighbours by balloting for the Supplementary Militia caused concern among some local gentlemen. 'He is a bolder man than I am who will undertake to carry it through', the Marquis of Buckingham told Pitt. In some areas, to prevent the trouble which a ballot might cause, subscriptions were raised to pay a bounty for volunteers to make up the Supplementary Militia. Elsewhere the ballots did provoke disturbances, notably in Lincolnshire. The Attorney General was informed that the 'lower sort of people' were reasoning:

> This is for the protection of Property against an invasion, but it is imposing the burthen of defending property most heavily on those who have least. A rich man can procure a substitute by payment of £10 or £15 out of £20,000. A poor man can only procure a substitute by paying half the price out of £10 or £20, and if he has not the amount of half the price, he *must* serve personally, whatever his situation may be.

It was reported that some of the poor believed that the new levy was· introducing conscription for the regular army.[29] An official advertisement carried in most newspapers protested that such rumours were spread by the factious and asked what man could refuse the short period of training required (twenty days) for his country's safety. Eventually, in spite of the fears and the disorders, the ballots were held. While the Supplementary Militia did not reach its projected strength, the government and its military advisors regarded the measure as a success.

Organising the ballots was a burden for parish officials; it cost them time and possibly money and did little for their popularity in their parish. Probably, given this situation, some unofficial arrangements were made. It was reported that in southern Yorkshire local officials were limiting the size of the Provisional Cavalry by listing for the horse tax only 'those whom *they thought ought to pay*'. The Lancashire justices fined Thomas Tetlow, a constable for Chadderton, five pounds for preparing false lists for the Supplementary Militia ballot and thus shielding his son; the fine was subsequently reduced to two pounds.[30] The expenses incurred in the execution of the legislation were paid out of the county rates; some counties were fairly generous, but the expenses could be a long time coming. These expenses added to the burden on the rates of the wives and families of regular soldiers and seamen who could not support themselves, and the relief permitted to the wives and families of all embodied militiamen. Legislation in 1795 attempted to clarify the confusion which still existed over the payment of the militia allowance. The act emphasised that the families of substitutes, hired men and volunteers for the militia were all entitled to relief. It also brought a degree of greater centralisation to local government by regularising the system of contributions to the county rates out of which this relief was paid. Hitherto certain independent local authorities had not contributed to the county rates of their home county; the town of Cambridge and the Isle of Ely, for example, had not contributed to the rates of Cambridgeshire. The Cambridgeshire Militia consisted of 480 men, 163 of whom came from the Isle and 51 of whom came from the town; yet relief came out of the county rates. In January 1798 the county treasurer of Cambridge was directed by the quarter-sessions to require payment under this act of £184 1s. from the Isle and £57 3s. from the town towards the £542 10s. which he had paid out during the previous year as militia allowances. But even if it resolved this anomaly the act was unable to speed up payment either from parishes to the county chest, or from one county to another. The Northumberland Militia had not been in Hull since December 1793, but in November 1796 John Davidson, the clerk of the peace for Northumberland, received a letter from Hull requesting that he call on his county treasurer and ask him to pay promptly the two accounts sent from Hull for reimbursing militia families 'which ought to have been done a considerable time ago. I shall also thank you to state to him the extreme hardship this town labours under, by the Treasurers of different counties being so very backward in their remittance.'[31]

Other legislation introduced during 1795 and 1796 was designed to make servicemen and their families more amenable to life in the armed forces. Seamen and marines of non-commissioned rank and below were permitted to allocate part of their pay for the maintenance of their wives and families. The content of the act was to be made known to ship's companies by the captain when he read them the articles of war. As usual the authorities charged with making the act work on the ground were the part-time parish officers whose job it became to handle the payment (35 Geo. III. 28). Probably the act eased the burden of the parish rates in seaports, since the wives and children whose principal breadwinner was serving in the navy were not so dependent on parish relief. A subsequent act (35 Geo. III. 95) extended the benefit to boatswains, gunners and carpenters; a third (35 Geo. III. 53) permitted servicemen of non-commissioned rank and below to send and receive letters at the reduced rate of one penny. Improvements were made in other areas. The War Office, now with the capable Duke of York as Commander-in-Chief, sought to put an end to some of the worst abuses in the army. Most notable in his first few months as Commander-in-Chief was the Duke's assault on recruiting abuses. Only *bona fide* military personnel were now to be permitted to recruit and the London police magistrates were empowered to investigate all recruiting centres in the metropolis. In spite of this the cry of crimping remained a potent one in London; during July 1795 crimping provoked a new wave of rioting and on one occasion the inflamed crowds pelted 10 Downing Street. Nor was it only in the metropolis where recruiting could lead to a disturbance.[32]

As 1796 drew to a close a majority in the country appears to have been dissatisfied and disillusioned with the war, which was costing so much and yielding so little. Pitt and his ministers were not unaware of these sentiments and in October Lord Malmesbury was dispatched to Paris to open peace negotiations with the Directory. But Directory remained deeply suspicious of Britain, and Carnot, the Jacobins' 'Organiser of Victory' and now a Director, together with General Hoche, still hoped to exact revenge for Britain's support of the royalist forces in the west. Carnot and Hoche planned to land raiders, with a high proportion of ex-convicts among them, in England.[33] On 19 December 1796 Malmesbury and his staff were ordered to leave Paris; four days earlier Hoche had set sail from Brest for Ireland with an invasion force of 15,000 veterans.

II   Invasion and Mutiny: 1797

Hoche's force was not intercepted by the Royal Navy but, fortunately for the governments of Dublin and Westminster, it was dispersed by gales and eventually returned to Brest. Two months later however Colonel William Tate and the *Légion Noire* (a force made up almost entirely of convicts) did effect a landing on the Pembrokeshire coast. Tate's landing was the only part of the Carnot–Hoche plan which materialised, but his attempts to attract Welshmen to his standards failed, and the entire *légion* surrendered just three days after landing. In spite of their military failure both Hoche's and Tate's expeditions produced serious repercussions. For weeks after Tate's landing alarms of new invasions sprang up with the appearance of unidentified ships off the coasts; in general these ships were innocent merchantmen or fishing vessels, but it was a Royal Naval squadron off Strumble Head which provoked the fear of a second landing at Fishguard. A Somerset man noted how 'new news come[s] in two or three times a day. I believe every person's imagination [sic] after spoken once or twice are put down for fact.' These fears help to explain why, some months later, the people of Alfoxton assumed from the antics of Wordsworth and Coleridge that they were French spies and Portland was sufficiently impressed to direct an agent to investigate. The west coast of England and Wales was the last area where the government and its military advisers had expected an invasion attempt; now men flocked to the colours of the local volunteers and the government was inundated with requests for additional protection by land and sea. The landing intensified the fears about the large numbers of French prisoners of war: the Mayor of Liverpool requested a bigger guard for the 1200 prisoners held within his jurisdiction; General John Morrison suggested turning the Isle of Lundy into one great prison camp, while the Honourable Charles Greville proposed the Isle of Man, or, better still, exchanging the French for British prisoners in French hands.[34]

More importantly Hoche's abortive invasion and Tate's actual landing brought to a head the deteriorating cash position of the Bank of England. In 1795 nearly £8 million was held by the Bank in specie; by February 1797, largely as a result of substantial advances to the government to help finance the war, this amount had dwindled to £1,272,000.[35] The appearance of Hoche's fleet in Bantry Bay prompted the Irish government to apply for a loan of £1,500,000 and while Pitt represented this loan to the Bank directors as vital for defence purposes the directors themselves feared that it would involve a further loss of specie and perhaps ultimately lead to the Bank being forced to shut its doors. Furthermore the appearance of Hoche's fleet, together with the expectancy of, and preparations for, invasion, led to many people demanding cash from the country banks; these banks in turn sought specie in London. The first news of Tate's landing reached the Admiralty on Friday 24 February and possibly the news leaked out to some members of the public before the *Extraordinary Gazette* of the following day made the official announcement. Crowds rushed to withdraw money from the Bank, and the government was forced to intervene. On 26 February a meeting of the Privy Council issued an order empowering the directors of the Bank to refuse cash payments. The Order in Council only applied to the Bank of England, but country banks were compelled to follow suit and to continue this policy by tendering Bank of England notes in place of gold when Parliament confirmed the order on 3 May with the Bank Restriction Act (which also, technically, only applied to the Bank of England). This act itself was seen as a temporary measure and was designed to continue only until 24 June; in the event it was renewed by Pitt and by successive governments until 1821.

Such a drastic change in the financial habits of the nation was bound to cause concern and protest. Two days after the Order in Council Fox and his parliamentary supporters roundly condemned Pitt for this profligacy in loans to foreign powers and for bringing Britain to the brink of bankruptcy. Pitt carried the day, but with a smaller majority than usual. Possibly partly as a result of this the amount paid in loans and subsidies to foreign powers was reduced over the next two years, though Britain's lack of powerful allies during this period may account more readily for the reduction. Less than a week after the order, Gloucestershire clothiers feared that the cloth-workers in the county would riot as they could get no cash with which to pay them. A Cornish gentleman wrote to his steward from London urging him to keep at least £300 in cash by him, 'for really no one can judge to what extremities mankind may be drove', and he had visions of his family and himself being forced 'to fly to our family mansions and seek our bread there'. The suspension of cash payments was a common complaint in the petitions which the *Annual Register* described as 'having been presented from almost every county, city and town in England, to his Majesty for peace and the dismissal of his ministers'. Among the most outspoken of these petitions drawn up in the spring of 1797 was that of the nobility, gentry, clergy, yeomanry and freeholders of Middlesex, who declared the Order in Council to be 'an illegal and arbitrary act' and warned

> that the pretended necessity of reserving for the public service the specie deposited by individuals in the Bank . . . may be pleaded at any time, and applied, with equal reason, to any private property whatsoever, which an arbitrary government may be able to seize and appropriate to their own purposes, under colour of the public service.

Yet for all the concern and criticism the transition to the paper pound was effected with little confusion and disturbance. Resolutions to accept banknotes were passed at a meeting of merchants and bankers in London the day following the Order in Council; these were eventually signed by 4000. Looking back on the crisis in 1803 the Scottish banker Sir William Forbes recorded:

> It was a matter of agreeable surprise to see in how short a time after the suspension of paying in specie, the run on us ceased. . . . It was remarkable, also after the first surprise and alarm was over, how quietly the country submitted, as they still do, to transact all business by means of bank notes for which the issuers give no specie as formerly.

As far as Forbes knew, no one sought to force a Scottish bank to pay *in specie*, and on the one occasion that this had happened in England the judge handling the case had managed to have it shelved. However the shortage of specie was to continue to create problems throughout the war years, particularly with regard to the payment of weekly wages.[36]

The situation in the late spring and early summer was so gloomy for the government that the young George Canning was prompted to compose some stanzas for Windham urging him to hold a celebration on a 'day of *no* disaster'.[37] For while Britain reeled before the invasion alarms and gentlemen up and down the country petitioned George III to dismiss his ministers for their prosecution of 'a long, disastrous, unjust and unnecessary war',[38] the armies of her principal European ally, Austria, were crumbling before the French. In April came another shattering blow when the fleet at Spithead mutinied.

Since the outbreak the war there had been a steady stream of petitions for an increase in navy pay and for the payment of long overdue prize money. Ship's officers were aware of the discontent below decks, and at the end of 1796 one of them urged the First Sea Lord to take some steps to improve the seamen's pay before the men took steps themselves – lieutenants had just received an increase and captains were damandinga a similar increase, but the seamen's pay remained unchanged. The Spithead mutineers demanded higher pay, security against embezzlement by pursers – especially with reference to provisions – an improved medical service, shore leave at the end of a voyage; subsequently they also demanded the removal of unpopular officers. The government was compelled to accept the demands (it raised the pay of the other ranks of the army at the same time to forestall any trouble in that service) and Parliament authorised a supplementary estimate of £372,000 to be added to the war budget. Yet procrastination in Parliament and suspicion of both the Admiralty and the government led to some bloodshed at Spithead before the mutiny ended, and also contributed to a major outbreak of mutiny at the Nore anchorage in the Thames estuary. In general the mutiny at Spithead had been conducted in an orderly fashion; the ships were run as usual, punishments were inflicted, only the commissioned officers were lacking. The Nore mutineers appear to have believed that the concessions won at Spithead did not apply to them, in particular the pardon for the seamen's leaders; but the aims of the Nore mutineers were confused. The moderation shown at Spithead by both mutineers and the authorities was not in evidence at the Nore: supplies to the mutinous ships were cut off, the mutineers retaliated by blockading the Thames; thousands of troops stood by on shore and London gentlemen volunteered to defend the capital; the East India Company and private merchants put their ships at the government's disposal. When the mutiny eventually collapsed those ringleaders who were singled out and caught (some appear to have escaped to France), notably Richard Parker, the 'President' of the Fleet, were court-martialled. Parker and twenty-eight others were executed.

Many believed that there was Jacobin involvement in the mutinies. The Duke of Portland authorised the opening of letters to and from seamen at the Nore and directed to stipendary magistrates from the London police officers, Aaron Graham and Daniel Williams, to enquire into the involvement of corresponding societies in both mutinies. Graham conducted the Spithead investigation alone, and found no links: 'I am persuaded from the conversation I had had with so many of the sailors that if any man upon earth had dared openly to avow his intentions of using them as instruments to distress the country, his life would have paid the forfeit.' From the Nore he and Williams felt that they could 'with the greatest safety pronounce that no such connexion or correspondence ever did exist'. They believed that 'wicked and designing men' had been among the mutineers, but they also thought that the seamen were perfectly capable of having conducted the whole mutiny by themselves, especially since the recent increase by the Quota Acts, for 'many good writers . . . must have been found among the quota-men'. No evidence has been discovered which contradicts this conclusion, but no 'wicked and designing men' have ever been identified. Some naval officers suggested that quota men, who had been members of the popular societies, were largely to blame for the mutinies. Historians have come to similar conclusions. Richard Parker was a quota man. Valentine Joyce, one of the leaders at Spithead, may have been one, but he was also a capable and experienced seaman to be holding the rank of quartermaster's mate in his mid-twenties. The past of most of the mutineers' 'delegates', like the pasts of the overwhelming majority of the seamen in the fleet, remains a mystery. Some of the mutineers were educated – they could match Shakespearian quotations with correspondents of the *Sun* newspaper; possibly some of these were quota men, but the quota men's certificates of enrolment suggest little more than that they were a cross-section of young men from the lower orders of society. Perhaps however, the appearance of these men in the fleet, generally untrained but often in receipt of ten times the bounty offered to able seamen at the beginning of the war, aggravated the existing discontent over pay and conditions. Significantly the Admiralty received its first warning of trouble when the 1796 quota was being raised and the mutiny at Spithead began shortly after the men raised under this quota had been drafted into the fleet.[39]

The mutineers had sympathisers on shore, some of whom adopted a position far from that of the majority of the seamen. John Leverit was brought before the Northumberland Summer Assizes in 1797 charged with uttering seditious words in North Shields:

It is no matter to me who is King or who is Queen. Damn their eyes, I have no freehold or estate to lose. I may have a chance to get some, and it is no matter to me how soon we begin to have a revolution. Blast them, they want to starve the sailors at the Nore. Damn their eyes, they had more need to pay their wages; they have four years pay due, and the blasted government has no money to pay them; the poor fellows are all naked on board, and it is high time for them to get their eyes opened.

Leverit was sentenced to one year in prison and was required to find sureties for his good behaviour for three years. Some individuals saw the seamen's actions as an example for others in the country to follow. In Liverpool a ballad was circulated called *Injur'd Freedom; or, Brethren Unite*; it urged Britons to take a stand against tyranny, emphasised the growing trouble in Ireland, and concluded:

> Then rouse from your sloth and resolve to be free,
> Be firm, yet be moderate too;
> In your SEAMEN a noble example you see
> Their conduct a pattern for you.

The author, Thomas Lloyd, and the printer, John Thacker Saxton, were arrested, tried, and sentenced to two years and one year in prison respectively. Efforts were made to subvert the army; seditious handbills appeared in military barracks and quarters up and down the country asking: 'Were not the sailors, like us mocked for want of thought, though not so much despised for poverty as we are? Have they not proved that they can think and act for themselves and preserve every useful point of discipline, full as well, or better than when under the tyranny of their officers?' There was a small disturbance among the artillery at Woolwich and there were rumours of unrest among the Guards, but it is impossible to say whether it was connected in any way with the sailors' example or the handbills. The reaction of most corps receiving such bills in their quarters was reassuring; they offered rewards out of their pay for the apprehension and conviction of the printers and distributors. Only one such offender, Henry Fellows of Maidstone, was arrested and convicted; he was sentenced to two years in Maidstone Gaol and, before his release, he was to find sureties for his good behaviour for seven years.[40] A bill was rushed through parliament in the aftermath of the mutinies making any attempt to foment mutiny in the armed services punishable by death. Like so much of the legislation during these years it was designed as a temporary measure to continue only until the beginning of the next session, but was renewed annually until 1800, when it was extended for seven years.

There are extant copies of twenty-nine letters to and from mutineers at the Nore which were opened and copied by post office personnel on Portland's warrant. The eighteen sent by civilians to men involved in the mutiny give an insight into the attitudes of seamen's families and friends which, in general, are very different from the fury of Leverit and the exhortations of Lloyd and Saxton. One letter may have encouraged the fears of Jacobin subversion: Thomas West, on board the fifty-gun *Isis*, which had deserted Admiral Duncan's blockade of the Texel to join the mutiny, was informed by his brother and sister in Chertsey that they were sorry to hear of the 'confused state' of the mutiny, but they expected that it would 'soon be as bad by land as it is by Sea', adding that 'the lower class of People in general wish the Sailors good success'. Three letters from Ireland discuss at length the deteriorating situation of that country, but make no, or only passing, reference to events at the Nore; a fourth letter from London, probably written by one Irishman to another, speaks of two delegates from France arriving in Ireland. Most of the letters however express loyalty to the King and, when they mention the mutiny, criticise the seamen's conduct. Joseph Pritchett, on board the store-ship *Seraphis*, which had been forced into the mutiny, was urged by his brother to 'Consider your Country weeping, remember her Songs in praise of the Sons of the Waves which you have often delighted in; think of the exultation of her inveterate enemies; feel for your relations and friends, and for God's sake begin to feel for yourself.' Peter Cudlip, on board another deserter from Duncan's squadron, the sixty-four-gun *Belliqueux*, was lectured by his brother John on the excellence of the British Constitution. John protested that he was

> no friend to War, but trust should I ever be called forth to bear Arms, would sacrifice my life in support of my King and Country. Let me beg of you also to obey your officers, doing your duty in every thing which is ordered you (and above all pray to God to keep you from joining those rebellious seamen, who are endeavouring to overturn our happy and glorious Constitution). I conclude with informing you that if my advice is not immediately taken in practice, never expect for me to countenance you any more as a Brother, if on the contrary you behave loyal and true to your King, nothing in my power shall be wanting to make you happy. . . .

John Cudlip lived in Deptford, about thirty miles upstream from the Nore and it might be expected that the mutiny would have a greater impact in such an area, especially after the mutineers' blockade of the Thames. James Bainbridge, on board Parker's ship HMS *Sandwich*, received a letter expressing similar, if less vehement, criticism from his father in London. But expressions of loyalty to the King and Constitution came from much further afield. Agnes Clark of Campbeltown told her son John on the sixty-four-gun *Standard* (another of Duncan's deserters) of the upsurge of loyalty in Scotland; she hoped that the 'Commanders and you Sailors are all quite reconciled together; and may the British Arms prosper'. From the other end of the kingdom Philip Vincent of Camborn, near Truro, wrote to Edward Tippet on the twenty-eight-gun *Tysiphone* expecting verdicts of execution to be passed on the Nore delegates – a prospect which, he believed, must 'give pleasure to every man that has his country at heart'. Like Agnes Clark he commented on the loyalty of his locality. 'I suppose there is not so loyal a Place in the King's Dominions as this. I suppose they would turn out to a Man for their King and Country.' But, he added significantly, 'at the same time [they] wish for Peace'.[41]

The LCS, while it did not combine with men from other social groups as it had done in the campaign against the treason and sedition bills, sought to capitalise on the demand for peace. As early as March 1797 it circularised county correspondents suggesting that meetings be held simultaneously in every town in the kingdom and outlining its own intention of sending a remonstrance to the King calling for peace and the removal of the ministers 'who have lost the confidence of the nation'. But of course, the letter went on, 'we want more than a change of *men*, we must have a change of measures'. The LCS organised its London meeting for July. It made some attempt to keep wthin the legislation of 1795, but the meeting, held at St Pancras, was closed by the Bow Street magistrates. The Home Office warned local authorities of the possibility of simultaneous meetings, but only in Nottingham, where the liberal-minded corporation gave tacit approval, did such a meeting take place. In radical Sheffield all remained quiet.[42]

Pitt himself wanted peace. The crises, together with the petitions for his removal, had shaken him. His private life was equally troubled; loans to his mother and brothers had left him financially embarrassed and led him to give up the prospect of marriage. At the beginning of June the Cabinet was split between Pitt with eight supporters, who wanted to negotiate peace, and Lord Grenville, backed by Portland, Windham and Earl Spencer, the First Lord of the Admiralty. Windham absented himself from two long and crucial Cabinet debates which resulted in the acceptance of Pitt's proposals; Grenville informed the King that but for the critical nature of the times he would offer his resignation; and in July Malmesbury set off again for France. There was a period during August when peace seemed possible, with Britain agreeing to French control of Holland and Belgium and restoring some of her colonial conquests, but the *coup d'état* of Fructidor put new men in charge of the negotiations. In the middle of September Malmesbury was presented with what was tantamount to an ultimatum; he left once again, for London. When Parliament met again in November Pitt roundly blamed the French for the failure of the negotiations. He warned the Commons that the French were no longer content with seeking the destruction of British commerce and wealth: 'but [it is] against the very essence of your liberty, against the foundation of your independence, against the citadel of your happiness, against your constitution itself, that their hostilities are directed'.[43] Admittedly Pitt had another naval triumph (Duncan's destruction of the Dutch fleet at Camperdown) to ease his situation, but the great majority in Parliament and the propertied classes were now resolved to fight on. At times this resolution was tempered with self-interest. Pitt's proposal to impose an additional tax on home-produced iron was withdrawn after a rapid mobilisation of the nation's ironmasters and a deputation to Whitehall. A tax on watches was almost impossible to collect, but more importantly it produced a buyer's strike and plunged watch-making centres into crisis and depression; this tax was repealed in March 1798 after less than a year. The opposition *Morning Chronicle* commented on the growing tax burden in 'A Loyal Song':

> If your Money he take – why your Breeches remain;
> And the flaps of your Shirts, if your Breeches he gain;
> And your Skin, if your Shirts; and if Shoes, your bare feet.
> Then, never mind TAXES – *We've beat the Dutch fleet!*[44]

Yet such grumbles and protests over taxes gave the opposition little cause for elation. The Dutch fleet had been defeated and the demands for peace had subsided. Fox and his friends were depressed and disillusioned. Once again Charles Grey had seen his motion for parliamentary reform rejected. 'It is too plain', he told Whitbread in October, 'that the public take no deep interest in our reforms or in any other public measure which does not affect their pockets.' A few weeks later he commented: 'Any exertions we can make at present I am sure are hopeless'.[45] Fox, Grey and most of their supporters seceded from Parliament and for the next three years there was no consistent opposition at Westminster.

4. From Rebellion to Respite: 1798–1801

I   Anti-Jacobins and Croppies: 1798

Between October 1797 and May 1798 Bonaparte's Army of England was encamped on the French coasts opposite Britain. For the first time during the war Britain was alone against a victorious France; Prussia had long since made peace, so too had Spain, who was now a French ally; in October 1797 Austria had signed the Treaty of Campo Formio. Pitt's government was faced with the problems of maintaining and boosting morale and, as ever, raising money and men for the conflict.

On 20 November 1797 the first edition of the *Anti-Jacobin* appeared. The new weekly journal's prospectus announced that its enemy was 'JACOBINISM in all its shapes, and in all its degrees, political and moral, public and private, whether as it openly threatens the subversion of States, or gradually saps the foundations of domestic happiness'. Upholding the ministry, the King and the Constitution, the *Anti-Jacobin* mercilessly criticised and satirised the Foxites and the opposition press. It upheld the war as 'just and necessary', especially now since the rulers of France 'Against our Constitution, and form of Government . . . have declared open and irreconcileable War. It is motive enough for them to *hate* it, that they see in it everything which should teach us to *love*, to *revere*, and to *defend* it.' Patriotic songs were published to fire the readers' ardour:

> Let France in savage accents sing
>   Her bloody Revolution;
> We prize our Country, love our King,
>   Adore our Constitution;
> For these we'll every danger face,
>   And quit our rustic labours;
> Our ploughs to firelocks shall give place,
>   Our scithes be chang'd to sabres.
> And, clad in arms, our Song shall be,
>   'O give us Death – or Victory!'

As the battle hymn of the Marseilles battalion promised to manure the fields of France with enemies' blood, this new *British War Song* promised the same fertilisation of British fields. The inspiration behind the *Anti-Jacobin* was George Canning, the young Under-Secretary at the Foreign Office. Contributions were made, on occasions, by Pitt, Grenville and Jenkinson; and while authors were not named and secret editorial quarters were established, there was no attempt to conceal that the journal received information from highly placed members of the government. The aggressive loyalty of the *Anti-Jacobin* struck the right note for a substantial section of the literate classes; the day following the second edition Canning noted 'we sell well'. In its final edition – it stopped at the end of the parliamentary session as it had always claimed it would – based on some dubious arithmetic, the journal claimed a readership of 50,000. It had had a weekly sale of 2500 copies, but a complete run of the journal, published in two volumes, reached a fourth edition during 1799.[1]

Loyal sentiments bombarded the eyes and ears of the whole population. 'The Snug Little Island', the only song from a patriotic play, *The British Raft*, first performed in 1797, gained wide popularity:

> Since Freedom and Neptune have hitherto kept time,
> In each saying, 'this shall be my land';
> Should the army of *England*, or all they could bring land,
> We'd show 'em some play for the island.

> We'll fight for our right to the island,
> We'll give them enough of the island,
> Invaders should just bite at the dust,
> But not a bit more of the island!

Handbills and prints appealed to the spirit which had defeated the French at Crécy and Poitiers, and overcome the Spanish Armada. The year 1798 was James Gillray's most active year for political cartooning; he attacked the French and the Foxites and emphasised Nelson's triumphs. Canning acquired his services to illustrate some of the *Anti-Jacobin*'s squibs while Sir John Dalrymple persuaded him to embark on a series of prints illustrating the *Consquences of a Successful French Invasion*. If Gillray ridiculed the wealthy gentlemen who made up the St George's Volunteers in London, and the army officers who 'recruited' at Kelsey's sweet shop, he left the spectators of his prints in Mrs Humphrey's shop window (and everywhere else where they were circulated in the country) in little doubt about the horrors that could result from a successful invasion.[2]

In many respects the galvanising effect of war was the same for Britain in 1798 as it had been for France in 1792. The threat from the French and the inspiration of the *Anti-Jacobin* together with other patriotic prints and papers all served to contribute to an upsurge in patriotism. In April 1798 Pitt could write that 'the spirit and courage of the country has risen so as to be fairly equal to the crisis', while the radical and anti-war *Sheffield Iris* could not 'but respect the patriotism and unanimity, which seem to inspire our fellow subjects'. In the following month Mallet du Pan, an *émigré* who had earlier concluded that war had caused the transformation of the French Revolution into the Jacobin's 'military republic', perceived a transformation in British society.

> Here we are in the full tide of war, crushed by taxation, and exposed to the fury of the most desperate of enemies, but nevertheless security, abundance and energy reign supreme, alike in cottage and palace. . . . The spectacle presented by public opinion has far surpassed my expectation. The nation had not yet learnt to know its own strength or its resources. The Government has taught it the secret, and inspired it with an unbounded confidence almost amounting to presumption.[3]

As patriotic Frenchmen had turned ferociously on the 'Austrian Committee' at court, the monarchy and all counter-revolutionary elements within France during 1792 so, in 1798, the British government could turn on what it considered to be pro-French, subversive elements, with the positive support of overwhelming majorities in Parliament and the tacit support of the rest of the population. At a dinner to celebrate Fox's birthday in London the Duke of Norfolk compared Fox to George Washington, who, with a small number of supporters, had made America 'free'; he went on to toast 'Our Sovereign, the Majesty of the People'. Pitt considered the words close to treason; the Duke was dismissed from his post as Lord Lieutenant of the West Riding. Early in May Fox repeated the toast. Pitt was urged to prosecute; he contemplated sending Fox to the Tower for the remainder of the parliamentary session, but eventually settled upon having his name struck off the Privy Council. The *Anti-Jacobin* saw justice in the punishment.

> We cannot but acknowledge . . . that there has been a struggle for some time past . . . whether or no the Government of the Country should assert itself against growing insults and attacks; and whether there should be *one* Man in the Kingdom, privileged to defy all animadversion, and to disregard all authority. The government *has* asserted itself; and We believe the Country feels itself in this, as in a

former instance [i.e. the dismissal of Norfolk], the stronger, and safer, for the proof which It receives of the spirit and energy with which the Government is capable of acting.

Pitt was reluctant to prosecute Fox because of 'the chance of an acquittal and a triumph'.[4] Although there was an upsurge of loyalty the government was cautious in how far this might be tested; the measures taken provoked no outcry.

In February a group of Irishmen were arrested at Margate endeavouring to take ship for France; among them were Arthur O'Connor, the editor of *The Press*, the semi-official newspaper of the United Irishmen, John Binns, a leading member of the London Corresponding Society, and Father James Quigley, in whose pocket was found a letter from the 'Secret Committee of England' to the French Directory inviting an invasion by Bonaparte, 'the hero of Italy and his invincible legions'. Rumours circulated of new conspiracies in Britain; some United Scotsmen had been arrested at the end of 1797; United Englishmen were arrested in Manchester in April 1798. In April the government authorised the arrest of LCS divisions. In the space of one evening both Houses of Parliament agreed to the suspension of the Habeas Corpus Act, and the suspension received royal assent the following morning. The Aliens Act was renewed and strengthened. Enquiries were initiated through the Post Office about the circulation of newspapers, both loyalist and opposition, throughout the country. In October the men arrested at Margate were tried. Fox and his friends travelled to Maidstone to speak for O'Connor; only Quigley was found guilty of high treason and executed. The acquittals of Binns, O'Connor and the others probably discouraged the government from prosecuting any of the LCS leaders or United Englishmen held under the suspension of Habeas Corpus. But the government took a much tougher line than it had done after the acquittals of four years before; many of those arrested under the suspension of Habeas Corpus in 1798 were held until the Peace of Amiens. Hostility to this draconian measure again was muted. Fox lamented to Grey that he could see 'little or no love of true liberty in the country, or perhaps in the world'.[5]

In spite of the government's concern it is unlikely that a French invasion force in 1798 would have received much support from Britons, no matter how opposed they were to Pitt's administration. The Duke of Northumberland resigned his post as Lord Lieutenant of Northumberland after a confrontation with some of his deputies about his absence from the county. The Duke had no time for Pitt, but in 1798 he raised his tenants as a volunteer corps at his own expense. The Reverend

Christopher Wyvill was the motivating force in organising his district of the North Riding to resist an invasion. While remaining critical of the war, the two leading provincial newspapers which took a consistent anti-government and anti-war line showed little sympathy for the French. The *Sheffield Iris*, whose editor and printer, James Montgomery, had served two terms of imprisonment for seditious libel and for libelling a local magistrate and volunteer officer, criticised war on humanitarian grounds; but it had no desire to see Britain 'bowing the neck to that yoke, which humbled Holland and Switzerland and Italy'. Benjamin Flower, the editor of the influential *Cambridge Intelligencer*, also criticised the war, but, he maintained, the initial ideals of the French Revolution had been perverted by Brissot and Robespierre. The final debates of the LCS General Committee in April 1798 centred on the question of what policy to pursue in the event of invasion but, thanks to the intervention of the Bow Street police officers, the heated debates were never concluded. Six months later Alexander Galloway, imprisoned in Newgate under the suspension of Habeas Corpus, informed Portland that the LCS had been arming but this was to fight French invaders: 'Tyranny in the Eyes of that Society has been, and I hope ever will continue to be equally obnoxious from whatever quarter it may originate or against whomsoever it may be directed.' A few men were accused of publicly wishing success to Bonaparte and his army. As usual in cases of seditious words, the government was hesitant about prosecuting such men if they had uttered the words while drunk or drinking. Popular radicals who harboured hopes of a successful French invasion were more careful in their public utterances, and it is difficult to untangle the genuine revolutionary or insurrectionary plans within the popular underground since all that remains are the reports of government spies whose own loyalties to the Crown, to their personal financial situation, or malice towards those they spied on, may have coloured what they reported.[6]

The classical scholar Gilbert Wakefield published a reply to a defence of Pitt's administration by the Bishop of Llandaff. Wakefield believed that the government had not negotiated with the French in good faith and that the only problem facing 'Bonaparte and his columns (unrivalled captain! unconquerable heroes!)' was exactly how to invade. He scoffed at the notion that the militia and volunteers were keen to fight and contrasted the British regular army, 'a collection of the vagabonds and outcasts of society, mere profligate mercenaries', with the French, 'a selection from all orders of citizens by a rigorous requisition . . . [and thus] an adequate and fair representative of the whole community'. He suggested that the poverty and wretchedness of the lower orders would help the French as it had done on the continent and that those who had an interest in defending the corrupt state should defend it alone. He recounted the fable of the sensible ass to reinforce his point:

> An old fellow was feeding an ass in a fine green meadow; and, being alarmed with the sudden approach of the enemy was impatient with the ass to put himself forward, and fly with all the speed that he was able. The ass asked him, whether or no he thought the enemy would clap two pairs of panniers on his back? The man said, No; there was no fear of that. Why then, says the ass, I will not stir an inch: for what is it to me, who my master is, since I shall but carry my panniers, as usual?

After reflection Wakefield brought out another edition of the *Reply*, omitting both his mockery of the auxiliary forces and the fable, toning down several of the passages and expressing himself against any French invasion. It was in vain; he was prosecuted for seditious libel, together with three booksellers who had sold the book; all four were found guilty. Fox and his friends were outraged; they believed that the liberty of the press was destroyed.[7] Yet prosecutions had not silenced the radical press at the beginning of the 1790s, nor were they to silence the press at the beginning of the nineteenth century. The prevailing loyal climate of 1798 was probably as much a cause of the stopping of radical presses as overt repression.

Loyalty permitted actions which encroached on the Englishman's boasted liberties, but it could be strained when, as Grey had told Whitbread, public measures affected people's pockets. At the end of 1797, as part of a budget intended to defray the expenses of the following year, Pitt introduced a bill to treble the assessed taxes; these taxes, on inhabited houses, windows, male servants, horses and carriages, were paid (and often evaded) principally by the well-to-do. The proposal caused division and outrage; it was condemned as inquisitorial. Pitt was warned that the poor would suffer since the wealthy would no longer be able to employ them. The City of London was furious. Tenant farmers in the North-east were concerned: as one land agent expressed it, 'If the taxes upon Husbandry accumulate in this manner I am very much mistaken if the distresses of the Farmer will not disable him from paying his rent – for within the last 7 years iron is advanced $\frac{1}{3}$, Labourage, Carpenters and poor rates in the same proportion'. Not all the opposition was as shrill or pessimistic. Charles Dundas, MP for Berkshire, reported that his constituents were not particularly discontented, except for those of limited fortune or those who had hitherto lived up to an income derived from annuities. Charles Mostin, a Roman

Catholic farmer in neighbouring Oxfordshire, moreover praised Pitt 'for his firmness and resolution the more so as he seems . . . to be risking if not sacrificing his own popularity which is usually the last thing statesmen wish to part with, for the safety of the country'. Momentarily the opposition and Pitt's unpopularity gave his few parliamentary opponents cause for jubilation, but on 5 January the Commons passed the measure, and the Lords followed suit four days later.[8]

In contrast to the pained outcry against the trebling of assessed taxes was the reaction to the Voluntary Contribution. During the heated debates on the new tax bill Addington suggested that anyone who chose should be allowed to make his own 'voluntary contribution' to the war effort in place of, and of course in excess of, his assessed taxes. Grenville did not approve of the scheme, believing that the contribution would not be truly voluntary 'but in reality extorted by popular clamour and prejudice'. But the idea caught on; Pitt, Addington and Dundas promptly subscribed £2000 each; George III gave £20,000 from his Privy Purse; and what had begun as a self-sacrificing substitute for an unpopular measure soon became an end in itself. Counties, towns, parishes, friendly societies, schools, military corps and ship's crews all began subscribing. Contributions came from all ranks of society: from national politicians and county worthies who subscribed thousands of pounds each, to the twenty-one persons in Keele (Staffordshire) who could only donate one penny each to their parish subscription; and from wealthy factory owners like Robert Peel who gave £10,000, to the workmen of John Mackmillan's horn-button manufactory at Rowley Regis in Staffordshire who added £3 14s. 5d. to their employer's £50.[9]

Patriotic contributions and trebled assessed taxes however were insufficient for the government's needs. In April Pitt introduced new fiscal measures. The Land Tax was voted annually; at the rate of four shillings in the pound it produced about two millions each year. Pitt proposed to make the tax a perpetual charge upon parishes but, at the same time, he encouraged those liable to the tax to redeem each pound due annually by the payment of a capital sum which would go towards the reduction of the National Debt. This, he believed, would not only assist the public revenue, but would also boost public credit. The principal objection, that there had been no Land Tax assessment since 1692 and consequently large tracts of land, especially in the North, which had then been assessed as barren moors were now prosperous manufacturing areas, was answered bluntly by Pitt: 'during a century which has now elapsed, no proposal for a more equal partition has been ever entertained. Is it more likely, then, looking to the future, that the anomaly would be corrected, even if the tax continued to depend upon a yearly vote?' A corollary of this anachronistic assessment was that the landed interest, as opposed to the mercantile and new manufacturing interests, bore the heaviest burden. By 1800 less than one-half, and perhaps even as little as a quarter, of the tax had been redeemed, which suggests that the landed interest was too weighed down to profit from the opportunity. Pitt's bill passed both Houses with large majorities; but while it was in progress Pitt told Parliament that he required a new loan of three millions, and to meet the interest requirements new taxes were levied on salt, on best quality tea and on armorial bearings.[10]

To meet the needs of the Royal Navy, seamen's protections were temporarily suspended and a 'hot press' swept through the seaports. To reinforce the troops available for home defence the Supplementary Militia was embodied, half in February and the remainder in April. The formation of the Scottish Militia in the summer of 1797 had provoked serious disorders; 'Scotland went stark mad' wrote Sir Gilbert Elliot, 'as if she had been bit by Corsica'. But the disturbances had been suppressed by the end of that year and great emphasis was put on the material benefits that Scots militiamen would enjoy both during and after service – the pay was said to be better than that received by labourers and many tradesmen, and the men were promised that after service they could practise any trade in a corporate town without having to pay a fee. The quotas for the Scottish Militia were eventually fixed by an Order in Council in March 1798, but it was not until seven months later that all of the 6000 men were mobilised.[11]

'A Friend to the King and Country', whose desire for economic reform and moderate parliamentary reform suggests a gentleman of Wyvillite persuasion, urged a *levée en masse* to meet the French threat. After a moderate parliamentary reform, 'Let Parliament tell us we are menaced with the attack of a terrible enemy, and that we must all arm, and learn to defend ourselves; thus let us form an armed nation, the whole country a camp, and every cottage a barrack. . . .' William Clavell, the High Sheriff of Dorset, resolved to act along similar lines, but without any preconditions. As High Sheriff Clavell had the right in common law to raise the *posse comitatus* of the county, this body dated back to Alfred the Great and Clavell can have had little or no information about it, nevertheless he directed the county magistrates and constables to make lists of all the men aged between fifteen and sixty capable of bearing arms, with the exceptions of clergy, Quakers, and men already serving in military corps. The men were to be divided into companies, those without firearms being armed with pikes. Further lists were made of all vehicles and horses which could be used for moving troops or driving the country. Clavell's activities were publicised by

William Morton Pitt, MP for Dorset, in *Thoughts on the Defence of these Kingdoms and the Raising of the Posse Comitatus*. The Marquis of Buckingham, the Lord Lieutenant of Buckinghamshire, was impressed with the measures and early in February 1798 he directed the Bucks Quarter Sessions to follow Clavell's lead. The government was also impressed; Dundas praised Clavell in the Commons and in April a bill, which owed much to Clavell, was passed [38 Geo. III c. 27] authorising the recruitment of Armed Associations.[12]

Volunteering into part-time army corps and sea fencibles during 1798, like the voluntary contribution, reflected a general surge of patriotism in the country. Yet in many instances this patriotism was bounded or limited by self-interest. Some men probably volunteered to escape the militia ballots which were held regularly to replace men who had been discharged or who had deserted. The sea fencibles were protected from the press-gang, a sure incentive for volunteers, though there could be local factors impeding recruitment. Some fishing boats in Essex, for example, were crewed by two men and a boy, and if one man volunteered fishing was impossible during that day of the week when he was called for training. Furthermore, men with a tradition of smuggling and wrecking were suspicious of the revenue cutters which ferried them to men of war for training. When factory owners organised their employees into volunteer corps, as in the case of Messrs Harley, Greens & Co. of a pottery near Leeds, or Messrs Peel, Yates & Co., calico printers near Blackburn, it would have been very difficult for an employee not to join. Some men were probably swept into volunteer corps, reluctantly, by their peers. A young Catholic law student in London explained to his father that he had not actually joined a corps of volunteers 'but was in a manner obliged to join a party of Catholic young men who meet at the Crown and Anchor to learn the exercise'. Another Catholic, Simon Scroope of Yarm, was reluctant to assist in organising an armed association because of the political bars against Catholics: 'if I cannot act as a free citizen I do not wish to come forward'. Scroope may have taken his cue from the protest of Sir James Lawson, another Catholic gentleman in the North Riding, during the raising of the Provisional Cavalry the year before. The apparent seriousness of the situation however led them both to relent; Scroope helped Wyvill to organise both an armed association and preparations to drive the country, and Lawson became commander of the Catterick Volunteers. Some gentlemen were reluctant to volunteer, fearing that their farms or business might suffer if they were called away any distance. The Lord Lieutenant of the North Riding warned that the organisation of armed associations in his county must be prudent, 'by that meaning, not to Interfere with

Husbandry'. In Lancashire, following a suggestion from Dundas, the Deputy Clerk of the Peace wrote to gamekeepers in the county to enquire whether they were prepared to come forward to train in case of invasion. Most of those who were fit were prepared, but some were not. Thomas Robinson even 'at this important crisis . . . cannot by any means be spared from his family and farm'; John Emett, who was also the works manager of a large cotton factory, considered that he could not be spared either, 'but at the same time in case of actual invasion I will come forward with every man in the employ, they profess their readiness, in support of king and country should occasion require them'. In contrast to these reluctant volunteers it is probable that many more men, who saw no need to commit their motives to paper, were encouraged to come forward purely for the sake of king and country, and that they were fully prepared to march wherever they were needed in case of invasion or the imminent threat of such.[13]

While the volunteers were never called upon to serve for any length of time far from their farms, businesses or workshops, the recruitment of men into the regular forces and the militia, and the embodiment of the Supplementary Militia, was beginning to have an impact in some areas of the country. In 1797 a Manchester calico printer, angered by the desertion of one of his apprentices into the army, protested:

> If his majesty's service, and the real interest of the country were attended to, every calico printer in the army would be flogged from the ranks, and conveyed home by a file of soldiers, as by remaining a useless soldier he receives sixpence per day from his country, and when he is attending to this natural business, this country gains near forty shillings per day by the duties on the cloth which the man prints.

As early as the harvest of 1796 a gentleman in Nottinghamshire was reporting that labourers were scarce and their wages high. 'Some farmers have been obliged to mow their wheat for want of reapers.' At harvest time the following year farmers in Bedfordshire were finding labourers expensive and hard to come by, 'thanks to Mr Pitt for having been the cause of destroying so many of our fellow countrymen and of making those few that remain at home soldiers'. In June 1798 Dundas was reminded 'of the necessity of permitting the different corps of military having permission to assist the farmers not only in their Corn, but in their Hay Harvest'. Commanding officers of regular and militia regiments were consequently authorised to grant six weeks' leave, at their own discretion, to no more than one-third of their effectives to help with the harvest. In some areas the deficiency in male labour began to be made up by the employment of women in heavy agricultural work, while in the North-west women and children were moving into the largely male preserve of handloom weaving. A Wigan correspondent told the Home Office:

> Although numbers of our people are gone for soldiers and sailors there is still an increase of looms, for if a man enlists his wife turns weaver (for here the women are weavers as well as the men) and instructs her children in the art of weaving; and I have heard many declare that they lived better since their husband enlisted than before.[14]

The fluctuations in the weavers' trade make it most unlikely that any women taking it up in the absence of soldier or sailor husbands were better off throughout all of the war years. Also there were many women and children, whose husbands and fathers had enlisted, who were unable to profit from agricultural labour shortages or expanding industry and who depended heavily upon their parishes. In July 1798 the wives of men in the East Riding Militia petitioned the quarter sessions for an increase in their allowance from one shilling to one shilling and sixpence a head each week. The magistrates, however, felt that no increase could be made. The hungry wife and children of servicemen became a subject for poets who described the contemporary social scene. In *Margaret; or, the Ruined Cottage* (later incorporated into book one of *The Excursion*) Wordsworth portrayed the increasing distress of a wife with two young children, after her husband had enlisted leaving her his bounty money. Among the pitiful poor described by an anonymous versifier in the *Cambridge Intelligencer* was another mother with two young children:

> She told us that her husband serv'd
> A soldier far away
> And therefore to her parish she
> Was begging back her way.[15]

In spite of the distress of some servicemen's families, the resentment probably felt by some of those embodied in the Supplementary Militia and the Scottish Militia, and the reluctance of some men to join volunteer corps, the general mood in England, Scotland and Wales during 1798 appears to have been one of loyalty to the Crown and a determination to resist the French. Ireland however seethed with disaffection and disorder. Roman Catholic gentlemen resented the political bars imposed on them because of their religion; the largely Catholic peasantry hated their landlords for both their exactions and their heretical religion; in the north Catholic tenants, called Defenders, fought Protestant tenants known as the Peep-o-Day-Boys; young nationalists and radicals, inspired by the ideas of the French Revolution, had formed the United Irishmen in an attempt to unite Catholic and Protestant behind demands for political reform. The government at Westminster and the Viceroy's administration in Dublin were well aware of these problems. Pitt was sympathetic to some of the Irish complaints, far more so than the authorities in Dublin. In 1793, during the early months of the war, the Irish Parliament was pressurised by Pitt into passing a Catholic Relief Act; this removed some of the bars against Catholics, giving them the right to vote, to sit on juries and to hold minor civil posts and junior army ranks, but they remained barred from Parliament and senior administrative posts. One of the fruits of the Pitt–Portland coalition in 1794 was Earl Fitzwilliam's appointment as Viceroy. Fitzwilliam's behaviour in the three months that he held the post (January to March 1795) implied that he intended revolutionary changes; he was forced to resign, but his actions aggravated the situation on both sides. The United Irishmen began negotiating for French assistance and organising themselves militarily; this lost them much support from Ulster Presbyterians, but won them increased popularity among the Catholic peasantry. The Dublin authorities struck at the United Irishmen early in 1798. In March the Leinster Directory was arrested in Dublin; but this did not prevent the Catholic south from spluttering into rebellion in May, and areas of the north-east rising in early June. In the south Catholicism became the motivating force behind the peasant pikemen; in the north-east Catholic suspicion of the Presbyterian leadership weakened the rebel forces. Both the rebels and the government forces fought with unbridled savagery; prisoners of both sexes and of all ages were massacred. The northern rising was over in a few days, the southern rebels were finally swept away by the artillery bombardment of Vinegar Hill on 21 June. Two months later 1000 veterans from the campaigns in Italy and the Rhineland commanded by a young general who had fought beside Hoche in the Vendée landed at Killala. General Humbert's invasion force was too few in numbers, and too late, but with a number of Irish levies he fought a brief, impressive campaign against the British forces opposing him before surrendering on 8 September. Six weeks later a second invasion force was intercepted by Sir John Borlase Warren's squadron; Warren took seven out of the nine French ships with 2500 soldiers on board including Wolfe Tone, a founder of the United Irishmen, now in the uniform of a French colonel. Rather than face execution Tone cut his throat; with his death the rebellion was at an end.

The defeat of the rebellion did not solve matters. Loyalists in Britain regarded Irishmen, especially Catholic Irishmen, as traitors. Attempts to renew the naval mutinies in 1798 were blamed, with some justice, on United Irishmen serving in the navy, although the ringleader of the plot on HMS *Diomede*, a marine named George Tomms, was a former member of the Nottingham Corresponding Society who allegedly 'enlisted . . . to have an opportunity of assisting in a future Mutiny'. On at least two occasions after the rebellion loyal Irish regiments serving in England were provoked into violence by civilian taunts of 'Croppies', 'Irish Rebels' and 'Irish Rascals'.[16] In Ireland itself the memories of the rebels' ferocity burned itself into the recollection of the Protestant minority, while the Catholic peasantry remembered, with equal hatred and horror, the savage repression. Catholic gentlemen remained frustrated over the political barriers before them; a few United Irishmen who had survived the holocaust continued to plan insurrection. More than ever Pitt recognised the necessity of pacifying Ireland; his attempts were to lead to his fall.

II *Peace Becomes a Necessity: 1799–1801*

At the close of 1798 British prospects for a successful conclusion to the war looked good. 'Our late successes', wrote the Reverend John Hawtrey, 'and the prospect before us, is very exhilarating; it must end, I shld. hope in peace. The French have nothing before them but misery.'[17] Besides the successes in Ireland the threat of a landing on English coasts had long since disappeared with Bonaparte's expedition to Egypt. Nelson had missed the French fleet in the Mediterranean, but had made up for this ill-luck by annihilating it in Aboukir Bay. The news of the victory of the Nile, like the news of other naval successes, had been the cue for wild popular demonstrations and illuminations throughout Britain. From Egypt, Nelson had sailed back to Italy where he persuaded the Neopolitan court to launch an abortive attack on the French. Sir Charles Stuart with a tiny force of British troops had seized Minorca. The whole of the Mediterranean seemed to be about to turn against France. Portuguese warships had taken up station alongside British ships off Malta, while an unlikely alliance of Russian and Turkish fleets attacked French forces in the Ionian Islands. Encouraged by victories, and by the possibility of a new coalition against France, Pitt's government resolved to make every effort to bring the war to a successful conclusion; again they called upon the population for more money and more men.

In December 1798 Pitt outlined a proposal for replacing the assessed taxes with a new tax which no longer fell upon expenditure but upon incomes. As in the previous year Pitt hope to raise sufficient money in one year to meet the expenses of that year. He emphasised that the economy was prospering in spite of six years of war and had the satisfaction of stating 'that the total amount of our exports and imports exceeds, in a large degree, the largest sum that any man yet ventured to state upon the subject'. There were only rough estimates of the nation's resources available (these were in the published works of economists like Adam Smith and agricultural improvers like Arthur Young); but building on these Pitt estimated that the total national income which he might tax was £102 million. He proposed a general tax of two shillings in the pound on all annual incomes of £200 or more. Income under £60 a year were exempt, and those between £60 and £200 were to pay on a graduated scale. Individuals were to draw up their own assessments of their annual income, and swear an oath as to their accuracy. Anyone declining to make a disclosure would be assessed by the Crown commissioners; these latter were sworn to confidentiality. The methods of disclosure, with ultimate coercion, Pitt hoped, would cut down the frauds practised under the assessed taxes. Such of the opposition as were present to hear the proposals were outraged. The fiery George Tierney, whose nagging opposition had led Pitt to fight a duel with him in May 1798, accused Pitt of pursuing similar policies to the French. 'This measure puts a tenth of the property of England in a state of requisition', he proclaimed, 'a measure which the French have followed, in their career of revolutionary rapine, and which the chancellor of the exchequer has, with all his eloquence, justly branded with the hardest epithets.' It was suggested that the tax would impair investment in both trade and industry. But the Commons authorised Pitt to bring in his bill. During the subsequent debates on the bill Pitt was accused of permitting spies to become acquainted with men's private concerns through the measure. Time after time opponents protested that the bill would encourage the indolent at the expense of the hardworking. William Smith, the radical member for Sudbury, quoted Adam Smith against capitation taxes, against taxes on profits, and relied on his analysis to urge that, as incomes might fluctuate from year to year especially at the lower end of the income brackets, the new system was totally unfair. Fox, still in secession, considered 'that if people will not resist this inquisition, they will resist nothing'. Yet Spencer Perceval, a loyal supporter of the government who had recently been appointed to a £300 a year 'place' and marked by Pitt as a possible successor, could sum up on the third reading with the assertion that only five or six in the Commons disapproved of the measure, and only a few outside. The new

tax would, he maintained, prove to the French that Britain still had
financial resources for an emergency, and the general approval of it
would show them 'that they had a whole country unanimous against
them'. The bill passed its third reading by ninety-three votes to two.[18]

Already the propertied classes, especially those on low, fixed incomes,
were feeling the pinch of war taxation. In May 1798 Mrs Michelson was
complaining to a friend in Cumberland of the plight of those who, like
herself, leased respectable, but modest accommodation in London:

> I cannot think this country in a prosperous way, for Bankruptcy
> stares us very full in the face; the present taxes are considered by most
> people and felt by many as a great grievance; and how is it possible for
> us to meet the future, for more heavy ones there must yet be. Perhaps
> you will be surprised to hear that in our small way the last assessment
> falls upon us to the amount of thirty nine pounds a year, besides all the
> old ones. I wish my dear friend I had a snug habitation as you as added
> to the pleasure of enjoying your society I should feel so much easier
> and happier respecting income, for really supporting this old, dirty,
> small house in Ormond Street is to us very inconvenient; but having
> three years to wear out the lease we do not know how to help
> ourselves; there are no hopes of parting with it, for you would be
> frightened to see the number of houses that are to be Lett in this
> Town. I believe if the war continues, and taxes increase, the grass will
> grow in London streets.[19]

The new burden of income tax squeezed such people more.

Fox believed that the tax would fall heaviest on those with incomes
between £200 and £600 a year. A correspondent of Dundas warned of
the ill effects of the measure on Scottish farmers in this bracket; 'it must
finally terminate in the ruin of many'. As the income tax entered its
second year John Higgins, a Bedfordshire farmer, heard that his rent
was to be raised, 'which joined to the consequent advance on Income
Tax on the rent of the Farm not only precludes all prospect of gain but
amounts to the certainty of my being a considerable looser by it'. He was
able to dissuade his landlord from raising the rent for a few months.
Higgins's sister, living in Carshalton, had also felt the impact of the tax.
She had hoped to make a short journey for convalescence, 'but this
Income Tax bears hard upon the pocket and absorbs a sum which might
otherwise be devoted to travelling'. Some of these complaints, of course,
may be attributed to a dislike of new and seemingly more efficient tax
methods; one naval surgeon was outraged by the possibility of 'the
pimply minions of Bureaucracy' picking over 'the fruits of his labour
and toil'. As with any new measure, there was some confusion. People in

Bury expressed their inability to estimate their income and consequently a handbill was circulated to assist them 'being an exact copy of what has been issued from the Office of Commercial Commissioners for the City of London, and its vicinity'. Henry Huddleston presumed that his father meant to deduct his own and his sisters' allowances from his tax statement, and enquired what his allowance was going to be supposing that he himself would have to declare it:

> Mr. Chambre an eminent barrister said the other day that under the head of deductions a person may deduct the rent of chambers taken for the purpose of business, if so I shall have to pay about a guinea as I certainly shall not return more than I am in receipt of, it will be wiser to be rather under than over the mark.

Probably many agreed with the wisdom of this concluding remark; others gave totally false statements. In October 1800 Michah Gibbs, a gentleman of Wellow, was found guilty of fraud by the Somerset Quarter Sessions, having produced false certificates to the commissioners at Bath; he was fined £200 and sentenced to four months in Ilchester gaol, where he was to remain until the fine was paid. It is an open question how many other frauds were not discovered.[20]

The new tax did not raise the amount which Pitt had estimated. In June 1800, when Tierney proposed to bring in a motion that would end the tax the following April, it had only raised seven millions out of the estimated ten. Tierney and Smith rehearsed the same arguments as before. R. J. Buxton, member for Great Bedwin, who prided himself on being a 'landed gentleman', sprang to the defence of the tax. He was prepared to give up one-tenth of his income for ten years, twenty years, indeed for ever, 'if the remainder of his property was secured from the inroad of French pikes and French principles'. Pitt replied in a more moderate tone suggesting that the final amount raised by the tax could not yet be assessed positively, and insisting that in general the tax was a success. Tierney's motion was defeated by 114 votes to 24.[21]

Besides raising money Pitt had also expressed his hope, in proposing the income tax, that it would act as an example to the rest of Europe. George Canning, when he rose to answer Tierney's motion for peace just a week after the initial discussion on the tax, emphasised that it was essential for Britain's safety to fight on, and that Britain must seek to raise the rest of Europe against France. This reply led at least one member, Joseph Jekyll, the member for Calne, to expect new and significant subsidies; his fears were soon justified. In June 1799 it was announced that £825,000 was being set aside for the Tsar to assist in 'the deliverance of Europe'. In the following year over one million was paid to Austria, over £500,000 to the Tsar, and another million was divided between Bavaria and other smaller German states. But the British government also wanted to employ British troops in the armies of the Second Coalition; the problem was that there were none available. 'At present', wrote Addington in February 1799, 'our means of internal defence are abundant, and our means of attack, next to nothing. The climate of the West Indies . . . has destroyed the Armies of Great Britain.'[22]

Between 1793 and 1798 close on 150,000 recruits had been raised for the regular army excluding the artillery. Disease, especially in the West Indies, and desertion had taken an enormous toll, far greater than enemy action, and in 1799 the total effective strength of the army was only about 130,000 officers and men. Even those regiments stationed on British soil were seriously under strength; the returns of June 1799 revealed that sixteen battalions of the Line in England had an average strength of 409 men out of an establishment of 712. Training an effective strike force from scratch obviously would take time, but there was a trained military force in the country which was not part of the regular army; in June 1799 the English Militia alone was about 90,000 strong.[23]

In 1798 the government had called upon English Militia regiments to volunteer to serve in Ireland, partly because there were so few regular troops available but also because there was some concern, at least on the part of the Duke of York, over the large number of Irishmen serving in the regulars. Several militia regiments volunteered for service in Ireland; possibly some pressure was brought to bear on the men to volunteer by their officers, but there is at least one example of the other ranks pressurising an officer.[24] The families of those who went profited to the tune of eightpence a week for each wife and child under ten in addition to the normal militia allowance; but the men continued to worry about their families, the service in Ireland was arduous and unpleasant, and as 1799 wore on the militia regiments there grew more and more reluctant to remain. In general, however, the measure was regarded as a success, certainly much more so than an attempt to augment the regular army by recruiting from the militia which had been tried in 1798. The recruiting had been left to regular regiments, which seems to have alienated the Lords Lieutenant and militia officers from the scheme. The government learned from this mistake and in looking for their strike force in 1799 they proposed to leave such recruiting to the militia regiments themselves; furthermore such militia officers who wished, providing they brought a set quota of men with them, also could transfer to the Line. Some Lords Lieutenant were opposed to the idea, and there were complaints that the militia was being misused, but in June 1799 a bill passed rapidly through Parliament reducing the militia to 66,000 men and authorising up to one quarter of the new quotas to join the army, their service being limited to Europe and to five years or the duration of the war plus six months; 15,712 men enlisted. Then in October Dundas believed it would be safe to reduce the militia to its 1793 level; Parliament agreed, allowing the surplus men to enlist into the army, or else to be disembodied subject to recall. This time the army got 10,414 recruits. The volunteers into the army appear to have come principally from long-serving militiamen who had grown accustomed to military life. In addition a higher proportion of the men caught by the Supplementary Militia Ballot in 1796 and embodied in 1798 were family men; enlisting into the regular army meant an end to the family allowances. Finally an industrial boom in some areas of Lancashire and the West Riding appears to have encouraged men from these areas to seek disembodiment and a return to civilian life in preference to regular service. But 26,000 trained volunteers were a great asset to the army; the measures were regarded as a resounding success, and were to be tried again in the next stage of the war.[25]

At the beginning of 1799 the British economy was on an upswing. There had been a phenomenal expansion of exports to the West Indies; there was an increasing demand for British manufactured goods in the United States; and grinding steadily along beneath the fluctuations in foreign trade, the war itself continued to boost some sectors of the economy and offer substantial profits to certain kinds of businessman. Mr Trotter of Soho Square had virtually cornered the market in military supplies and equipment, from tents to camp kettles to the individual soldier's knapsack and canteen. His account ran into millions; but while he occasionally had to wait up to a year for payment he was able to fix his own prices. Military tailors had an enormous market, with regulars, militia and volunteer corps to outfit. In October 1798 James Duberley's bill for clothing one militia regiment over the previous twelve months was £1369. 9s. 5¾d. Wool merchants from both the West Riding and the west country supplied the cloth for these uniforms. The firm of York and Sheepshanks in Leeds had supplied the Cambridgeshire Militia with cloth to the value of £658. 16s. 9d. over the six months ending in October 1798. In the same year Samuel and Nathaniel Wathen of Hampton in Gloucestershire were trying eagerly to win the contract for supplying the West Riding Yeomanry Cavalry. They were manufacturers of best superfine broadcloth, material of a very different quality from that supplied for regulars and militia. The cost was 22s 6d. a yard – the scarlet supplied for the sergeants of the Cambridgeshires was only 10s 3d. a yard, the 'red' for the ordinary militiaman a mere 5s 6d., but then the Yeomanry were the pinnacle of provincial society. Wool for uniforms was a steady demand, independent of the fluctuations of foreign markets, except when dyestuffs, notably cochineal from Spain for the scarlet of officers', sergeants' and the yeomanry's coats, were impeded by war. Warships were continually being put out to tender. These provided steady work in the shipyards, but there was an element of risk for the shipbuilder since a seventy-four-gun man-of-war took three or four years to build and costs were rising throughout the 1790s. In 1801 the Navy Board offered an allowance to make good at least part of any loss made on a fixed contract, but only after the ship was delivered. Block makers and coopers could do well, though the days of the former were numbered; reports into frauds and abuses in the naval dockyards begun at the end of 1802 revealed how work had remained with the same families over a period of years with no control over standing contracts. Neither did the profits to be made out of the war go unnoticed in parliament. 'Contractors and loan-mongers are the only persons who have not been impoverished by the war' declared Thomas Jones, the member for Denbigh borough, in December 1800. 'War is life to the contractor, and death to the landed man. War is life to the loan-jobber, and death to the peasant; life to the jobber, and death to the mechanic; life to the remitter, and death to the shopkeeper; life to the clothier and death to the labourer.'[26]

Jones had a point, yet the craftsmen and labourers employed in certain areas were also doing well out of the war, or at least were able to use the demand for their labour to keep abreast of wartime inflation. By the turn of the century seamen on the north-east colliers were receiving as much as eleven guineas a voyage. Tailors were needed to make the army uniforms. In the early years of the nineteenth century some of the larger businesses recruited cheap female labour, yet in London at least the highly skilled 'flints' and the less skilled 'dungs' were doing well at the end of the century. In October 1798 Lord Hardwicke was looking for a skilled tailor to serve with the Cambridgeshire Militia, but no London journeyman could be found to enlist 'for less than £100 per year'. He was informed that 'all the journeymen, good or bad, receive £1.0s 5d. weekly but in the country their wages are considerably lower and therefore charges should be less'. The tailors in London were able to develop an efficient and powerful trade union during the war, and in spite of the new Combination Act the 'flints' were able to conduct a long and moderately successful strike at the end of 1800. Dockyard workers, essential to the war effort, developed a powerful organisation. In Portsmouth about one-third of the rapidly expanding population worked in the dockyards. In 1796 several hundred of the dockyard workmen organised themselves, on strictly egalitarian lines, into a cooperative to destroy what they considered to be a monopoly among the millers and bakers. They erected their own mill and bakehouse, and their society continued throughout the second stage of the war and beyond. During the provision shortages at the turn of the century the dockyard-workers attempted to organise a boycott of foodstuffs at prices which they considered exhorbitant. At the same time the commissioner of Plymouth dockyard was so alarmed by the organisation amongst his workforce that he spiked the dockyard guns. This unity and organisation spread outside the individual yards and by 1801 the workers of all the royal dockyards at Deptford, Woolwich, Chatham, Portsmouth and Plymouth were linked in one single combination and seeking pay increases. Circumstances eventually enabled the Navy Board to divide the work-force, though it went some way towards granting the combination's demand. But after the departure of the Baltic expedition at the beginning of 1801 there was no serious pressure on the yards and men, especially those deeply involved in the combination, could be discharged. When war broke out again in 1803 however, the work-force had the whip hand.[27]

But organisation was not simply the prerogative of those workers in war industries or industries demonstrably affected by the war. Governmental and parliamentary circles appear to have been growing increasingly aware of workers' combinations at the turn of the century. Although there were no figures for days lost through strike action, there may be a parallel for the historian in that the incidence of strike activity in Britain increased significantly as the two world wars of the twentieth century wore on and the pressures of labour dilution, the demands for men, for money and austerity increased. In the late spring and early summer of 1799 cotton weavers in the North-west were organising on a massive scale to petition for the regulation of their wages. This organisation was probably the spur prompting the government to introduce the Combination Act of 1799, which rendered trials for combinations by workmen more speedy by permitting them to be heard before one or more justices. The act, and the amending legislation of the following year, however, did not put an end to trade union activity. In February 1800, arguing for Parliament to impose a minimum wage, Whitbread replied to those who insisted that labour should find its own level: 'If labourers found they were not sufficiently paid, they combined, and the price of their labour was raised.' Four years later Spencer Perceval noted: 'it is . . . too notorious . . . that combinations exist in almost every trade in the Kingdom'.[28]

The Combination Acts have also to be seen in conjunction with the other repressive legislation of the 1790s. The authorities were suspicious of all forms of organisation among the lower classes, and when the first Combination Act provoked further organisation in the North-west to petition for its repeal, there was concern about emissaries from 'unlawful and *seditious* Societies' becoming involved. The fear of Jacobinism was still very much in evidence. Early in 1799 another Commons Committee of Secrecy presented a report tracing insurrectionary behaviour among some British radicals, their links with the United Irishman and through them, with the French. It would appear from a letter to Pitt from William Wickham, the Permanent Under-Secretary at the Home Office, who had only recently finished a secret service career in Europe, that not all of the evidence available to the government was laid before the committee.[29] An act of Parliament passed in the summer of 1799, which banned the United Societies and the London Corresponding Society by name, was the logical conclusion to the Irish rebellion and the report of the Committee of Secrecy. It seems probable that this assault on industrial and political organisation among the lower classes worsened the internal crises of the last three years of the war against revolutionary France by driving such organisations further underground and heightening their members' sense of injustice.

The harvests of 1799 and 1800 were again deficient. The diversion of lower-class purchasing power to meet the increased cost of bread led to a collapse of the home market for textiles. This was most noticeable in the West Riding wool industry, and master manufactures began to lay men off precisely at a time when the soaring cost of provisions put the textile workers in desperate need of money. Similar problems appear to have hit Lancashire cotton. In May 1801 William Rowbottom noted that 'a deal of families have sold their household goods to exist.' Again the shortages seem to have reduced the poor's resistance to disease. As usual the high cost and shortage of provisions was a cue for widespread popular disorder.[30]

Alarmist minds were quick to spot Jacobin agitators behind the disorders. One gentleman informed Portland that 'this spirit of Monopoly is kept up by a set of designing men who wish to throw all the odium on the Government that they may with more facility bring on a revolution by their destructive principles of Jacobinism'. Sir John Wrottesley, head of the influential Staffordshire family, MP for Lichfield and a county magistrate, suspected that colliers who had plundered farms in the neighbourhood of Bilston and Sedgeley in April 1800 had been 'prevailed upon by others to commit these depredations'. Less than a month later Mr Legge of Aston Hall, near Birmingham, commented that 'there are certainly many very active and ill disposed persons, who instigate the Boys and Women to be riotous, in hopes of promoting general confusion'. In November the Reverend John Hawtrey advised his brother: 'You may depend upon it the Democrats are now turning to account the convetousness of the Farmers.' J. Wescomb Emmerton noted that the poor of Nottinghamshire were 'not at all inclined to believe that there is a deficiency in the last year's crop, and the Jacobins, who are for taking advantage of the times, encourage that notion'.

Some people may have at least half-welcomed the shortages and the disturbances as an additional pressure upon the government to make peace with France. The Reverend Thomas Bancroft, collecting subscriptions for the poor in Bolton in December 1800, found some 'respectable but disaffected persons' refusing to give even one farthing, saying 'that the Poor must speak and act for themselves, that their Distresses would bring it about at last and that this compulsion was necessary to effect a peace'. But no British Jacobin or French agent was ever arrested for stirring up provision disorders. At the East Kent Quarter Sessions in 1801 William Scott, a labourer of Wye, was sentenced to two years in gaol and to find sureties for two years' good behaviour, himself in £50 and two others in £10 each. Scott's offence was 'sedition'; he had incited others to 'insurrection and rebellion' in order to lower the price of provisions. In fact people had not rallied to Scott's call, nor did he employ the overtly political language David Masters had used six years before.[31]

However if there is no evidence proving that French agents or British Jacobins directly encouraged the provision disturbances of 1799 to 1801, language derived from, and alluding to, the French Revolution was employed widely by the authors of threatening letters and notices throughout the shortages. 'Bread or Blood', ran one notice, 'have not Frenchmen shewn you a pattern to fight for liberty.' An anonymous versifier in the neighbourhood of Maldon warned 'Broth Makers and Flower Risers':

> On Swill and Grains you wish the poor to be fed
> And underneath the Gullintine we could wish to see your heads.

While another in Somerset urged 'half Starv'd Britons':

> Then raise yr drooping spirits up
> Nor starve by Pitt's decree
> Fix up the sacred Guillotine
> Proclaim – French liberty!

Some notices called also for an end to the war:

Peace
and Large Bread
or
a King without a head.

A notice posted on a Wiltshire church door combined criticism of the war with criticism of the social structure:

Dear Brother Britons North and South Younite your selves in one Body and stand true Downe with your Luxzuaras Government both Spirital and temperal or you starve with Hunger they have stript you of bread Chees Meate etc etc etc etc etc Nay even your Lives have they taken thousands on their expeditions let the Burbon Family defend their owne cause and let us true Britons loock to our selves let us Banish some to Hannover where they came from Downe with your Constitucion Arect a rebublick . . .

There were criticisms of the social order elsewhere. The officers of the West Bromwich Volunteers were damned as 'big Devils as wear that damnation bloody bloody rag about your damnd paunch bellys'. The privates, however, were consoled as 'poor fellows' in whom the officers had no interest: 'What they want you for is to protect their lives and their liver, and their ill gained property and to dam you to death, and when you have done all you are able you may go to hell for all they care'.[32] The incidence of such language was far greater than during the provision shortages of 1795 and 1796; possibly the short period between these shortages and those of 1799 and 1800, together with the general increase in prices because of inflation and war taxes, and the demands for new military levies, combined to make the second round of shortages weigh more heavily on the lower classes. This, in turn, may have been one cause of the violence of these written threats. Perhaps, too, some of the threats were written by extremists from the now outlawed popular societies, who did hope, and even plan, for an uprising and a republic.

In *The Making of the English Working Class* E. P. Thompson argued for the existence of an underground revolutionary tradition in Britain, beginning during the 1790s and breaking the surface occasionally – the disorders of 1799 to 1801 being one such occasion. Debate has since been joined by historians both in support of, and critical of, Thompson; it has been particularly keen over how serious the insurrectionary element should be taken at the turn of the century.

There were mass nocturnal meetings. During one such, just outside Sheffield in December 1800, it was reported that some of the crowd advocated striking at the 'root of the evil', namely the government. 'Mr. Pitt and all his measures were execrable to Human Nature . . . nothing could prosper in the present hands, he would starve them all to death, . . . nothing would relieve them but a change of ministers exterminating Mr. Pitt and putting Charles Fox in his place.' There were connections between London, the West Riding and Lancashire, and, more seriously, connections between United Irishmen and extremists in Britain. Earl Fitzwilliam, the Lord Lieutenant of Yorkshire, confessed to Portland that 'Loose Conversation, taking its rise from the pressure of the Times, from scarcity and dearness of provisions, and from want of employment, has certainly been holden by the lower Orders of the People, and they talk'd of revolution, as the remedy for famine.' But the local magistrates had no concrete evidence and they did not 'seem to give much importance to any suppos'd Conspiracies, or Combinations, or to be in alarm on account of the Temper of the People'.[33] At the end of 1800 the government was concerned about the area around Birmingham; a stipendary magistrate was sent to investigate and troops were poured into the district. The sudden arrival of the troops surprised the magistrates, though they did not object to having them available in case of disorder; they believed the troops would be more reliable than volunteer corps. Several other volunteer corps were suspected of being unreliable in case of provision disorders, and officers of the Brixham Volunteers were involved in a price riot in Plymouth Dock. But there is no evidence that they would have backed any disorder of any other sort. Colonel Bastard suggested to Addington that if it was intended to recall the Supplementary Militia it should be done rapidly, as 'the sooner they are separated from the mob the better'. He believed that some militia regiments were in 'a bad state', but that they would continue to obey orders. An anonymous group of soldiers in the Bristol area threatened not to interfere in any popular disturbance: 'France has succeeded In her grand undertaking, and got every Article Cheap and Reasonable and we will follow her Example.'[34] The government received reports of troops being involved with the disaffected, the subsequent involvement of Grenadier Guardsmen in Despard's 'conspiracy' suggests that these reports were not wholly without foundation; but there is no example of regular troops or militiamen joining rioters or refusing to act in a police situation during the provision disorders.

Against this background of popular disorder and revolutionary threats Thomas Spence published *Restorer of Society to its Natural State*. Spence, a former schoolmaster from Newcastle, now wrote and sold cheap radical pamphlets in London; he was a member of the LCS and had been imprisoned under the suspension of Habeas Corpus.

Restorer was far more radical than anything Paine had produced in its analysis of, and programme for, society. Spence argued that to rid society of evil, it was necessary to destroy hereditary and personal lordship and the private property on which it depended. He recognised the revolutionary nature of his proposals, but considered that it was only necessary for the people to make their demands and the lords would have to capitulate. He drew this conclusion from recent wartime events.

> Are the Landlords in the parishes more numerous and powerful in proportion to the People than the brave warlike officers in our Mutinous Fleets were to their Crews? Certainly not. Then Landsmen have nothing to fear more than the seamen, and indeed, much less, for after such a mutiny on land, the Masters of the People would never become their Masters again, whereas the poor soldiers had to submit again to their former masters as they well knew to their cost, and as they accomplish their mutinies without bloodshed, so may Landsmen be assured if unanimous, of accomplishing their deliverance in the same harmless manner.

As for the war itself, he asked what he could reply to a French invasion force:

> If they jeeringly ask me what I am fighting for? Must I tell them for my country? For my dear country in which I dare not pluck a nut? Would they not laugh at me? Yes, and do you think I would hear it? No, certainly I would not. I would throw down my musket saying let such as the Duke of Portland, who claims the country fight for it, for I am a stranger and sojourner, and have neither part nor lot amongst them.

Unlike Wakefield, Spence aimed his pamphlets at the lower classes, and understandably the government reacted rapidly. *Restorer* was published on 10 April 1801; Spence was tried on 27 May for seditious libel and sentenced to twelve months in gaol, a £20 fine and he was required to find £500 sureties for five years' good behaviour on his release.[35]

While sedition and popular disorder were, or at least appeared to be, a threat in Britain, the situation in Ireland also remained serious. Lord Cornwallis, who had become viceroy in the aftermath of the rebellion, pursued a conciliatory policy, much to the disgust of many die-hard Irish aristocrats and gentlemen. Cornwallis, Lord Castlereagh the Chief Secretary for Ireland, and Pitt were all convinced that for the better preservation of security Britain and Ireland should be united under the same legislature, and that there should be a removal of the political bars against Catholics; without such measures it seemed that as long as there was conflict with France, Britain was going to have to keep a watchful eye upon Ireland. Much of Pitt's time during 1799 and 1800 was taken up with arranging the union. It was a difficult task. The Dublin Parliament had to be cajoled and bribed into giving up its sovereignty; the promise of Catholic emancipation had to be made in a veiled way, so that it would not alienate Protestants and so that Catholics would support the union. In the spring of 1800 the Irish Parliament was finally persuaded to vote itself into liquidation and Pitt prepared for the more difficult task of emancipation. Paradoxically the very thing which urged Pitt to pursue union and emancipation, the rebellion of 1798, accentuated old fears and bigotry among others. His attempt to hammer out an acceptable proposal in Cabinet meetings – before the ticklish task of approaching George III on the question – was thwarted by Lord Loughborough's underhand memoranda to the King, outlining the ministers' discussions. Though several members of the Cabinet were opposed to the scheme it was George III who took the decisive steps which led to Pitt's resignation. At his levee on 28 January 1801 he informed Dundas that emancipation was 'The most Jacobinical thing I ever heard of! I shall reckon any man my personal enemy who proposes any such measure'. Three days later he asked the Speaker, Henry Addington, if he could form a ministry; and on 14 March Addington replaced Pitt. The proposals for Catholic emancipation were shelved, but they were to be brought out again during the next war when they were to contribute again to the collapse of actual, or potential, administrations.

The new Cabinet was weak in debating power, and Addington generally comes out poorly in comparison with Pitt; yet he took over as Prime Minister at a difficult time and within seven months he had secured the preliminaries of the temporary, but much needed, Peace of Amiens. The war of the Second Coalition had begun well for the Allies; there had been some successes during 1799. Early in 1800 Bonaparte, now installed as one of three consuls by the *coup* of Brumaire, had suggested peace negotiations. The suggestions were rejected. Lord Grenville told the Lords that 'to negociate with the government of France now, would be to incur all the risks of an uncertain truce, without attaining the benefits even of a temporary peace'; he urged war 'until he could tell Europe, that he saw in the temper and conduct of the enemy the return of moderation and good principles'. Fox believed that if the country as a whole accepted this it was 'a complete proof that they will bear anything'. The country did not make demands for negotiations as had happened in 1797, but some gentlemen had their doubts about the wisdom of rejecting Bonaparte's offer.[36] In the event the victorious offensive of the Second Coalition was short-lived. At the end of 1800 it was in ruins. Austria, smashed at Marengo and Hohenlinden, was preparing to sign the Treaty of Lunéville. Russia, under the unstable Tsar Paul, had already withdrawn and, infuriated by the British capture of Malta (Paul was Grand Master of the Knights of St John), was leading Denmark, Sweden and Prussia into a League of Armed Neutrality. The league implied combined naval action against Britain and, more seriously, given the provision shortages, it threatened Britain's corn imports from the Baltic. Conscious of both the dangerous foreign situation and the unrest at home, Addington's first speech as Prime Minister promised to take steps for a restoration of peace, no matter what regime ruled France. Bonaparte responded by instructing Louis Guillaume Otto to return to London; ostensibly Otto had been charged with arranging an exchange of prisoners of war, but he was authorised secretly to take steps towards negotiating a settlement. In the weeks following Addington's appointment as first minister the pressure on Britain was relieved: Paul was assassinated at the end of March, and his successor, Alexander, came to an amicable understanding with Britain; at the beginning of April Nelson administered a death blow to the League of Armed Neutrality with his destruction of the Danish fleet. In the early summer came news of successes by General Abercromby against the remnants of Bonaparte's Army of Egypt. Bonaparte himself sought to maintain the tension in Britain with an elaborate bluff of new invasion preparations. The War Office warned its generals of the danger of a landing, and once again the part-time local authorities were busied with plans and preparations for driving the country. Lord Braybrooke, the Lord Lieutenant of Essex, explained to his brother-in-law how, throughout the summer, correspondence from Whitehall and preparations for an invasion kept him from his family 'every other week at least'.[37] Against this background Otto and Lord Hawkesbury, now Foreign Secretary, secretly discussed peace terms. On 1 October 1801 the Treaty of London was signed, the preliminary to the Treaty of Amiens; the issue being forced finally by Bonaparte before the news of Abercromby's triumph at Alexandria should reach London.

In general the terms of the peace were more favourable to France than to Britain. The old war-hawks of Pitt's Cabinet, Grenville and Windham, disapproved. In some loyalist newspapers and pamphlets doubts were expressed about the durability of the peace. Addington himself, according to Lord Glenbervie, was 'strongly defensive and apologetic' when discussing the peace and emphasised its necessity.

He said if we had refused these terms, and on continuing the war had laid them before the public, and the country had thought they should have been accepted, it would have been impossible to go on. He also intimated that the necessary supplies for two years' war could not have been found, and that the income tax is becoming daily less productive and unpopular. He says the plentiful harvest and crop of barley will enable him to take to the public the additional halfpenny the brewers imposed last year on their beer, and that Jackson of the Excise has drawn out a scheme which shows that this year at least (perhaps permanently if we have no return of scarcity) £1,800,000 may be expected from that additional duty.

But if a few were hostile to the peace, and Addington was apologetic, the majority in the country was overjoyed. 'The world are delighted with the Peace', wrote Braybrooke, 'being heartily tired of the War, and none of the people have as yet thought a moment of the terms.' In Cornwall the Quaker Jenkin wrote disapprovingly of the 'Illuminations, Shouting, Bawling, Huzzaing, Cursing, Drinking' which was occasioned by the end of 'the scourge of War and famine'. At the other end of the country the simple expectations of the majority were expressed by Dr Pearson who, on the day of celebration in Newcastle-upon-Tyne, exposed a real skeleton in one window with the motto 'the effects of war', and in another a large loaf and a large cheese – 'the benefits of peace'. In Durham, Wyvill's friend John Fenwick, commander of a volunteer company, displayed an illuminated Britannia with a cap of liberty and 'No Income Tax'. Across the Pennines, besides similar delight in the North-west, William Rowbottom recorded 'one Blessing observable' at Oldham fair: 'their [sic] was no Recruiting Sergeant nor air renting Militiaria Drum'.[38]

5. The Amiens Interlude

The cessation of hostilities was a bitter-sweet occasion for many. Thousands had seen a husband, father, brother or son set off for war and could only guess at his fate. When John Stevenson returned in an exchange of prisoners of war in 1796 both his regiment and his mother were greatly surprised, believing that he had been killed in the Low Countries two years before; it was not until 1797 that the Duke of York ordered commanding officers to report the dead by name, and even then there was no way of officially informing a family of a death. The new life-style of the armed forces might disrupt family life in other ways. Possibly the relatively idle life of militia regiments stationed at home disinclined some men to work. Martha King of Fulbourn protested to Lord Hardwicke that, rather than return to her when on leave, her husband, in the Cambridgeshire Militia, preferred to pursue 'base ways' with a married woman in Norwich. But in general peace was joyous news and probably few expected that it would be of such short duration. Many families were reunited; merchants and manufacturers looked forward to the reopening of many European markets; everyone believed that taxes and poor rates could be cut. The pressure of war had led to some improvements in individual local government administrations; from the summer of 1797 the Worcestershire bench imposed a much tighter control over the county treasurer; the county treasurer of Durham was removed after an enquiry into his shambolic accounts in 1800. The new controls and the new personnel remained, but with no more militia doles and no more preparations for invasion local government could sink back into its more comfortable, pre-war pattern of administration.[1]

Addington's government did what was expected of it, and in some instances more. Although the income tax had received large majorities in Parliament it was generally unpopular. When Addington introduced his first budget in 1802, five days after the signing of the peace treaty, the tax was repealed on the grounds that it 'should not be left to rest on the shoulders of the public in time of peace, because it should be reserved for the more important occasions, which, he trusted, would not soon recur'. There were still enormous war-time expenses to pay off and to do this Addington raised a massive loan, together with new permanent taxes on malt and beer, assessed taxes, imports and exports which were to defray the interest on the loan. The budget was generally popular and Addington, far more capable in financial matters than Pitt, followed it up with a series of improvements to the machinery of the Exchequer which benefited both the public and the Treasury.[2]

The armed forces were drastically reduced. The militia regiments were stood down and the military establishment of Britain and Ireland was more than halved from 288,786 men in 1801 to 132,308 the following year. This reduction left an army far larger than many people had expected, but Addington remained wary of the First Consul. No such concerns restrained Earl St Vincent at the Admiralty. Two months after the signing of the treaty the navy had been cut from 130,000 to 70,000 men, and there were plans to reduce it to a mere 30,000; the number of battleships in commission was cut from over one hundred to less than forty. St Vincent's reductions were popular with taxpayers, who were delighted to see £2 million sliced off naval expenditure in two years; but the economies were false and meant only greater expenditure when war was resumed. In addition to the cuts the old admiral was convinced that the administration of the navy was riddled with abuses and financial extravagance and mismanagement. In August and September 1802 a series of official visitations unearthed a number of malpractices in the royal dockyards. In December, in spite of the reluctance of his Cabinet colleagues, St Vincent insisted on the creation of a commission, reporting only to Parliament and able to call for documents and to examine witnesses under oath, which was to enquire into the affairs of the Navy Board. The commission began presenting its reports in the summer of 1803. They did reveal abuses; they also provoked acrimonious debate at a time of national emergency.

The fear of Jacobinism was still present; indeed during the general election held in the summer of 1802 many gentlemen believed that Jacobinism was reviving. Westcomb Emmerton was alarmed by election parades in Nottingham.

Besides the violent outrages of the Jacobins during the Election; when they chaired their member, he was preceded by the Tri-coloured Flag, and four and twenty Vestals (modern ones) cloathed in white, and singing 'Millions be free' and other revolutionary songs – his friends having green Ribbons and Laurel wreaths in their hats – and some, it is said, with Bandeaws [sic] bearing this inscription 'No Church. No King'.

William Windham lost his seat to 'Jacobins' in Norwich. John Bowles, especially alarmed by the lively contest in Middlesex which was won by the radical young Sir Francis Burdett, produced a pamphlet with the self-explanatory title of *Thoughts on the late General Election, as demonstrative of the progress of Jacobinism*. But the very few victories of constitutional radicals presented no threat to Addington, nor to the existing parliamentary system. A more serious threat existed in the secret conspiracies of British Jacobin extremists and United Irishmen. Peace, and a reasonable harvest, probably did much to ease the situation which was developing during the last year of the war, but in November 1802 Colonel E. M. Despard was arrested in London on a charge of high treason. Despard's 'conspiracy' appears to have been one link in a revolutionary plot directed from Ireland and depending on French assistance. There were links elsewhere in England, but the main thrust of insurrection was planned for Ireland. This too went off at half cock with Emmet's disastrous rising in Dublin the following year. Despard and six associates were executed, as were Emmet and his fellow rebels; William Lee and William Ronkesley, two Sheffield men, were sentenced to seven years' transportation for administering secret oaths in the West Riding – probably just one link in the English side of the conspiracy. But Addington did not use the discovery of the plots as an excuse for unleashing an anti-Jacobin witch-hunt. He was no liberal, but both Whig and radical opponents admitted that under his governmet the wounds left by Pitt's repressive policies were soothed. Men imprisoned under the suspension of the Habeas Corpus Act were released and the suspension was not renewed.[3]

Peace had been welcomed as promising prosperity and easing the tax burden, but peace also brought economic disorder and imposed burdens of another sort. Within a month of the signing of the treaty of London *The Times* was reporting lay-offs in the naval dockyards: 500 labourers from the Deptford yard, and 300 shipwrights; in addition 325 men were being paid off at Woolwich Warren, and 150 coopers and packers were being discharged from the Victualling Office Yard at Deptford. The newspaper noted that the men discharged from the dockyards would receive 'a certain sum, not yet ascertained . . . to subsist them to their respective places of residence'; furthermore they were to be given first preference in employment on any future occasion. But there was no guarantee of work when men reached their homes and the promise of possible future employment was of no help to the present. Moreover an increase in the number of men available for work in private yards meant that shipbuilders could start cutting wages in what was now a plentiful labour market. In December 1801 shipwrights in South Shields struck over a reduction in wages and trouble continued along the Thames for much of the peace interlude.[4]

Some soldiers and sailors returned to find their local industries flourishing. In the textile districts of the North-west men appear to have been reabsorbed in spite of the overall increase in handloom weavers. Samuel Bamford recalled a serving soldier who, during an extended leave in 1802, earned sufficient from handloom weaving to purchase his discharge. Rowbottom noted reasonable prices and good wages throughout 1802. Indeed in August 'trade was never in a more flourishing state in the memory of the oldest person living'. But other demobilised servicemen found no such prosperity. Disorders became especially serious in the west of England clothing districts, where factories were attacked and new machinery destroyed. James Read, the chief magistrate of Bow Street, who was sent to investigate the trouble, reported:

> The disbanding of the army and navy has occasioned an increase of workmen before the manufacturers were ready for them, which is, I believe, the present temporary grievance, although almost every labouring manufacturer, but particularly the shearmen, are impressed with an opinion that the use of machinery is the only cause of their being out of employ.

At least one master noted former soldiers stiffening the union organisation; it was 'not an assembly of a common Mob, but a body of armed, regulated, and systematical people composed principally of Militia Men and Marines'. Benjamin Hobhouse, the MP for Hinden, received a letter from 'a Soldier Returned to his Wife and weeping Orphans', who protested: 'Some of us may perhaps more or less [have] served in His Majesty's Service some Six, Eight or ten years in Defence of him and his Country. Now the Contending Nations are at Peace with each other we are send [sic] home to starve.' The West Country shearmen had close connection with the West Riding croppers (who followed the same trade under the different name). Possibly some former soldiers and sailors stiffened the less violent, but powerful and effective combination which emerged in the Leeds area.[5]

It was neither Jacobinism nor industrial disorder which produced the most serious problems for Addington's government, but the highly charged diplomatic situation. Thomas Hardy wrote admiringly to the First Consul recording the LCS's attachment to France in 1792 and declaring that now 'peace reigns on earth and this is the work of Frenchmen'. A stream of radicals and Foxite Whigs crossed the Channel for a glance at the new France and its youthful leader; but there were others in Britain who continued to regard the Republic with hostility. Robert Wilmot, the rector of Morley in east Derbyshire, confided in his parish register that he feared the peace would be only temporary for he could not imagine Bonaparte would 'rest quiet when he has once obtained a reduction of our fleets and armies and [had] a little time to recruit his own, no doubt he will then attack us again for so long as he beholds a rival in Britain he never will be satisfied'. John Bowles gave his similar fears a more public airing: France was now territorially much larger, she was 'a Revolutionary Power, a Military Despotism' and as such her interest and ambition might lead her to try to emulate Rome. Bowles believed that there could be no peace until the Bourbons were restored.[6] Sections of the British press were caustic and malicious about the new government of France, about Bonaparte and his family, though Addington's government went as far as it dare in urging moderation. A French *émigré* journalist, Jean Peltier, was prosecuted for libelling the First Consul; the prosecution was conducted by Spencer Perceval, the Attorney General. But the freedom of the press was a proud boast of the freeborn Englishman, and when Addington had the editor of the *True Briton* warned about one such 'abominable paragraph', John Heriot replied, agreeing that he should not have allowed the paragraph to be published, but trusting that Addington was not intending to attempt to threaten any man into submission. It fell to Lord Whitworth, the ambassador in Paris, to explain to a furious Bonaparte and his calculating Foreign Minister, Talleyrand, that the British government, unlike the French, had no control over its press, and had no intention of imposing such control.[7]

The press war was only one element in the developing hostility between the two countries. Bonaparte continued to enlarge his battle fleet. Lord Braybrooke suggested that peace would last only 'until the French navy is superior to our own, which *may* happen, as they are launching every day in all their ports'.[8] There was concern about French colonial expansion: part of South Australia was claimed as *Terre Napoléon* in April 1802; General Leclerc sailed to resubjugate Haiti; early in 1803 General Victor prepared an expedition for the Mississippi and General Decaen departed for India. Most serious, in British eyes, was Colonel Sebastiani's much publicised mission to the eastern Mediterranean which implied a renewed French military presence there. The economic prosperity which many British merchants and manufacturers had hoped would emerge from the peace was hampered by Bonaparte's protectionist policies; not only were the ports of France and Belgium (now incorporated into *la grande nation*) closed to British merchandise, but also those of Holland and Italy. Bonaparte criticised

Britain's tardy evacuation of Egypt and her failure to evacuate Malta, dismissing British protests about the French presence in Holland and Piedmont and the occupation of Switzerland. Juridicially his position was the stronger, as his diplomacy had manoeuvred Britain into accepting a treaty which required two British evacuations while making no mention of the European territories where the First Consul was strengthening his position. But if Bonaparte was girding himself for a second conflict with Britain he was not yet ready when in April 1803 Whitworth presented his government's ultimatum. Bonaparte's subsequent efforts to patch up the quarrel, without conceding to British demands, were met with a stubborn silence which he had not expected from Addington's Cabinet. On 18 May 1803 Britain formally declared war.

6. Wooden Walls and Volunteers: 1803–5

I The Sinews of War

The years 1803 to 1805 saw the greatest danger of invasion by the French. France could count on the support of her satellites from the outset, and in December 1804 Spain, too, joined the conflict on her side. Britain was alone, without allies for most of the period; her weather-beaten warships blockaded their enemy counterparts, while thousands of soliders – regulars, militiamen and volunteers – stood by awaiting a landing should the 'wooden walls' of Britain be breached or bypassed. The period saw Pitt restored as Prime Minister in May 1804 – 'the one great opponent whom the French Revolution and Napoleon encountered'[1] – and Bonaparte crowned as the Emperor of the French in December 1804. It concluded with a reassertion of British naval power at Trafalgar, and of Napoleonic land superiority at Ulm and Austerlitz.

Britain had begun mobilising before the declaration of war. In March the militia was embodied; at the end of the month circulars were issued inviting volunteers to come forward. Regulating officers reopened rendezvous houses in the seaports in April. Addington saw the possibility of a long war; in a private memorandum on finance he even predicted that it might last twelve years. His intention was to fight a defensive war. Offensive operations were permitted in the West Indies, where the remnants of Leclerc's army were made prisoner and enemy territories seized; but principally the plan was to remain inactive, trying Bonaparte's patience until he attempted an invasion. After defeating such an attempt, Addington believed, it might be worth re-creating a European coalition against France.[2]

St Vincent's manpower reductions made naval recruitment a priority. As before, bounties were offered for volunteers and magistrates handed over some petty felons and vagrants as well as being instructed to seize 'straggling seamen'. But volunteers and men sent by the magistrates were insufficient; the naval estimates of June 1803 provided for 77,600 men. Some press-gangs became over-zealous in their search. A serious riot in Chester prompted the city's magistrates to draw up a memorandum protesting that the local gang had broken down doors and pressed tradesmen, freemen, and apprentices who had never been seamen; even farmers' servants coming to market had been seized. There was rioting elsewhere and the number of reports to the Home Office suggest that the trouble was more prevalent than at the beginning of the revolutionary War. Women, many of whom may have spent most of the previous ten years without their seaman husbands, were reported as playing a prominent part in disorders in Carmarthen. When a gang from HMS *Squirrel* seized some Irishmen near Barking in Essex they brought the full weight of the Irish community down upon themselves, and lost their victims; and the cohesion and comradeship which developed among the volunteer corps could also be turned against the press-gang, as happened in Chester. Tyneside keelmen went on strike, bringing the coal trade to a standstill, when fifty-three of their number were pressed; negotiations between local coal-owners, supported by local MPs, and the Admiralty resulted in the keelmen agreeing to a quota of men being supplied for the navy, proportional to the numbers employed on the Tyne. This appears to have been what the Admiralty had hoped for in the first place. A few similar agreements were made elsewhere. South Shields and Portland Bill became refuges for seamen, with organised systems of lookouts which made it difficult for the impress service to function in them.[3] Elsewhere seamen went into hiding and adopted landsmen's trades. Enough sailors were reported working in Kingswood colliery, just outside Bristol, to man a 'seventy-four'; others were apparently working in quarries near Bath. The 'deserters' reported to be hiding in the Merthyr Tydfil ironworks in June 1803 were also probably seamen. John Nicol avoided the press in a similar fashion. He had been discharged after the Treaty of Amiens, had married and set himself up as a cooper in Edinburgh. When war broke out again he recalled: 'My wife was like a distracted woman, and gave me no rest until I sold off my stock in trade and the greater part of my furniture, and retired into the country. Even until I got this accomplished I dared not to sleep in my own house, as I had more than one call from the gang.' It was only possible to be a cooper in a large seaport or town, so Nicol went to work in the lime-quarries near Cranston. He slept at Dalkeith or Musselburgh and became nervous whenever a stranger visited the quarry. Those of his workmates who were no friends to the government taunted him.

One would ask what I thought of British freedom; another if I could defend a government which did such things? I was at no loss for my answer. I told them 'Necessity had no law'. Could the government make perfect seamen as easily as they could soldiers, there would be no such thing as the pressing of seamen, and that I was happy to be of more value than them all put together, for they would not impress any of them, they were of so little value compared to me.[4]

Recruiting for the regular army was left, more or less, to look after itself. Between June and December 1803, 360 regular recruiting parties raised less than ten men each; they could only offer bounties of £7 12s. 6d., while some substitutes for the auxiliary forces were getting six times that amount. The government's principal concerns were the auxiliary forces for home defence, as is evidenced by the flood of legislation introduced in the summer of 1803. On 11 June one act was passed to speed up the completion of the militia (43 Geo. III c. 50), and another (43 Geo. III c. 55) which required a full report from the counties of all able-bodied men between the ages of fifteen and sixty distinguishing those in the volunteers, those willing to serve, to drive waggons or act as guides, together with details of waggons, boats, horses, cattle, food and forage. Less than a fortnight later, militia regiments were authorised to discharge any seafaring men for the navy, filling the gaps with volunteers raised by beat of drum, and a ten guineas bounty from the navy (43 Geo. III c. 62). An act passed in the beginning of July (43 Geo. III c. 71) provided for the augmentation of officers for the Supplementary Militia which had been enrolling since May. On 27 July the Levy en Masse Act (43 Geo. III c. 96) was passed requiring the Lords Lieutenant and their deputies to draw up lists of all men between the ages of seventeen and fifty-five excluding clergymen, Quakers, schoolmasters and the infirm. The men were to be divided into four classes: unmarried men under thirty with no living child under ten years; unmarried men between thirty and fifty, with no living child under ten; married men between seventeen and thirty, with not more than two living children under ten; and all the remainder. Provision was then made for training them, arming them and, in case of invasion, calling them out and sending them anywhere in the British Isles. In the event the enormous number of volunteer corps rendered this act superfluous and the Levy en Masse was never raised for training. Besides these auxiliaries, the government also sought to raise the Army of Reserve, 50,000 men raised by ballot – 34,000 from England and Wales, 6000 from Scotland and 10,000 from Ireland. The men were to serve in the British Isles only; principals serving for five years and substitutes for five years or until six months after a final peace. They could be drafted into the second battalions of regular regiments stationed in Britain, and from these they could enlist into front line battalions. About 19,500 men from the Army of Reserve (about two-thirds of those eventually assembled into it) did transfer for general service in this way.[5]

The ballots for the militia, the Supplementary Militia and the Army of Reserve caused hardship and resentment. If a man had found a substitute, or paid a fine, after being balloted for either militia, he was still liable to the Army of Reserve ballot. As the Duke of Richmond commented, for ordinary men 'a ballot is a ballot . . . and when they have bought exemption from one they cannot understand how they are liable to another'. The price of substitutes soared as individuals, insurance societies and local authorities sought their services. Some men were lucky. A North Riding gentleman enquired of his friend, Francis Cholmeley: 'Have you escaped all the different drawings for Militia, Supplementary, Army of Reserve etc? I was drawn for the Supplementary but came off very well, being the only one drawn out of a Club of near 40 who had agreed to support one another.' Cholmeley's mother however, at Brandsby, ten miles north of York, recorded that the ballots fell 'terribly hard' on the poor, 'nor do they submit with a perfect good grace even in these quiet parts'. The local gentry subscribed for the poor's substitutes, 'and . . . self interest must now prompt this generosity for after all the poorest class would certainly suffer the least and might eventually benefit the most by a revolution'. But elsewhere the poor could not always rely on the self-interest or paternalism of the gentry. A shepherd of Bute sold everything he had, raising £26 to provide a substitute for the Army of Reserve; an administrative error meant that his sacrifice was unnecessary, but in spite of protests on his behalf by the local authorities, he received no recompense. Nor was there any recompense if a substitute let down a balloted man. John Gough, a grocer of Princes Risborough in Buckinghamshire, asked Butler Stevens, a labourer of Bledlow who had served with the Bucks Militia in Ireland, to serve in his place in the Army of Reserve. Gough agreed to pay a bounty of twenty-two guineas, giving Stevens five shillings in advance and three shillingsworth of ribbons, as well as treating him to drinks in the pub where he had met him. But when it came to enrolment, Stevens refused to go to Aylesbury to be sworn in.[6]

One way to avoid the ballots was to join a volunteer corps; the government's decision to exempt these corps from the ballots contributed to the enormous number of offers of service. William Upcott, the antiquary and autograph collector, was working for a London bookseller in 1803 and confessed in his diary to being 'in a continual state of ferment and trouble' over the prospect of being ballotted. Eventually a wealthy friend paid for him to enrol in the St James Loyal Volunteers. For three weeks he rose at 6 a.m. to learn his drill; some enjoyed this, together with the name of volunteer, but for Upcott "twas more from necessity than inclination, more with a view to perfect myself, the sooner to receive the certificate from the adjutant declaring me able to join the rest of the corps, and to render regular attendance unnecessary'. In the *Political Register* William Cobbett savaged the volunteers, maintaining that many had enlisted, if not to avoid ballots, then to avoid 'low company'. But not all volunteers were from the better off groups in society and had to pay for admission like Upcott; many were day-labourers volunteering, possibly to avoid the ballots, but also out of patriotism. As in the earlier war most of the volunteers were infantry; the wealthier country gentlemen made up the yeomanry cavalry regiments. There were also sea fencibles, and a corps was organised by the magistrates of the Thames Police Office, selected from the best men who volunteered among the work-force on the river.[7]

The initial organisation and administration of the volunteers was chaotic. Some had agreed to serve under a set of regulations laid down in June, others under different regulations laid down in August. Henry Dundas, now elevated to the peerage as Lord Melville, believed that the government should accept all offers of service rather than disappoint volunteers and a ruling was made to this effect in August. Nevertheless some offers were rejected. In December 1803 the men of Liskeard in Cornwall were continuing to parade and drill even though their offer of a corps had been rejected. The Lord Lieutenant was directed to advise them that they were breaking the law and would be prosecuted if they continued. Officers often failed to get their commissions, except after a long delay; Fortescue has blamed the casualness of government clerks for this, but these clerks were few in number, had the usual business of their office to conduct, and were never prepared for the flood of volunteer offers. But perhaps most serious was the lack of weapons for the volunteers. At the beginning of the war the ordnance had a reserve stock of 150,000 muskets and bayonets. Recruits for the regulars and deficiencies in the regulars and militia naturally had first call on these. A proposal to hand out twenty-five muskets for training among each 1000 volunteers was never acted upon, and the weapons began to be distributed haphazardly, sometimes to individual corps, sometimes to the Lords Lieutenant. The lack of muskets was temporarily made up with pikes. Lord Mulgrave, preparing the defences of the East Riding, was disgusted; armed in such a way against French veterans, he stated, his men would be massacred. He was subsequently sent ammunition for fowling pieces, though not a man under his command was armed with such a weapon.[8] By the end of 1803 there were some 450,000 volunteers in Great Britain and Ireland; it is problematic how formidable an opposition they would have presented to the French at this stage, but the inspecting field officers appointed by the Duke of York were beginning to hammer them into shape and had they faced an invasion in 1804 or 1805 some corps at least would have performed creditably.

When Pitt replaced Addington in May 1804 his government sorted out some of the remaining problems in the volunteer army with the Volunteer Consolidation Act (44 Geo. III c. 54). He enlarged the regular army by persuading some 9000 men to transfer from the militia. He then set about trying to raise an additional regular force for home defence by a combination of the quota system of 1795–6 and the Army of Reserve Act of 1803. The Permanent Additional Force Acts (44 Geo. III c. 56 (England and Wales), c. 66 (Scotland) and c. 74 (Ireland)) required each county to raise quotas in their parishes. The men were to be levied by offering bounties, but the parishes were forbidden to accept men from more than twenty miles away in their own county and more than ten miles away in a neighbouring county. The parishes were to pay a fine of £20 into a national recruiting fund for each man they were deficient. The men's service was limited to the British Isles and to a period of five years or till six months after the end of the war; they were to be used to build up second battalions from which, it was hoped, they would volunteer for general service. The acts were a miserable failure. Pitt proposed to raise 20,000 men in under two months, it took twenty-three months to raise 13,000. The majority of parish officers, it seems, would not try to enforce it, or even to understand the tasks set them.[9] Probably when the Permanent Additional Force Act was passed, many of the part-time officials of local government had had enough of the burdens which the government had placed upon them and were not prepared to go to the trouble of interpreting and acting upon a new act for a new kind of recruit.

Every tier of local government felt the pressure of the wartime emergency on the resumption of the conflict with France. The Lords Lieutenant had to oversee the organisation of auxiliary forces and the arrangements for driving the country in case of invasion. In August 1803 the Duke of Marlborough felt himself 'wholly unequal' to the task owing to 'a nervous indisposition', from which he had been suffering for some time. He passed on his duties temporarily to the Earl of Macclesfield. Not every weak or inefficient Lord Lieutenant yielded his authority, but several stood out for their determination to take tough, uncompromis-

PLATE 1 'Flannel Coats of Mail against the cold', Isaac Cruikshank.

PLATE 2 'A General Fast, in Consequence of the War', Isaac Cruikshank.

PLATE 3 'Kidnaping, or a disgrace to Old England', Isaac Cruikshank.

PLATE 4 'The State Waggoner and John Bull', James Gillray.

PLATE 5 'The Friend of the People and his Petty-New-Tax-Gatherer', James Gillray.

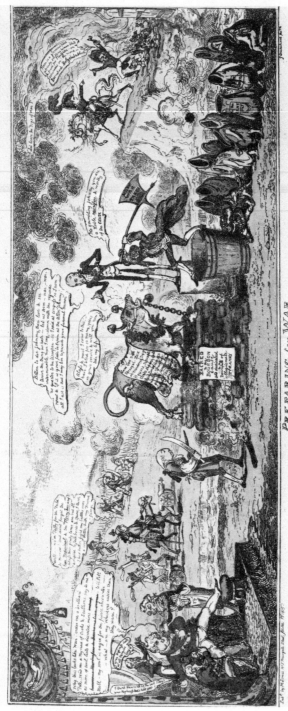

PLATE 6 'Preparing for War', George Cruikshank.

II —MARTELLO TOWERS, EASTBOURNE BAY.

PLATE 7 An early 19th Century engraving of Martello towers at Eastbourne. These towers, (christened 'Bull-dogs' by the French) were among seventy-nine on the coasts of Kent and Sussex after the ruptured Peace of Amiens; twenty-nine others, of an improved design, were built north of the Thames in 1810–12. Each tower, built by local contractors (many of whom made substantial profits), required some 700,000 bricks. They were thirty-four feet high, and were designed to withstand heavy bombardment.

Office for receiving Certificates of Payments of the Duties on Dividends, Annuities, &c.

No.

DELIVERED into this Office the 6th ___ Day of December 1803 ___ a Bank Certificate of the Payment of the Sum of £11..0..0 ___ into the Bank of England, under the Provifions of an Act paffed in the 43d Year of His prefent Majefty's Reign, for granting a Contribution on the Profits arifing from Property, Profeffions, &c. which Certificate will difcharge the Affeffment upon the Dividends due on the undermentioned Stock, viz.

Name in which the Stock ftands in the Books of the Bank.	Stock of Annuities.	Amount.	
Sir John Bridger	Long Annuities	200 —	100 —
	Short Ditto	100 —	50 —
Combe Place	4 ℔ Cent Annuit	400 —	8 —
Suffex	5 ℔ Cent 1797	2500 —	62..10
			220..10

G. Beach Infpector.

T. Burton, Little Queen Street, Printer to the Tax-Office.

R. Bridger Efq Bank

PLATE 8a   An Income Tax Receipt belonging to Sir John Bridger, December 1803.

STAMP OFFICE CERTIFICATE.

Hair Powder Annual Duty, 1796.

Mr. Willm. Dixon

Nº 12 —

1796.

2d April

of Holton-Le-Moor

Lincolnshire

House-keeper

This Certificate will expire on the fifth Day of April 1797.

Office Castor

For the Year 1796

North Lincolnshire District.

Geo. Capes for John Ansell Efqr.

PLATE 8b   A Licence for wearing hair powder for William Dixon, 1796.

ing measures. In July 1803 Lord Fortescue, the Lord Lieutenant of Devon, who required his wife to act as his clerk, disbanded a battalion of inefficient volunteers and balloted them all for the Army of Reserve; as a result an efficient corps of volunteers was soon established in Devon. Lord Braybrooke's determination and energy in Essex were apparent. In December 1803 he commented on 'the labours of my vocation' having kept him very busy since June. The deputy lieutenants also varied in efficiency, but the best expended a considerable amount of time, energy and expense (they often had to pay the postage on letters delivered to them on affairs of state) on their labours. Before becoming the Inspecting Field Officer of the Home District, Sir Nathaniel Dukinfield was Lord Radnor's deputy in the eastern division of Berkshire. Dukinfield took his duties seriously; in October 1803 he wrote no less than eighteen letters of lieutenancy business to Radnor alone. Charles Mostyn declined to serve as a lieutenant-colonel of the volunteers – 'I was by no means equal to the drudgery of [it], supposing even that I had any military knowledge' – but he agreed to serve as a deputy lieutenant for Oxfordshire. In March 1804 he protested that he was almost the only active deputy in his district: 'The rest being either absent or prefer to throw the fagg of it upon me. The Militia and Army of Reserve business give employ for at least one whole day weekly. . . .' He was sickened by some of the abuse of authority and extortion which he had seen. As in the revolutionary war the various militia, volunteer and defence acts gave opportunities to the petty tyrant and the corrupt official at all levels of local administration. It fell to the magistrates at quarter sessions to oversee much of the business of the militia, in particular the treasurers' accounts of payments to militia families. They had to swear in recruits and enforce the Alien Act which, in the situation of 1803 to 1805, once again appeared essential. At the bottom of the administration of local government came the parish officials to whom fell the tasks of collecting the lists for ballots and the different defence acts. These were rarely popular or easy, and they could run into complications undreamt of at Westminster. The lists of men required by the Levy en Masse Act were being collected in August, and at harvest time in some areas men left their parish of settlement for the good wages paid by grain farmers at that time of year. John Carrington ran a small farm in Bramfield in Hertfordshire; he was one of the thousands of parish officials who felt the burden of war through his new tasks. In July 1803 he recorded in his diary: 'The Armey of Reserve Raised this Month besides the old Militia and supplementary Do., the Devell to pay'. Faced with the problem of making lists of men aged between fifteen and sixty for the June defence act and between seventeen and fifty-five for the July Levy en Masse Act, he wrote: 'So Nothing but Soldiering three times a week'.[10]

As during the revolutionary war the government did not only demand men, it also required more money to finance the conflict. During the debate reviewing the diplomatic events which had preceded the war Fox suggested that the income tax would soon return, and at a much higher rate: 'let no man now look to his holding a pound without giving possibly fifteen shillings of it to government towards the support of the war'. In mid-June Addington introduced a war budget which did revive the tax, now generally described as the property tax, but his proposals were not merely a repetition of Pitt's tax, nor were they as severe as Fox had suggested. Incomes under £60 a year were exempt, and there was a sliding scale ranging from threepence in the pound up to the full rate of one shilling, only half of that demanded by Pitt, on incomes of £150 or more. People were no longer required to make a general return of their income, a requirement which had caused so much offence to those who objected to having to make a full disclosure of their fortunes. Instead there were to be five schedules under which the tax was declared and collected: Schedule A charged tax on the amount of land and buildings; Schedule B taxed the produce of the land; Schedule C taxed the interest received by the holders of government funds; Schedule D taxed the profits derived from trade, commerce, professional earnings and salaries; and Schedule E taxed the incomes from offices, annuities, pensions and stipends. A second major innovation provided for the deduction of tax at source for interest, dividends, rent, income from government funds and the emoluments of government employees. As was to be expected the tax met opposition like its predecessor, and among the critics was Pitt himself, who opposed both the major innovations. However Addington got the necessary majorities and his new system proved to be far more successful than its predecessor. He estimated that it should raise £4.5 million in its first year; in fact it raised £4.76 million. In his budget for 1804 Addington estimated £4.8 million from the tax, and collected £4.9 million. Pitt was convinced by the success, and in his budget for 1805 he stuck to the new system with a few minor changes in administration and an increase in the rate to 1s. 3d. in the pound. One historian has described the income tax simply as 'the tax that beat Napoleon', noting that while Pitt made the major breakthrough with a tax on incomes rather than expenditure, Addington's two principal innovations were almost as important. The system which developed, especially after 1803, was a significant extension of the administrative powers of the British government. In his monograph on income tax during the Napoleonic wars Arthur Hope-Jones observed:

'For the first time in England the servant of the Crown, not in the person of the county magistrate, but as the paid official of a centralised administrative department, was coming into the everyday life and activity of a majority of the people'. Furthermore the tax required, and secured, a new departure in Civil Service organisation: a staff of experts under strict control.[11]

Reforms in the Treasury did not stop with the section which dealt with the income tax. The old structure, all but overwhelmed by the increase of business between 1793 and 1801, was, in August 1805, subjected to major, if belated, reorganisation. This led to a new professionalism in the Treasury. Six distinct administrative divisions were created, in addition to the revenue department, whose principal concern was tax collection. At the top of the administrative hierarchy was a new permanent Civil Service post, that of under-secretary and law clerk; significantly the man holding the post was forbidden to seek election to Parliament; he was to be outside politics. George Harrison, the highly capable man appointed to the post, continued to hold it after Pitt's death, during the Talents' ministry and beyond. Chief clerks lost responsibility for the overall supervision of the Treasury office under the reorganisation, but they became men with a specialist knowledge of their own administrative division; highly qualified politicians and academics, like the mathematicians called in by Perceval in 1808, had to rely on the guidance of these experts through the increasingly complex financial situation of the country. Even junior clerks could now be entrusted with responsible work; they had opportunities for advancement, but inefficient and dishonest men could now do serious harm in these posts and the introduction of a three-month probationary period for all Treasury officials was Perceval's logical extension to Pitt's 1805 reform.[12]

The Ordnance also began to extend its operations. The increased demand for weapons was good news for the private arms manufacturers, but the Ordnance was determined to improve upon the practice of the earlier war. In 1804 it established an office in Birmingham to increase supplies of muskets and to test them before they were dispatched. The department also went in for the manufacture of arms on its own account with the setting up of an assembly plant at the Tower of London, again in 1804, where parts purchased in Birmingham were put together. Four years later a factory was established at Lewisham where the process of musket manufacture could be overseen from beginning to end. The artisans employed at the Tower and at Lewisham were paid the piece-work rates prevailing at Birmingham.[13]

The Ordnance's insistence on carefully vetting weapons before they left Birmingham was probably unpopular with the local gunsmiths, but they did not have the economic power of the 'Timber Trust', the contractors who had a virtual monopoly of the supply of timber to the navy. Among St Vincent's measures for improving the administration of the navy and cutting costs was the introduction of timber masters into the dockyards whose job it was to examine and look after all the wood stocks. The masters infuriated the contractors in the trust who protested that their oak was now being rejected for trivial defects and that this would wipe out their profits. They cut off supplies. St Vincent was unable to break their monopoly; his efforts to find timber elsewhere met with little success; even had the measure been contemplated, Parliament would never have agreed to a general requisition of oak which denied the market price to its owners. At the beginning of 1804 the shortage of timber was acute. The situation eased when with Pitt's return to the premiership St Vincent was replaced by Lord Melville, who rendered the timber masters innocuous and agreed to the trust's demands for higher prices. One year later, with the revelations by the Comission of Naval Enquiry of Melville's very lax administration of naval finances during the previous war, he was replaced by the aged but extremely capable Middleton. The latter made every effort to ensure that the fleets blockading French ports were up to strength, nevertheless Nelson's ships at Trafalgar were leaking, rotting, wracking out of shape and many of their repairs had been made with unseasoned wood or pine.[14]

Nelson's fleet may have been in poor shape, yet the battleship remained the most technologically advanced weapon of war during the period, and its production and maintenance kept the dockyards as much in the forefront of the industrialisation process as were the civilian textile mills. Especially significant was the introduction of Marc Brunel's block making machinery into Portsmouth Dockyard in 1803. These forty steam-powered machines provide the first instance of machine tools being employed for mass production. They were the first machine tools of a substantial size to be built entirely of metal, and they set the standard for subsequent machine-tool practice. The average battleship required about 1000 pulley blocks for its rigging; the Navy estimated its total requirement at 100,000 blocks a year. By 1808 the Portsmouth machinery had already recovered its capital outlay, and it was producing 130,000 blocks annually. But the machines had a detrimental effect on the livelihood of the civilian contractors and craftsmen who had traditionally provided for the Navy's needs; 10 men could now do the work of 110 skilled block makers.[15]

Elsewhere there was little change in the equipping and provisioning of the armed forces, though there was one interesting new departure. In

1804 the beginnings of the modern assembly line were in operation in the navy's Victualling Office at Deptford to meet the demand for ship's biscuit. The work was divided into phases, and the hand operations of the workers were timed to one another. A contemporary described the 'curious and interesting' process:

> The dough, which consists of flour and water only, is worked by a large machine. . . . It is handed over to a second workman, who slices them [the biscuits] with a large knife for the bakers, of whom there are five. The first, or the *moulder*, forms the biscuit two at a time, the second, or *marker*, stamps and throws them to the *splitter*, who separates the two pieces and puts them under the hand of the *chucker*, the man who supplies the oven, whose work of throwing the bread on the peel must be so exact, that *he cannot look off for a moment*. The fifth, or the *depositor*, receives the biscuits on the peel and arranges them in the oven. The business is to deposit in the oven *seventy biscuits in a minute* and *this is accomplished with the regularity of a clock*, the clacking of the peel, operating like the motion of the pendulum.

Twelve ovens furnished biscuit for 2040 men each day.[16] Wool merchants, master tailors and shoemakers continued to make arrangements with regimental colonels or their agents, and they all continued to make profits though sometimes still at the expense of the common soldier. Many troops were supplied with poor quality shoes and did not have clothing warm enough or capable of protecting them against the damp on cold nights keeping watch for a French invasion. During the wet winter of 1803 to 1804 many of the Oxfordshire Militia became ill after exposure to the damp nights on guard at Dover; the only remedy was for the officers to subscribe one month's pay to provide their men with flannel waistcoats. Some troops appear to have purchased their own equipment. In April 1804 William Jackman was travelling among troops in Sussex selling gaiters; it was not this which occasioned surprise and alarm, but his foreign origins. Ironmasters, like the timber contractors and other suppliers of military equipment, also profited from the renewal of the war. The impetus derived from recent developments in the iron industry had carried most of the big ironmasters through the Amiens interlude without much disruption to their trade. From 1803 however they received an additional boost when the navy and the Ordnance decided that British iron was of good enough quality to replace the Russian and Swedish product upon which they had depended previously. As the war dragged on Britain established and consolidated a position as the world's foremost producer of iron.[17]

Again the boost given to these sectors of the economy by the war on occasions profited the workforce. Iron workers were in demand – no wonder 'deserters' were 'hiding' in the Merthyr iron works – so too were the miners who provided the works with coal. The Lord Lieutenant of Carmarthen reported that one reason for the failure of Pitt's Permanent Additional Force was the high wages paid in the county's coalmines. In Shropshire going down the pits became almost a voluntary activity; twenty years after the war the colliers looked back with nostalgia to the time when they could earn more than adequate wages by working only three or four days a week. St Vincent's reforms in the dockyards, especially a general tightening up of paperwork and the manner in which wages were paid, considerably reduced the perquisites of the artificers in the yards. It became possible to earn more than twice as much in the merchant shipyards on the Thames rather than in the naval dockyards, providing a man was prepared to go without the security of regular employment, sick pay and possible superannuation. The need to attract men into the naval dockyards when the war recommenced led to the raising of the maximum age of entry to thirty-five years in 1803, to forty-five in the following year, and to the complete removal of the limit in 1805. The shortage of unskilled men was partly made up by the use of convicts. Some skilled men were poached from civilian employers many miles from the yards. Simon Goodrich, the Engineer of Portsmouth Dockyard, wanted skilled men for his new metal mills, and he got them by offering higher wages, free coal and free travel for the new workers and their families down to Portsmouth. Civilian employers protested; Goodrich was called before the Navy Board, but he remained unrepentant and continued to poach. Goodrich was in a special position; he wanted skilled men to perform tasks new to the dockyards. The Navy Board had no authority to increase the permanent expenses of the yards by raising rates of pay up to those of the civilian yards, but it did seek other means of improving the artificers' wages. The growing incidence of absenteeism in the dockyards as the war progressed, like the absenteeism in the Shropshire mines, probably was related to a continuing rise in what the men could earn; in 1810 the absenteeism rate at Portsmouth Dockyard was twice what it had been in 1793. Also the Navy Board adopted a conciliatory policy in work and pay disputes, agreeing to the workers' demands in six out of seven instances in 1804 and 1805.[18]

In some areas it appears that recruitment into the armed forces, rather than simply a demand for a product, was a major cause of labour shortages. The Lord Lieutenant of Somerset, commenting on the failure of the Permanent Additional Force, reported that recruiting for the forces had already left a scarcity of men in his county and those who remained were in receipt of high wages. Cumberland was thinly populated and in April 1803 John Bateman, the manager of Whitehaven colliery, found twenty-three of his men, sixteen of whom were hewers, taken by the militia. Until an agreement was reached by the colliery owners in June there was cut-throat competition to recruit miners. Even after this miners who were so inclined could cross to Newcastle where coal owners were prepared to pay three times as much binding money on a man signing articles for eleven months' work. There was a shortage of miners in the Northumberland coalfield also, and it was not until October 1805 that the owners signed an agreement not to poach each other's men. William Fairbairn, the great Victorian engineer, began his working life in the Northumberland coalfield at this time. In later life he recalled how 'wages were high and men were scarce', not only in the coal-mines but also on the coal ships where 'able-bodied seamen were in receipt of eleven to twelve guineas per voyage (to London and back), and some of them, if they had the good fortune to escape the press gang, made as many as ten voyages in the year'. The average weekly earnings of farm labourers increased markedly during the years 1803 to 1805. Labourers were reported to be scarce in Essex after the rupture of the Peace of Amiens 'in consequence of the drafts for the army'. In March 1805 some husbandmen in Northumberland refused to sign on for their former masters at wages of fifteen or eighteen shillings a week, until they had gone into Morpeth on hiring day to see the state of the market for themselves. In some parts of Bedfordshire threshing mills appear to have been introduced to cope with the labour shortage. Once again troops helped bring in the harvests, but the government was cautious in this practice in those coastal areas most vulnerable to invasion; during the Sussex harvest of 1805 troops were ordered out of the fields and back to their military posts to the chagrin and bewilderment of the farmers.[19]

In districts where there was plenty of work the news of a ballot for the militia or the Army of Reserve must have been received with despair by the poorer sections of society who might enjoy an adequate wage for their living expenses, but insufficient to allow them funds for providing a substitute. On the other hand in areas where work was hard to find or where the war had an unfavourable effect on trade, recruitment into the armed forces provided a way out for the unemployed. This did not go unnoticed by contemporaries. *The Times* remarked that 'men enter as substitutes in the militia, or as recruits in the Line, because they want employment'. The textile industry of the North-west began another downward slide when war was declared. Surveying the situation from the other side of the Pennines after two months of war, the *Newcastle*

Chronicle could write: 'Five large houses have already stopped business in Manchester. Twenty thousand people are there said to be out of employ: but recruiting sergeants stand ready day and night, to offer them "ready pay and good quarters"'. William Rowbottom noted how the price of labour dropped in his locality with the reopening of hostilities; by the time of the Oldham Rushbearing at the end of August the recruiting sergeants had so drained the area of men that he believed there were 'three nymphs to one swain' at the festivities.[20]

II Attitudes and Propaganda

The population was well aware of the invasion threat, especially those on vulnerable coasts who could see artisans, both civilian and military, labouring over new fortifications, like the squat Martello towers with their five-feet-thick walls, and their gun platforms from which invasion beaches could be swept with grapeshot; or like the Royal Military Canal, designed to create an insurmountable obstacle to any enemy landing on the beaches beyond Romney Marsh and deemed preferable to destroying valuable agricultural land by flooding it with sea-water (and also recognised as a useful transport route for the local civilian economy). The enemy could even be seen massing on the French Coast. Richard Huddleston, encamped with his regiment at Lympne in Kent, explained to his sister that he could see 'quite distinctly' the French camp at Boulogne: 'the tents, houses etc. . . . a wood and church beyond their camp is likewise very discernable'. Some civilians packed up and left coastal districts; Eastbourne was almost deserted in August 1803 when it was rumoured that the French would land in the vicinity; two months later Thomas Twining confessed to leaving Colchester because he was afraid to stay in it – 'many have left, more are prepared to leave it'. Among others however the martial spirit reigned supreme. Women of fashion paraded in 'rifle' dresses of dark green velvet with matching 'rifle' hats. Every district had a corps of volunteers in training; in some instances they hastily assembled to meet false alarms. Old or very young men watched on the coasts at night from the shelter of turf huts ready to fire warning beacons if the French should come: paradoxically, if the popular recollection passed on to the novelist Thomas Hardy may be believed, they were often warned by spirits smuggled from the enemy shore. Enormous military camps were assembled, especially on the coasts, which delighted Jane Austen's Catherine and Lydia Bennet and the village girls of Hardy's Wessex, but gave local landowners cause for concern about their game, their grain or vegetables and their fences. Where the troops had no barracks and no tents, again it was the innkeeper who suffered; early in 1804 Lord Mulgrave reported the difficulties of the innkeepers of Hull who were unable to cope with the men, and especially the horses, quartered on them.[21]

Fear of invasion meant that foreigners were again eyed with suspicion, particularly in coastal areas. The Home Office was advised of several men travelling and even sketching, probably quite innocently, on the coasts. A gentleman journeying through Wales in September 1803 was nearly arrested in Radnor where the local population took him for the First Consul. Nuns in Dorset were suspected of harbouring a brother of Bonaparte who, it was alleged, had come to assess the feelings of the English towards the invasion. A local magistrate organised a search which was all the more ironic for the nuns, since their convent in France had been subjected to a similar search at the beginning of the French Reign of Terror, by men convinced that they were harbouring Pitt. William Cobbett criticised those London newspapers which had condemned *émigrés* returning to Bonaparte's France; these condemnations were, he believed, simply hints for 'the mob' and the papers were principally motivated by '*malignity against those Emigrants who remain here*, and not anger against those who have returned'. Some foreigners suffered in the new climate. The Earl of Clanricarde dismissed a French footman for 'absurdly indiscreet words'; but at once rumours began circulating about his butler who, the Earl believed, was perfectly loyal. The government itself was sufficiently alarmed to close the Thames to foreign shipping above Limehouse, an action which aroused resentment among neutrals, especially Americans.[22]

The war commenced with a show of patriotic fervour; a fact remarked upon by men not particularly sympathetic to the struggle. The *Sheffield Iris* perceived that 'a spirit of unanimity and patriotism, unexampled even in the annals of this favoured country, displays itself among all ranks of people'. Several men who had opposed the conflict with revolutionary France now supported the struggle against consular France. William Frend published *Patriotism, or the Love of our Country* which concluded calling for volunteers for the militia. Wordsworth eulogised the 'men of Kent' now the front line against the French:

> In Britain is one breath;
> We all are with you now from shore to shore; –
> Ye men of Kent, 'tis victory or death!

Loyal sentiments ran through all ranks of society. Stephen Morley wrote of everyone showing an 'enthusiastic ardour in defence of their country' during 1803, but with the deference common to many of his class, he would not presume to say that he was influenced by such in joining the Army of Reserve. John Hodgkinson, a naval rating, arrived at Spithead at the end of May 1803; he was sorry 'that we hare going to war with the french so soon, but howheaver I keep my spirits up in hopes of seeing peace one day or the other'. Hodgkinson had probably missed a discharge with the Peace of Amiens by being taken sick at the Cape of Good Hope. In October 1803 however, happy with his ship and officers, he was awaiting the French at Spithead. 'We are prepared for them and if they make that bold attempt to land upon our little spot of ground I am afraid they will forget to find there way back.' Women offered their services as volunteers. Lady Jerningham proposed a corps of 600 women to drive cattle in Norfolk in case of invasion. Addington received a letter from the women of Neath requesting that they be allowed

> to defend ourselves as well as the weaker women and children among us. There are in this town about two hundred women who have been used to hard labour all the days of their lifes, such as working in coal-pits, on the high roads, tilling the ground, etc. If you would grant us arms, that is *light pikes* . . . we do assure you that we could in a short time learn our exercise . . . I assure you we are not triffling with you, but *serious* in our proposal.

The boys of Shrewsbury School exercised with wooden muskets and wrote home requesting their parents to buy them real, but light-weight weapons; they intended to get bayonets made near the school.[23]

Parliament began the war with a show of unanimity. Fox's call for a speedy restoration of peace and his suggestion of Russian mediation received a cool reception. Pitt powerfully defended the decision to go to war, but cautiously avoided linking himself directly with Addington's government. However as 1803 drew to a close men of both Houses of Parliament increasingly began to look upon the government as unequal to its task. Some looked to Pitt as a kind of natural leader. Grenville and Windham despised Addington's lowly origins; Grenville disliked the 'democratic' elements which he saw creeping into the country's defence organisation; Windham had very positive ideas for a total reorganisation of the army. Even the Cabinet, though still supported with large majorities, began to lose confidence in itself. Charles Yorke, who became Home Secretary in August 1803, lamented that all the best debating power was outside the government. By the beginning of 1804 intrigues were afoot to bring Addington down. Grenville approached Pitt in the hopes of producing a government 'comprehending as large a proportion as possible of the weight, talents, and character to be found in public men of all descriptions, and without any exception'.[24] Pitt refused to enter direct opposition, but Grenville had found an ally in Fox – an understanding which bewildered many for, as *The Times* noted on 5 March, Grenville's principles were 'almost in the highest strain of Toryism', while Fox had toasted 'the Sovereignty of the People'. As this alliance developed George III was struck down with temporary insanity; the plans to bring down Addington now became intermingled with talk of a regency and intrigues around the Prince of Wales. In April George recovered, but by now Pitt had decided to oppose the government on some issues relating to defence. Addington saw his majorities decreasing and, much to the King's regret, he decided to resign. Pitt promptly proposed forming an administration which would include the Grenville faction and the Foxites; precisely the kind of government that Grenville had suggested. But the King refused to have Fox among his ministers, and Grenville stuck by his new ally. The result was that Pitt's administration, which took office in May 1804, was not much stronger than the one which it replaced. Pitt temporarily healed the breach with Addington in January 1805 when Addington returned to the Cabinet as Viscount Sidmouth and with the post of Lord President of the Council. But when Melville was forced to resign after the revelations of the naval enquiry the split reopened; Sidmouth believed that one of his followers should have replaced Melville, and he and his followers voted for criminal proceedings to be instigated against the unfortunate Scot. On 5 July 1805 Sidmouth resigned. Pitt continued to get his measures through Parliament, but the strain of conducting the war with a weak administration and powerful parliamentary opponents told severely on his health.

The sentiments of the population as a whole were little affected by the intrigues and squabbles at Westminster. The loyalty and unanimity of the nation did not depend on the chief minister but on the external threat. Invasion cartoons and broadsides of the period rarely showed an heroic Addington or Pitt opposing the French; the heroic figure was generally John Bull, Jack Tar or a 'bold volunteer'. Even more than in 1798 the eyes and ears of the population were bombarded by propaganda; 1803 saw the first appearance of Gillray's 'Little Boney' in a print published before the war began. Once the conflict had commenced Gillray gave full reign to his new creation and the Lilliputian figure ferociously waving his sabre or attempting to sail his boat across the Channel became a stock character in the armoury of

British anti-Bonapartist satire. In the theatres patriotic plays were performed; Shakespeare's *Henry V*, subtitled 'The Conquest of France', was played at both the Theatre Royal, Haymarket, and at Covent Garden before the end of 1803. Other pieces were accompanied by patriotic songs and tableaux. The Bishop of Llandaff advised his clergy to preach against the French in their sermons; a Nonconformist in Colchester was said to have begun his prayers with an anti-Bonapartist request: 'O Lord God, be pleased to change his wicked heart or stop his wicked breath!' Pro-government newspapers in particular chronicled with care and outrage what they saw as new manifestations of the 'Corsican monster's tyranny': the internment of British males aged between sixteen and sixty in France and Holland on the ground that they could serve in the militia; the seizure on neutral territory and execution of the Duc d'Enghien; the arrests of conspirators against Bonaparte and the strange death of General Pichegru. According to *The Times* on 2 June 1804: 'In France, certainly every human crime is now perpetuated under the sanction of the Government; and no man's person is safe from assassination or poison'. Broadsides and pamphlets accused Bonaparte of poisoning his wounded so as not to be burdened with them at Jaffa; in others he was anti-Christ; his soldiers were hordes of butchers bent on murder, plunder and rape. Even the more bizarre charges appear to have been taken seriously by some; in July 1803 John Carrington confided to his diary: 'This month we are Thretned to be Invaded by one Boneparte, by the French, and England is to be Divided amongst the french And Every man to be Killed and the Women to be Saved.' Bonaparte became the bogeyman who would punish wicked children:

> Baby, baby, naughty baby,
>   Hush, you squalling thing, I say;
> Hush your squalling, or it may be
>   Bonaparte may pass this way.

Older children could learn their ABC from James Bisset's loyalist alphabet in which A stood for Albion's Isle and Z 'proved Englishmen's zeal to humble the zany of France'. Propaganda was directed at women. *Alfred's Address to the Ladies of England* urged them to rouse themselves and their menfolk against the enemy. *Old England to her Daughters* expressed similar sentiments with a careful regard for the social divisions of the period. 'Ladies' were urged not to scream or faint when the enemy appeared and not to cling to their menfolk and thus weaken their exertions; women of the middle classes, 'busy shopkeepers and active housewives', were directed to be sober and well behaved, to keep their doors locked and their servants in; labouring women 'may get in the Harvest, and feed the Horses tho' they cannot clean them'. In spite of these social differentiations it remained possible for all to be 'useful to the wounded Soldiers; *all* may employ Needles to work for *them*'.[25]

A large amount of this propaganda was directed towards the lower orders of society, urging them that they had just as much to fight for as their social superiors. *An Address to the People of the United Kingdom of Great Britain and Ireland on the threatened Invasion*, published in Edinburgh in 1803, warned that Bonaparte was 'as prodigal of human blood as Robespierre, Marat, and Danton', and explained that the French expected the people to be 'idle spectators' in the fighting should the invasion come. The author then exhorted his readers to ask themselves whether they were prepared 'to continue to receive from British Merchants and Farmers the reward of your labours, or to pay your last Farthing in contributions to your ancient enemies, and trust to them for your subsistence'. A similar point was made more colloquially in a dialogue between George and Tim, sheltering from a shower. George, the 'sensible' man, admits that he is not fond of soldiering, but he is prepared to fight for his country. He explains to Tim how, wherever the French have gone, the poor have been plundered, ravished and murdered, and he stresses that without rich men there would be no trade and no wages. Should the French be successful, George predicts, British workmen would become slaves with 'a French guard pricking them forward with bayonets at their A——'. William Burdon of Hartford House in Northumberland urged those who thought that they would be better off under the French to look at what had happened in Switzerland and Holland. He encouraged the poor to come forward 'in defence of what is dear to us all; let us stand or fall together, for we must mutually depend upon each other'. He continued with a passage which suggested that the unity of wartime could lead to a better society on the return of peace.

Remember that by thus coming forward to aid, not to defend your richer superiors, they will contract a debt of gratitude which, after the contest is over, they will not fail to repay: by being brought nearer to each other, they will be better acquainted with your wants, your virtues, and your condition; and by thus becoming more familiar the distance between you will be lessened, and they will treat you with more humanity and respect, if you conduct yourselves firmly, honestly and soberly.

Hannah More also took up her pen in the cause, but unlike Burdon she saw no material improvements necessary for the poor, and no improvements necessary to the relations between the different ranks of society. War veterans, she boasted in *A King or a Court*, were sheltered in the 'palaces' of Chelsea and Greenwich when the fighting was over. She also produced *The Ploughman's Ditty: Being an answer to that foolish question: 'What has the Poor to Lose?'* Her poor ploughman had a small house, a garden and an orchard, besides

> King, churches, babes and wife,
> Laws, liberty, life.

Even the poor's complaints about balloting for the militia and the Army of Reserve were answered by the propagandists. The author of *John Bull turned into a Galley Slave* maintained that if the French were successful, Bonaparte would want an English army to fight Austria, Prussia and Russia, and in such a case there 'would be no *volunteering*, no *balloting*'.[26]

Paradoxically the drive for lower-class support coincided with the publication of the second and much enlarged edition of Malthus's *Essay on the Principle of Population*. Although it was not his intention, Malthus provided the propertied classes, burdened with war taxes and increasing poor rates (themselves often aggravated by the war), with a powerful argument for reducing their outlay on the poor. Debate was joined as soon as the edition appeared in June 1803. One West Country doctor, highly critical of Malthus, stressed that the poor not only produced the country's wealth but also contributed most to the country's defence. 'They fight the battles by sea and land, to do which many of them are torn from their houses, their wives, and their children and undergo every kind of suffering that human nature can be afflicted with.' However it was Malthus who won the majority of converts, including Pitt, and probably few saw any contradiction between leaving the poor to the hard facts of economic survival, while urging them to face the hard facts of Britain's physical survival against Napoleon's threats. The large amount of propaganda urging the poor that they had as much to lose as anyone else suggests that, apart from the arguments of Malthus, the propertied classes were disturbed by the questions posed by men like Wakefield and Spence and that they were not sure how far they could trust lower-class patriotism. Some radicals remained disaffected in spite of the general trend towards loyalty. The government initiated prosecutions against men who dared to issue anti-war tracts. A few individuals were reported for praising Bonaparte, wishing success to French arms or uttering other similarly seditious sentiments. 'Notary', one of the government's most able spies, was confident enough to state in January 1804 that 'domestic treason' was destroyed. 'The Consul is no longer worshipped as the Hero of Liberty: his actions have decidedly proved him the Military Tyrant.'[27]

More alarming than the threat from English Jacobins appeared the threat from the Irish. Emmet's rebellion spluttered on to the streets of Dublin in July 1803. Fox did not believe that the French would attempt a landing on English coasts, but he was less sanguine about the coasts of Ireland. J. C. Curwen was urged to organise sea fencibles in Cumberland, not because the French were expected to land there but because his correspondent expected them to land in northern Ireland, 'a part fertile in disloyalty and sedition', and from there the Cumberland coast would be very vulnerable to raids. Irishmen in England were also suspect. In August 1803 Lord Braybrooke supported an Essex magistrate's disinclination to enrol the Irish around Barking, East and West Ham under the Levy en Masse Act. Ralph Fletcher, a magistrate living in Bolton, had spies spread all over the North-west and in August 1805 he was informed that the Irish in Manchester were 'more than usually full of expectation of a descent by the French upon Ireland'. Understandably British propaganda was directed at the Irish. 'An Irishman and a Soldier' urged his fellow countrymen in England not to be misled by 'French spies' and 'French perfidy' and to fight 'for *your King*, *your Country*, and *your God*'.[28] While in Dublin Denys Scully, Richard Huddleston's brother-in-law, wrote *The Irish Catholic's Advice to his Brethren how to estimate their present situation and repel French Invasion, Civil Wars, and Slavery*. The Catholic emancipation question itself was not entirely dormant during these years. Fox and Grenville espoused the cause. An Irish Catholic petition was presented to the Commons in 1805 which led to some highly charged partisan correspondence in the newspapers. But the issue did not create the problems of 1801, nor lead to the outburst of Protestant bigotry which was to mark the election campaign of 1807.

Ireland apart, the majority in Great Britain were loyal. But the governing classes were wary of the strain that an invasion could put on this loyalty. The government consulted both the deputy keeper of State Papers and the Crown law officers on precedents for martial law. The former unearthed the preparations for defence against the Spanish Armada, which he thought inappropriate but 'historically at least instructive'. Proclamations for the introduction of martial law were prepared; arrangements were also made to ensure that, in the event of invasion, troops would be paid in cash rather than in paper currency.

The concern at local level was well emphasised in a letter to the Home Office from the Mayor of Leicester. He feared that invasion would disrupt trade and create unemployment. He recognised that the overseers of the poor should help the unemployed, and could increase the poor rate, but, emphasising the current scarcity of copper coin, he wondered what would happen if paper money depreciated too much to purchase food; provisions could be requisitioned for troops, but could he requisition food for the poor? 'I think that if, whilst the enemy remains in force, the people of this town were to suffer from the want of Bread a *fourth of the population* would join the French Standard if they had an opportunity.' There is no record of the Home Office's reply.[29]

The shortage of coin mentioned by the mayor was becoming acute in some areas and, in spite of issues of silver by the Bank of England in both 1803 and 1804, it was not only copper coin that was in short supply. Towards the end of 1804 a Staffordshire magistrate reported that cards were being issued in his neighbourhood to make up the deficiency in silver coinage. 'The cards are now become so numerous', he maintained, 'that in the change of a guinea we can scarcely receive a tenth part of it in silver.' There were other problems also: unscrupulous tradesmen were defrauding illiterate workmen by giving them five shilling cards in place of ten; many of the cards were now counterfeited; there was the possibility that by issuing several thousand of them men of 'base principles' could raise false credit. The Crown law officers were consulted and concluded that the employers and other persons responsible for issuing these cards were guilty of an offence, and could be brought to summary justice before a magistrate. Within a matter of weeks the cards were suppressed, but this did not solve the problem of the coin scarcity. In February 1805 a second magistrate wrote on behalf of the manufacturers of Dudley who, since the suppression of the cards were suffering 'the greatest inconvenience and embarrassment'. In some instances they were paying two or more workmen with one large banknote, in others they were forced to postpone payment to their men for two or even three weeks, or else lend to them on account. 'All which practices are highly injurious to the inferior classes and occasion much discontent and often murmurs against their employers.' One reason for the shortage of coin was the increase of the metallic value over the face value; this had been a problem with gold and silver coins throughout the eighteenth century, but in the early years of the nineteenth century it also became a problem with copper. On 20 April 1805 the *York Herald* noted the virtual disappearance of one-penny and two-penny copper pieces and explained that these coins were being melted down since copper was worth two shillings a pound and sixteen one-penny pieces weighed one pound. When the Attorney General was informed of men buying twenty shillings' worth of copper coin for one guinea and melting it down he had to confess that, unlike the melting of gold and silver, this was not an offence.[30] An additional cause of the coin shortage was probably the predilection which some people had for hard cash after the Bank Restriction Act; and with the possibility of invasion many more people probably kept a secret hoard in case a French landing should lead to the destruction of the paper currency.

It was implicit in the Mayor of Leicester's letter that, at the moment, the lower classes could afford bread. Indeed, allowing for seasonal fluctuations, during the Amiens respite and the first eighteen months of war the price of bread fell. Unrest over provision shortages ceased, temporarily, to be a major concern of the government; but there was agitation from farmers concerned about their profits. Although prices were falling, Parliament had renewed the emergency legislation, passed just before the peace, which permitted the free import of grain and forbade export. Early in 1804 the Commons received petitions from landowners and farmers in Essex, Norfolk, Lincolnshire, Staffordshire, Suffolk and Warwickshire requesting a revision of the 1791 Corn Law. A new act, swiftly passed in the summer, became operative in the middle of November. It introduced no new principles, but altered the rates settled by its predecessor; thus corn exported when the price was forty-eight shillings a quarter or less received a bounty of five shillings a quarter; foreign imports paid a duty of twenty-four shillings and three pence a quarter when British wheat sold for less than sixty-three shillings, a duty of two shillings and sixpence when the British price was between sixty-three and sixty-six shillings, and a duty of sixpence when the British price exceeded sixty-six shillings. Wheat from the North American colonies was admitted on a similar, but more favourable scale, and there was additional protection for rye, peas, beans, barley and oats. Complaints were made and petitions raised, particularly in the new manufacturing areas of the north of England and the south-west of Scotland. The ever-active Fletcher reported that the agitation in the North-west was organised by men 'of the Jacobin cast'. Cobbett protested that the measure was passed for the benefit of certain classes, 'contractors and corn merchants [and] . . . that other race of beings who have sprung from the dunghill of paper money and who are called speculating farmers'. Opposition to the measure might have increased had the harvests continued to be good, but within a year, after a poor harvest in 1804, the act was suspended and, with a succession of bad harvests and the impact of the Continental System, the question of the

Corn Laws was to remain largely dormant until the conclusion of the war.[31]

After the poor harvest of 1804 was gathered in British policy changed. No longer was it a matter of sitting back behind the barriers of the Channel and the North Sea to wait for the enemy's invasion attempt. Pitt, as in the earlier war, now sought allies with the offer of subsidies. He first secured the backing of Russia, then in August 1805, worried by French influence in Italy and Germany, Austria agreed to join a third coalition. The following month the ageing Lord Liverpool predicted both the opening of war on the Continent 'on a great scale', and, equally important, the end of the invasion threat as French troops were withdrawn from the coast to meet the threat of the coalition's land powers. Battle was joined as Liverpool expected, and events moved fast. The French and Spanish fleets broke out of the British blockade only to be smashed by Nelson at Trafalgar. The news was received in Britain with a mixture of great joy at the victory and great sadness for the death of Nelson, who had captured the popular imagination as the hero of the hour. But within two months the Third Coalition, already smarting from the surrender of an Austrian army at Ulm, was shattered when Napoleon defeated the combined armies of Austria and Russia on the field of Austerlitz. Many feared that the victorious French would now return to their camps on the coasts. The *York Herald* urged that should the invasion now come Britons would remember 'the noble and auspicious words of the Hero Nelson – 'England expects every man to do his duty'. John Mottram, a gentleman resident in Pall Mall, regarded the situation with rather less bravado: 'the alarms of our "Brave Yeomen, whose limbs were made in England" will be none the lighter for his [Napoleon] having since the 6th Sept. marched 600 miles, his army halting but one half day, and having overthrown the most powerful military state in Europe'. However in spite of his gloomy fears that no European power would now dare to oppose France for fifty years and that the achievements of the 'flimsy, faithless and insolent' French had destroyed 'the economy of the world', he recognised that Napoleon could not mount an invasion until he built new ships and trained more seamen.[32]

The disastrous outcome of the Third Coalition killed Pitt. Against failing health he had struggled to bring it into being as well as hold his weak administration together. From 14 January 1806 he was unable either to leave his house or consult with any of his colleagues; on 23 January he died; he had been George III's chief minister for nearly twenty of his forty-six years. Bertie Greathead, a Foxite gentleman in Warwickshire who had only recently broken his parole and escaped from internment by the French, wrote a biting epitaph for Pitt in his diary, but concluded expressing the concerns of many: 'What changes in three short months! Trafalgar! Austerlitz! What will the next produce?'[33]

7. Blockade: 1806–9

I Ministers and Measures

Pitt's death was not a cue for national mourning; in Royton old Jacobins prepared for an illumination and a mock funeral; in Hull bets were taken that the war would soon be at an end.[1] Others were less sanguine about the prospects of peace, and even Fox had doubts. Rightly so, for during the next four years the war was to spread even further across the globe: British troops and fleets were engaged in Holland and Spain, the length and breadth of the Mediterranean, and from the Baltic to South America. The economic struggle between Britain and France was highlighted by Napoleon's Berlin and Milan Decrees and Britain's Orders in Council; neutrals were dragged into the conflict which led to a serious confrontation between Britain and the United States. Furthermore Britain continued the war without an outstanding national leadership, with a succession of bad harvests, and with several major sectors of the economy exerting pressure for peace.

Pitt's ministry did not survive him, and did not want to. It was replaced by the Ministry of All the Talents; a ministry rather like the one which Grenville had urged on Pitt two years before. Grenville himself was the new First Lord of the Treasury, Sidmouth was Lord Privy Seal, Windham was Secretary for War and Colonies, Grey (who became Viscount Howick in April 1806) was First Lord of the Admiralty, and later Foreign Secretary. Fox was the Talents' first Foreign Secretary, and his personality held the ministry together; after his death, in October 1806, the divisions became acute.

The new ministry was received with great enthusiasm by radicals and reformers. The freeholders of Middlesex sent a congratulatory address to George III 'for having . . . opened to the people a prospect of Counsels more congenial with the English Constitution than for many years past they have experienced, as well as the hope of a redress of grievances'. At the meeting which agreed to the address men looked forward to reform and particularly the reduction of sinecures.[2] They were to be bitterly disappointed. There was the usual 'jobbing' over appointments in the early days of the ministry. The election following Fox's death saw the usual Treasury involvement. The presence of Grenville, Sidmouth and Windham militated against any chance of parliamentary reform. A select committee was established to investigate sinecures and the receipt of official fees, but it was due only to the initiative of a back-bencher, Robert Biddulph, in February 1807, and was something of an embarrassment to the Talents for the Grenvilles held several lucrative sinecures. Lord Henry Petty, the Chancellor of the Exchequer who was entrusted with putting the government's line during the debates on Biddulph's motion, argued that sinecures were necessary to supplement low salaries. The one piece of legislation for which the Talents are remembered, the abolition of the slave trade, was not a government bill and the Cabinet was divided on the issue; Sidmouth feared that if Britain abolished the trade it would simply be taken over by her rivals; Windham opposed the motion, principally, it appears, from that hatred of all innovation which had gripped him since the outbreak of the French Revolution.[3]

The Talents' conduct of the war was disappointing to those who welcomed the ministry. Shortly after they had taken office Petty denied a rumour that there was to be an increase in income tax to 7 to 10 per cent; yet in his budget, presented at the end of March 1806, to meet the cost of the war, he increased the tax to two shillings in the pound. Pitt's old colleagues were astounded, recalling the scathing criticisms of their old leader's increase made in the previous year; criticisms which were then led by Fox. Furthermore Petty reduced the level of exemption, removed allowances for children and improved the collection of the tax by requiring exemptees to pay their tax and then claim back their exemptions. It was probably the case, as the old Whig Sir Philip Francis warned during the budget debate, that the latter proposal caused hardship to the less well off who had to scrape money together to pay the tax, and then suffer official delays before their abatement was returned. Gillray savaged the increases in his caricature of '*The Friend of the People and his Petty-New-Tax-Gatherer, paying John Bull a visit*', in which Fox demands new taxes of a bankrupt John Bull in a cruel parody of the speech he had made criticising Pitt's increase. Cobbett also used Fox's words against him in the *Political Register*; the tax was 'what Mr. Fox formerly described it, a tax which leaves no man anything in this world, that he can call his own'. Petty had also hoped to raise £500,000 by an excise of forty shillings a ton on home-produced iron, but as in 1797 the ironmasters were quick off the mark organising a committee to fight the proposal. Pamphlets and letters to the press were published explaining the adverse effects that the measure would have on everything from the nail trade to agriculture. Although the proposal had a majority of ten in the committee stage in the Commons, the ministry decided to drop it because of the opposition.[4] Petty and some of his colleagues hoped that, after their increases of 1806, they would not have to increase taxation again. In the following February they introduced a plan, principally for loans, both to raise money for a long war and also pay off the rapidly expanding National Debt. Not all of the Talents were convinced by the new proposal, in particular by the requirement to continue war taxation after the conclusion of peace. But the plan was never given a chance; it fell with the ministry.

The expense of the war probably was responsible for persuading Grenville to support Fox's attempt to negotiate with Napoleon. But the negotiations earned the ministry little credit. They were apparently oblivious of Lord Yarmouth's lack of principle when they appointed him as their plenipotentiary. Lord Lauderdale was sent to advise Yarmouth when his laxity was causing some alarm. Lauderdale found him using his inside information to speculate on the funds, and Yarmouth was recalled. Lauderdale then continued discussions with the French, even though the Talents appear to have recognised that Napoleon was playing a very shrewd diplomatic game to Britain's disadvantage. He had successfully entangled Britain in a war with Prussia before the Talents realised that his motive was to isolate Prussia before destroying her. By the time they decided to make peace and offer Frederick William a British subsidy, the Prussian army had already been destroyed in the brief Jena – Auerstadt campaign. Refusals to raid French and Dutch coasts to draw Napoleonic forces from eastern Europe and to allow the use of British credit for a loan, alienated Britain's last ally, the Tsar. Involvement in the eastern Mediterranean, to end a Russo-Turkish war in order to keep Russian troops in Poland and to prevent open hostility between Russia and Austria, led to an unsuccessful naval expedition to the Dardanelles and a pointless expedition to Egypt by a tiny force which was rapidly defeated. Such military successes as were achieved under the Talents were due primarily to the initiative of local commanders; but the most promising expedition, Sir John Stuart's brief descent on Calabria and his victory over a French army at Maida, was not followed up, while the most astonishing decision of Sir David Baird and Sir Home Popham to use part of their successful expedition to Cape Town for an attack on Buenos Aires, gave rise to impractical schemes in Windham's mind for a seizure of the entire continent of South America.

Windham also had imaginative ideas about the reorganisation of the army. Since the recommencement of the war he had been highly critical of the recruitment schemes employed; though he opposed reform in every other branch of the state his proposals for the army were revolutionary. The problem of enlistment as contemporaries saw it, was spelt out in a letter from the Duke of York in March 1806.

On the Continent where there is comparatively speaking little or no trade or manufactures and consequently little means for the Employment of the Population otherwise than in agriculture, the Pay and advantages of a soldier are equal to that of the Handicraftsman and therefore is a sufficient inducement for a man to enlist; besides which in most of the Continental Powers the Plan upon which their armies are formed by giving a Property to the Captain in their respective companies and obliging them under pecuniary Risk to keep them constantly complete makes it both an Object and Credit to them to use every exertion upon the Recruiting Service: – But in this Country where all Labour is so exceedingly high and where such inducements are held out to the Lower Class of the People either to engage in manufactures or to be employed at Sea, and where no temptation whatsoever is offered to the Officer to exert himself on the Recruiting Service . . . that branch of the Service must be materially impeded, and the continual drain which is unavoidable occasioned by the common casualties of the Army, particularly in Our Colonial Possessions, causes such an Annual deficiency, as has as yet at least never been supplied by ordinary recruiting. . . .[5]

Windham proposed to change the terms of enlistment. Instead of joining the army for life, a man was to enlist for seven years; if, at the end of that term he decided to re-enlist, his pay was to be increased from one shilling to one shilling and sixpence a day; if he re-enlisted for a third term, he would receive two shillings a day. In addition every two years' service in the West Indies was to be counted as three years' service, and there was the additional promise of a pension for all soldiers at the end of their army career. Supporters of the proposals saw numerous advantages. Like the Quota Acts of 1795 they appeared to promise an end to trickery and crimping in army recruitment; short service and a pension suggested that a better class of recruit would come forward. But Windham's measures, when they appeared on the statute book, do not seem to have been directly responsible for any increase in the size of the army and the administrative problems created by the abatements for service in the West Indies were beyond the bookkeeping arrangements of the period.

Windham's new legislation swept away Pitt's Permanent Additional Force Act and remitted all the fines outstanding from local authorities under this act. This, together with the suspension of the militia ballot and its replacement with a limited bounty for volunteer recruits, probably won some sympathy and support in the provinces among the officers responsible for organising Pitt's act and the ballot, and among those men liable to the ballot. But at the same time Windham succeeded in alienating most of the kingdom's volunteer forces. He did not approve of the volunteers; he savaged them in the Commons, reduced their allowances and abolished the inspecting field officers who had been so valuable in overseeing their training. Some volunteers resigned; Grenville and Sidmouth began to have doubts about Windham's activities in this area. Windham, however, was not to be diverted from his course; he hoped eventually to replace the volunteers entirely with a scheme to train all the able-bodied men in the country, in batches of 200,000 each year chosen by ballot. The Training Act (46 Geo. III c. 90) passed in July 1806; it was fraught with problems, not the least of which resulted from Windham's own reluctance to consider details. He believed that his mass army could be trained by sergeants with a constable standing by to ensure that the men behaved themselves; the men were to receive only twenty-four days' training and yet, in the event of an invasion, Windham expected them either to act as 'an armed peasantry' or to fill up any gaps in the regular army. There were problems for local government also. A West Riding magistrate feared that 'after endless trouble we shall not enroll half the compliment of men' because the lists upon which the ballots were to be based were collected in September 1806 and in his county about two-thirds of the farm labourers changed their employers at Martinmas (11 November); thus a man might be balloted after he had left the district for which he was listed. One of the first actions of Lord Castlereagh when he replaced Windham on the fall of the Talents was to repeal his predecessor's legislation.[6]

Army reform had been one of the two issues to which Foxites and Grenvillites were committed when they took office; the other was Catholic relief. The Talents did not come into office with any minister prepared to forge ahead on this issue in the way that Windham pursued army reform. Nothing was done until after Fox's death and then the ministers were driven to act in haste by growing unrest in Ireland and a renewed project to petition for relief. There was a belief that more Irishmen would enlist in the armed forces if the political bars against Catholics were removed, and the proposal which the Talents came up with at the beginning of 1807 was basically a revival of the 1793 law which had given Catholics special status in the Irish army, but which had disappeared with the Act of Union. The new proposal however, extended its predecessor, giving the rights to all of George III's Catholic subjects. Sidmouth reluctantly supported his colleagues, and even George III's agreement was secured; but both turned against the measure when it became clear that the majority in the Cabinet intended that staff appointments, as well as colonelcies, should be open to Catholics. The King was adamant in his opposition; the Talents resigned.

The ministry of All the Talents was the only experience of government for the main Foxite tradition of the Whigs between 1783 and 1827. It was subsequently lionised by nineteenth-century Whig historians, but it achieved little of any credit and few tears were shed when it fell in March 1807. In spite of its professed determination to reduce expenditure, it had almost doubled the income tax. Its military successes had been limited; it had failed to negotiate peace. Its pursuit of Catholic emancipation awoke all the latent Protestant bigotry in the country, and the election which followed its fall and the appointment of Portland's administration was marked by virulent 'No Popery' propaganda. Admittedly there was little mass support for parliamentary reform while the Talents were in power, but their failure to initiate any moves in this direction and their embarrassment over the investigation of sinecures encouraged reformers to support new men in Parliament who espoused reform, notably Burdett. Extra-parliamentary reformers of a popular stamp – men like Cobbett, who took up the cause of reform in 1806, 'Orator' Hunt and Francis Place – could now proclaim to the mass of the unenfranchised that clearly there was no difference between ministries, whether they called themselves Whig or Tory.

It appeared to many that an era had come to an end, with the deaths of Pitt and Fox following so soon on one another. The two men had dominated politics for over twenty years, the one, principally as the King's chief minister, the other proudly claiming to be the 'man of the people'. Early in 1807, with no single dominant personality to hold a Cabinet together, government depended on which of the factions at Westminster could come together with some common policies. The ministry which replaced the Talents was uninspiring. It was composed of former Pittites, but without that group who followed Sidmouth, and led by the aged and infirm Duke of Portland, who took the post of First Lord of the Treasury. The new ministers were united by a determination to continue the war, but there was division over other issues. Castlereagh, for example, Secretary for War and Colonies, was sympathetic to Catholic demands; Perceval, the Chancellor, was fervently opposed. Everyone recognised the brilliance of George Canning, the new Foreign Secretary, who boasted of being Pitt's true heir and who labelled, for the first time, Pitt's policies as 'Tory'. But few trusted Canning, and his intrigues to get Castlereagh removed from his post led to the two of them resigning in September 1809, to fight a duel. However, in spite of its weaknesses and divisions, the new government was more suited to its wartime task than its predecessor. Castlereagh, Canning and Perceval especially had a determination which appeared to have been lacking in Grenville at least since Pitt's death, and which was generally lacking in Howick, who was notorious for preferring his Northumberland estate to Westminster. Furthermore Castlereagh and Perceval possessed an efficiency and an attention to detail which was essential to the continuation of the war.

Contemporaries generally considered Portland's appointment of Perceval to be his worst, but the new Chancellor confounded his critics with his budgets for 1808 and 1809. Loans were negotiated on favourable terms but, apart from an additional £300,000 to be raised from the assessed taxes and stamp duties in his first budget, there was no increase in taxation. Perceval's principal weapons were reform and careful management. His reforms were not always well received. In 1808 the creation of travelling inspectors general to oversee the income tax brought the usual protests against 'SPIES and INFORMERS. . . . Beings who are to INSPECT and CANVASS . . . AGGRAVATE the distresses of the people, and attempt to DRAG the last farthing out of the pockets of the poor'. But most of his reforms were not as public. Together with William Huskisson, the Financial Secretary to the Treasury Board, he launched enquiries into the collection of taxes and investigated all reports of corruption. The reformation of the assessed taxes and the consolidation into one of nearly a hundred acts for collecting stamp duties saved some £350,000. The Bank of England was persuaded to reduce its management charges on the National Debt, and Treasury agents were persuaded to cut their commissions on exchequer bills. Government departments found their allowances for the purchase of almanacs, pocket books, court calendars and newspapers reduced. The Treasury Board was even persuaded to plant potatoes in Marylebone Park in order, as Perceval put it 'to bring revenue to the Crown and food to the nation'. In addition he performed the remarkable feat of limiting some of the extravagance of George III's spendthrift offspring.[7]

Perceval was subsequently criticised for his significant role in preparing the Orders in Council of November 1807, in retaliation for Napoleon's attempted economic blockade of Britain. After crushing the Prussians Napoleon had attempted to break the deadlock which had resulted from British naval supremacy and his own European land supremacy. His Berlin Decrees declared Britain to be in a state of blockade; they sought to keep British goods out of any French-controlled port and to bully the weaker neutrals by threatening to seize any ships trading with Britain. The Talents had replied in January 1807 with an Order in Council prohibiting sea-borne trade between ports controlled by France or her allies. Portland's administration wanted tougher measures, especially Perceval, who had been convinced by *War in Disguise, or the Frauds of the Neutral Flags* published two years before by his friend James Stephen, and Castlereagh, who urged his colleagues that the war was 'no longer a struggle for territory or for point of honour, but whether the existence of Gt. Britain as a naval power is compatible with that of France'.[8] The Orders in Council of November 1807, agreed to reluctantly by some members of the Cabinet, were an attempt to make all French trade pass through British hands and at the same time, as might be inferred from the title of Stephen's pamphlet, to stop any neutrals profiting at Britain's expense. Every harbour which excluded British ships was declared blockaded; neutral shipping could only trade with France or her allies if it called first at a British port and paid a duty. Napoleonic retaliation was swift; the Milan Decrees, proclaimed in December 1807, made all neutral ships calling at British ports or submitting to a British search liable to capture and confiscation by the French. The economic war hit both sides, and infuriated neutrals. The most powerful of the neutrals, the United States, retaliated with an embargo on trade with the belligerents, hoping that this would force them to adopt a more reasonable attitude to overseas trade.

Britain's demand for men was also souring relations with the United States. In 1807 and in the following two years Parliament voted for a naval force of 98,600 seamen and 31,400 marines. A few volunteers could still be found, others were seized by press-gangs coming ashore from warships, by the gangs of the rendezvous houses or by patrols of marines recruiting inland. Edward Costello and a friend, both recruits in the 95th Foot, were seized by a press-gang while asleep in a Liverpool cellar; they were released the following day when their sergeant claimed them. Samuel Bamford, absconding from the coal trade ships running between the North-east and London and making his way from London to Lancashire, narrowly avoided capture by marine recruiters in St Albans and again in Northampton. Bamford also described one of his coastal convoys being stripped of its best hands by the navy as the colliers sailed through Yarmouth Roads in 1808.

From the vessel which immediately proceeded [sic] ours several hands were pressed, but it so happened that when we came to pass, both the guard boats were full, and were taking their prizes to the ship appointed to receive them, whilst in the hurry of the moment we got clear through, and so escaped a most unpleasant visitation.

What angered the Americans was when British warships treated American ships in such a way. Neutral ships, the Americans argued, had neutral crews; while the British considered that they had a perfect right to seize a man born, bred and with a settlement in Britain. The situation was aggravated by the relative ease with which British seamen could acquire false certificates of American nationality from some customs men in the United States for Twenty-five cents, and even from the American Consul in London, for two shillings and sixpence.[9]

Recruiting for the regular army in 1807 was fairly successful. Castlereagh demanded another draft of volunteers from the militia and got all but 500 of the 28,000 that he called for. Two years later he secured another batch of roughly the same number. The deficiencies thus created in the militia regiments were made good with new ballots. Castlereagh also reorganised the auxiliary forces for home defence which had been left in such a shambles by Windham's vendetta against the volunteers and the Training Act, which was never implemented. It is customary to argue that the threat of invasion was over after Trafalgar, yet while this is relatively easy to argue from hindsight it was not so apparent to contemporaries, for Napoleon persevered with a significant shipbuilding programme which could only have been with the intention of defeating Britain at sea.[10] The British government persevered similarly with invasion precautions – the Harwich Redoubt was begun in 1808 and the Martello towers north of the Thames even later – and clearly believed that some kind of auxiliary force was necessary. Castlereagh gave the volunteers limited encouragement; then in the summer of 1808 he presented his proposals for a local militia. The Local Militia Acts were passed at the end of June that year (48 Geo. IIIc. 111 (England and Wales) and C. 150 (Scotland)). They provided for an auxiliary force of 300,000 men or six times the quotas of the militia set in 1802, divided, like these quotas, among the counties. Volunteer infantry corps could transfer to the local militia for a bounty, individuals could enlist, and deficiencies were to be made by a ballot of men aged between eighteen and thirty, there was to be no substitution and service was to be enforced by heavy fines or imprisonment. Service was for four years and, during which time and for two years afterwards, local militiamen were exempt from the ballot for the regular militia. The men had to undergo twenty-eight days training each year either in their own, or in a neighbouring county; in case of invasion they could be sent anywhere in the kingdom. They could also be called out by their Lord

Lieutenant in case of riot, but their assembly in this case was limited to fourteen days and was counted against their annual training. Within a year some 125,000 men came forward from the volunteers and between 50,000 and 60,000 others enlisted voluntarily. The local militia rapidly eclipsed the volunteers and in 1809 additional pressure was put on the volunteer infantry corps when the government withdrew their clothing allowance. In the early summer of 1809 the British population was supporting an armed force of 786,500 men excluding colonial corps and East India Company troops: there were nearly 300,000 regulars and embodied militia; 130,000 seamen and marines; nearly 198,500 local militia and 189,000 volunteers. Thus, even allowing for foreign-born soldiers and sailors, roughly one man in every nine or ten of military age in Great Britain and Ireland was serving in the regular forces of army, navy or regular militia; if volunteers and local militia are added the proportion rises to one man in every six.

The problem remained for the Cabinet: how best to deploy their forces against Napoleon. Portland's administration inherited the disastrous Egyptian campaign from the Talents, and the chance of a campaign in Italy had been lost through lack of men on the spot when they were needed. Castlereagh toyed with following up Windham's South American adventures, but news of General Whitelocke's disastrous assault on Buenos Aires gave him second thoughts. At Tilsit, in the summer of 1807, Napoleon patched up his quarrel with the Tsar and threatened to close those ports of Europe still prepared to accept British trade, notably in Denmark, Sweden and Portugal. Portland's young ministers acted with vigour. Copenhagen was bombarded into submission and such of the Danish fleet as remained seaworthy was captured and sailed to Britain. The Regent of Portugal and the Portuguese fleet were whisked away to Brazil by a British squadron as French troops entered Lisbon. Early in 1808 negotiations with Sweden collapsed when the unbalanced Gustavus IV placed General Sir John Moore under arrest. Moore escaped, and on his own authority brought his army back to Britain. But as Moore returned from the Baltic a new opportunity was opening up in southern Europe. Napoleon's meddling in Iberian politics provoked popular revolts and the Junta, speaking for the Spanish people, sought British help. The struggle in the Peninsula began with mixed fortunes for the British. Sir Arthur Wellesley's victory at Vimeiro in Portugal was thrown away when his superior officers declined to follow it up and then signed the Convention of Cintra permitting Junot's army to return to France. Sir John Moore's bold raid into Spain concluded with his death at Corunna and the temporary end of any significant British presence in the Peninsula, but the Cabinet was not prepared to let the opportunity slip and in April 1809 Wellesley returned to Lisbon as commander-in-chief of the British and Portuguese armies. In the summer of that year it looked as if success might also be found elsewhere in Europe; Austria again took the field, only to be beaten, again, at Wagram. A diversion was staged to assist the Austrians, and also to destroy the dockyards of Antwerp, which were so important to Napoleon's plans for a new navy; but the expedition sent to the Scheldt never got beyond Walcheren Island and half the men went down with sickness. The failure at Walcheren, the news of the bloody and exhausting battle of Talavera and Wellesley's retreat into Portugal brought a crisis in the Cabinet as Canning intrigued against Castlereagh and for a new chief minister – a role which Canning believed he would fill best. The result was the duel between the two ministers, Canning's temporary exit from politics with a thigh wound, and the complete breakup of Portland's ministry.

II   Reactions

During the years 1806 to 1809 there was not the same unanimity in opposing the French as there had been in the preceding years, when invasion seriously threatened. Nevertheless some of the attitudes prevalent in the earlier years remained. Foreigners were still objects of suspicion. *The Times* urged that only Englishmen and 'English-disposed foreigners' should find 'nourishment' in the country and one of its correspondents assailed the 'legions of foreigners' working as merchant's clerks, defrauding the income tax and making 'no scruple of declaring themselves decidedly the friends of our enemy'. The most bitter attacks of this sort were directed, understandably, at the French and their Emperor, who himself remained the butt of cartoonists and propagandists. In January 1808 Lord Hawkesbury was urged never to believe 'perfidious Gaul, now more than ever perfidious' by a correspondent who headed his letter with the assertion:

> The motto of France is
> *Vel Vi, Vel Fraude* – By Force or Fraud
> Britain's should be
> No peace can be with ye Wicked.

A few men still preserved an attachment to Napoleon; prominent among these were William Hazlitt and the pedagogue Dr Samuel Parr. A serious altercation blew up between Parr and Bertie Greathead over the latter's condemnation of the Emperor. 'Sir', protested the irate Parr, 'you have on the most partial and selfish grounds conceived an implacable aversion to one of the greatest characters either of ancient or modern times.' The internment of Greathead and his wife was the result of 'a wise and most luminous application of a coercion politically and morally necessary', while Napoleon had 'done more towards the practice of sound morality, the advancement of true learning, and the establishment of rational Piety than all the princes and potentates have done from the creation of the world to the present time'. In general, however, during these years reactions to the war were motivated less by the enemy themselves, and more by the economic impact of the struggle.[11]

Not every sector of the economy suffered from the economic struggle. In south Bedfordshire one industry profited significantly when the closure of the Italian straw-hat-making centres to British merchants combined with a preference in women's fashions for Leghorn hats and the invention of a new straw-splitting knife. Women in the rural parishes of south Bedfordshire could earn from six to twelve shillings a week for straw plaiting, children earned from three to four shillings, while on average the farm labourers in the county earned from eight to ten shillings. In the towns, chiefly Luton and Dunstable, which were convenient for the London market, women and a significant number of men were employed making hats from the plait. The plaiting industry of the Bristol area was not as fortunate, probably because it was nearly four times as far from the metropolis, though one of the leading tradesmen in the industry around Bristol blamed French prisoners of war for undercutting his work-force. The militia guarding the French in Stapleton prison smuggled straw in and smuggled plait out, splitting the profits with their captives. A protest to the government from the journeymen boot- and shoe-makers of Bristol suggests that leather was also finding its way into the prison in quantity. But the prisoners of war, while they took some of the market, were probably convenient scapegoats for other problems. The Bedfordshire straw industry also had to contend with a large prison camp at Norman Cross just outside Peterborough. An official investigation in 1812 concluded that about half of the 6000 prisoners there made straw plait, again in collusion with their guards, but the investigator believed that this did not interfere with full employment in Bedforshire and Hertfordshire, on the contrary it created work for those locals who transported the prisoners' work and made it up into hats. If anything there was a shortage of plait 'and the shop-keepers of Dunstable complain the difficulty of obtaining Straw Plait owing to the competition of the London Traders, who carry away early market morning the whole quantity brought for sale'.[12]

Other much larger industries were not as fortunate. The blockade made imports more expensive and foreign markets more difficult to find. The economy fluctuated furiously with the war situation. The news of Popham and Baird's adventure, together with the arrival of more than a million dollars seized by Popham, brought high hopes of trade with South America. Lloyds and the Stock Exchange rejoiced at the failure of the Talents' peace negotiations and, describing this to his aunt, Captain Thomas Wood went on to explain that the capture of Buenos Aires 'has opened a firm field of speculation' and that merchandise was already piling up in the London Customs House for export to South America. These early hopes were unfulfilled; the boom in trade with South America had to wait another two years, until Napoleon's involvement in Iberian politics threw Spanish and Portuguese colonies open to British merchants. Before this, the economy had to cope with the effects of the Tilsit treaty, particularly serious for the West Country's wool trade, which had sent much of its cloth to Russia, and the effects of the American embargo. Some merchants and industrialists found ways around the blockade through entrepôts in Sweden, Gibralta, Malta, and the Ionian Islands, and through a variety of frauds and deceptions practiced by both sides. The most unlikely goods found their way in. French troops campaigning in Poland wore greatcoats made of West Riding cloth and boots from Northampton. In September 1808 the *York Herald* boasted that West Riding clothiers had executed contracts for the French army to the value of forty thousand pounds, promptly paid. But there were obvious limits for this kind of illicit trade.[13]

The year 1808 was the bottom of a depression which had been gathering momentum since the beginnings of the blockade. Much of the West Riding's wool had been exported to the United States; the problems in that market and the recurrent fear during 1808 that the arguments with America would lead to war hit the Yorkshire wool industry hard. Throughout the year Joseph Rogerson, a fulling and scribbling miller of Bramley near Leeds, complained in his diary of a serious scarcity of money. Wakefield merchants who employed forty to fifty men reduced their work-force to between six and twelve, and still found stocks accumulating. West country clothiers also suffered. In March 1809 a gentleman of Tiverton told Whitbread:

the stock on hand here is very large, and totally unfit for home consumption, and only calculated for the Dutch and German markets, and independent of which, a large Number of Bales from this place have been in London from two to $2\frac{1}{2}$ years for the markets I have mentioned, most of which were shipped, but by distressing Events of the Times were again warehoused.

The workers in the West Country blamed the dislocation of trade on new machinery, a tangible offender which could be smashed, or else kept out by threatening the masters. Birmingham's variety of trades were hit; a high percentage of its metal buttons and buckles, wire thread and glass toys was bound for the United States. During 1808 a large number of the town's employed were reported to have found refuge by enlisting, and nearly 2000 houses were unoccupied. But the most vulnerable industry, and that which suffered most in the depression, was cotton. All its raw material came from overseas, and the bulk of its exports went to the United States or Europe. The Lancashire cotton industry was declining in 1805 and the downswing gathered momentum with the Berlin Decrees. Rowbottom noted the effects of the 'unparaled [sic] victories of the French Arms' at the end of November 1806; merchants were in 'the greatest consternation . . . and a universall gloom hangs over the lower class of people'. The situation was critical by the end of the following year and Rowbottom saw no hope but peace. In September 1808 he reported some factories at a standstill while others were on a four-day week; the following month some were only working three days. At the beginning of 1809 Whitbread was informed that of eighty-four mills in Manchester only nine were in full work and thirty-one were in partial work; the town's poor rate had doubled in a year. Some of the male weavers sought to preserve their work by endeavouring to prevent the employment of female labour. But as this critical moment arrived, the whole process of economic downswing was reversed as merchants began eagerly to speculate in South America and the United States lifted its embargo. From the spring of 1809 to the summer of 1810 the whole economy saw a remarkable revival; the cotton industry in particular soared from slump to boom.[14]

The detrimental effects of the economic warfare during 1807 and 1808 led to demands for peace, especially from the hard-hit industrial areas of the north. Petitions were drawn up in the cotton districts and discussed by mass meetings. Colonel Stanley, member for Lancashire, presented the Bolton petition to the Commons but declined to call for a debate on the grounds that it would 'place Peace at a still greater distance'. He did not bother to reply to a similar request from the Oldham petitioners. There were similar meetings in Yorkshire. Here a county member, Lord Milton, a scion of the Whig élite, addressed meetings of his electors in Huddesrsfield and Leeds urging them to refrain from petitioning on the grounds that this could only encourage the enemy 'by making a discovery of our distresses'. He reiterated that the Talents were unable to make peace, and how deeply he personally felt the loss of Fox; this won him the approbation of Grenville and Lord Grey (as Howick had become in November 1807) but little sympathy from the Yorkshire electors. 'A Woollen Merchant and Voter for Lord Milton at the late Election' who wrote to the *Manchester Gazette* on behalf of himself and 'a number of respectable and distressed tradesmen in he West Riding' considered the speeches 'disgraceful' and 'ungrateful to those constituents who placed him in that important situation'. The *Leeds Mercury* proclaimed that ninety-seven out of every hundred inhabitants of Yorkshire wanted peace, and the petitions were sent.[15] In spite of the opposition from Whig leaders like Grey andGrenville the petitioners did find support elsewhere in the party. Samuel Whitbread, who saw himself as the true heir of Fox, believed that peace, subject to appropriate concessions, might be had for the asking, even after the abortive negotiations of 1806. Critical of the Talents' failure, and even more critical of their successors, he found support among some sections of the opposition, as well as the provincial press. The *Morning Chronicle* lost the warlike attitude it had maintained under the Talents and began moving towards demands for a cessation of hostilities. The *Edinburgh Review*, assuming an increasingly political tone in 1807, began carrying articles in favour of peace. But perhaps most important in focusing and voicing the demands for peace outside Parliament were the pamphlets of William Roscoe, a liberal-minded Liverpool gentleman and banker who had been MP for the town during the Talents' ministry.

The demands for peace did not start as a party issue, but they rapidly became one. The *Leeds Mercury* saw the government and its 'minions' seeking to label those who sought peace 'as enemies to their Sovereign and his Government'. Whitbread's motion for peace at the end of February 1808 brought praise from some quarters, but condemnation from others who saw Whitbread as a traitor and assailed him with the kind of criticism levelled at the radicals of the 1790s. 'The shameful opposition to his Majisties Ministers', declared 'John Bull', 'proves you are an Enemy to your country and a Traitor to your King'. 'Billy Baker' of Anti-Jacobin Corner compared Whitbread with Santerre, the Parisian brewer who commanded that city's National Guard in 1792, and Legendre, another prosperous Parisian tradesman and ally of Danton.[16] Such criticisms and comparisons were unfair; Whitbread may have been blind to the problems of making peace, but he was no revolutionary. However in some areas political extremism did reappear. Ralph Fletcher and William Chippendale thought it significant that old Jacobins were prominent in the peace movement in Lancashire. In the aftermath of a peace meeting at Bolton a paper was found in the road:

To the Public
No King   No War

The downfall of the trade will be the downfall of the nation, if peace does not come soon we shall have Bloody work in a short time the present ministers are such as never was before nor never can come again but if things has not a turn in time we will not sit still much longer for we plainly see that tyranny and oppressions still keeps its station while the poor subjects are labouring under a heavy burthen of taxes such as we will not bear any longer, if there was no King and a new set of Ministers things might come forward a new way so that the working people might earn a living . . . .

James Ogden, an organiser of the peace petition in Oldham, believed that without peace there would be 'calamity and bloodshed' in Britain. While such fears were proved wrong and extremists probably had little support at this time, the peace petitions may have convinced some members of the northern working classes of the need for thorough-going reforms of the political system. The government, and a great majority in Parliament, had rejected the petitions and appeared insensitive to the sufferings created by the war. On the other hand the men who championed the petitions were Whigs of the Whitbread stamp and radicals like Sir Francis Burdett, men who were prominent in the demands for economic and political reform. In addition the organi-sation for the petitions probably gave to some members of the middle and working classes an idea of their potential strength if united. Alarmed by industrial disorders across the Pennines in the summer of 1808 William Cookson, a Leeds alderman, feared that the petitions had 'engendered a sort of Union amongst the working classes, and an idea of their collective weight to which all these disgraceful commotions may be imputed'.[17]

After the failure of the petitions some of the middle-class opponents of the war directed their attentions towards the Orders in Council. Perceval himself was having doubts about them because of the friction developing with the United States, but his Cabinet colleagues were not convinced by his proposals for amendments. Some outside parliament continued to share the opinion voiced by *The Times* that by the orders Britain was 'engaging in battle with the enemy'. But events in Spain also worked against the campaign for repeal; on the one hand there were new and exciting opportunities for British trade in the Spanish and Portuguese colonies, on the other Spain presented a cause for Britain to champion. The pro-government press made much of the unfortunate situation of 'the Roscoes of Spain' and emphasised how events in Spain confirmed once and for all that the enemies of France were 'more secure' than her friends. Whig leaders at Westminster were divided on the issue, but Sheridan's emotional speech to the Commons that Napoleon was now fighting a 'people' rather than 'princes without dignity and ministers without wisdom' found echoes among former opponents of the war. Whitbread remained firm in his demand for peace, but Francis Horner, a founder of the *Edinburgh Review*, informed him that the events in Spain had changed his mind on the question, and in January 1809 Roscoe told Whitbread that he believed peace was impossible at the present juncture since the government could not desert Spain. Samuel Parr could now write to Bertie Greathead referring to Napoleon as the 'oppressor' and the Spanish as the 'oppressed'.[18]

The radical *Independent Whig* was not convinced that Spain was a cause worth fighting for and suggested that it would be better to remember the starving workers of Britain. Doubtless many cotton operatives and wool-workers shared this sentiment even though they did not articulate it for posterity. When the news of the bloody *Dos de Mayo* in Madrid reached Britain, the cotton operatives of Lancashire were flexing their muscles in a cause which served to increase their hostility to the government and their dependence on their own organisation and efforts. Since the 1790s the weavers had sought a minimum wage bill on the lines of the act which enabled the magistrates of London and Westminster to fix the wages of Spitalfields weavers. At the same time as the petitions for peace were being prepared in the cotton districts there was also a campaign to petition Parliament for a minimum wage bill; as usual the dislocation of trade had been met with wage reductions for those lucky enough still to find work. The two kinds of petitions arrived together, but while the peace petitions were left to lie on the table, the minimum wage petitions were referred to a select committee which was to deliberate for a year. Several prominent master manufacturers supported, or at least paid lip-service to the requests and a group of nineteen masters visited Perceval urging the passing of such a law. Perceval believed that the price of labour should be left to find its own level, however he suggested that the masters might meet the operatives' leaders and negotiate a basic wage; if smaller and less scrupulous employers undercut this agreed wage then Perceval promised to bring in a bill during the next session. For some unknown reason the masters rejected this proposal. George Rose, the Treasurer of the Navy and Vice-president of the Board of Trade, had long shown himself sympathetic to the idea of a minimum wage, and on 19 May he proposed to bring a bill before the Commons. Rose was coldly received by the House; Perceval spoke against him, as did Sir Robert Peel, one of the masters who had visited Perceval. Rose withdrew his motion, and the news of this urged the cotton workers into action on their own behalf. There were mass meetings in Manchester on 24 and 25 May; the local authorities ordered troops against the crowds on the second day and one workman was killed. The men struck, demanding a one-third increase in their wages; those who declined to join the strike were intimidated or had their shuttles removed. The strike spread through the cotton districts of Lancashire, and Lancashire woollen workers joined them. Precise evidence of the outcome of the strike is lacking, but it appears that the men eventually secured their increase.[19]

During 1807 and 1808 the demands for a minimum wage, for peace, and even for some kind of reform of the political system were becoming intermingled in the consciousness of the northern textile workers. It is difficult to know what to make of Samuel Bayley's battle-cry during the rescue of strikers in Rochdale gaol: 'This is the Bastile of Paris. O Glorious Revo-lu-ti-on, this is what we have long wanted.' Bayley, a bookkeeper, may have been swept along by the enthusiasm of the moment, but his words may also have had a deeper significance. Handbills were circulated during the disorders which went beyond the call for a wage increase. One from Royton urged an end to the strike, but wanted increased peaceful agitation to end the cause of distress, 'which cause we have no hesitation in pronouncing is the WAR'. A handbill from Bolton was more outspoken; it condemned the war, and accused the Cabinet, 'that nest of adders', of causing it; 'reformation' was now needed and the handbill concluded by asking if it was not time 'to drag the British Constitution from its lurking hole, and to expose it in its original and naked purity . . . ?' At the same time the weavers' hero was a man deeply committed to an end to the war, as well as to their campaign for a minimum wage. Joseph Hanson had been Colonel of the Manchester and Salford Volunteers, but at the end of 1807 he was publicly critical of Lord Milton and urging peace because of the distress in the North. He rode among the crowds of weavers in Manchester on 25 May voicing his sympathy, though there is conflicting evidence about precisely what he said. The Court of King's Bench put the worst construction on his comments and Hanson was sentenced to six months in prison and a fine of £100. The weavers offered to open a penny subscription to help pay his fine; he declined, and they presented him with a silver cup instead. They turned up in hundreds to greet him on his release but, cautious of creating any disorder, Hanson avoided them and hurried home. His reputation spread however, and was adopted by the revolutionary underground during the more serious disorders of 1812. 'Ned Ludd's clerk' informed a Huddersfield manufacturer that in 'the Cotton Country . . . the brave Mr. Hanson will lead them on to Victory'. In fact Hanson had died the preceding September.[20]

Demands for reform did not just mean demands for changes in parliamentary representation, the extension of the franchise or the shortening of a parliament's life; indeed during these four years such demands took second place to those for economical reform. People had seen the requirements of war lead to an enormous increase in the indirect taxes that they paid as well as the introduction of a tax on their incomes; they wanted to be sure that the money was being spent properly and that new appointments were not simply sinecures. Even a newspaper sympathetic to the government like *The Times* could urge investigation into these areas.

> . . . it is irritating beyond expression for a patient people, parting, and willingly parting, almost with their life-blood, in support of the independence of their country, to be told by the highest authority, that what is so hardly wrung from them, under pretence of public service, has been converted into sources of private emoluments; yet, for God's sake, if these things are done, let them not escape comment, and especially in the proper place, the House of Commons.[21]

Gradually governments had been moving in the desired direction. The non-party civil servant, like Sir George Harrison at the Treasury, John Beckett at the Home Office, William Hamilton at the Foreign Office and Henry Bunbury at the War Office, besides fulfilling the need for administrative continuity, was one aspect of these changes. Over a period of five years the select committee appointed on Biddulph's initiative in February 1807 presented a series of reports which, together with some proposals for reform, suggested that the situation was not alarming. Yet the changes were not of the kind which the public could easily perceive, and in 1809 the exposure and destruction of corruption became a national preoccupation.

In the autumn of 1808 the *Independent Whig* rumoured 'corruption and undue influence' were at work in military promotions. The explosion came in January 1809 when Gwyllm Lloyd Wardle, MP for Okehampton and Colonel of Volunteers, brought charges before Parliament that the Duke of York had been conniving at the receipt of money by his mistress for her supposed influence in hastening promotions and procuring commissions. Wardle's own reputation was not of the best, but his revelations brought a public outcry and demands that corruption be rooted out. Votes of thanks poured in to him from the cities of London and Westminster, from Southwark, Bristol, Liverpool, Manchester, Nottingham, Sheffield, thirty smaller boroughs and eight counties. Radicals like Burdett backed him and reformist Whigs like Whitbread and Lord Folkestone, initially lukewarm, soon rallied to his side. A full-blooded attack on corruption rocked the ministry; in May, W. A. Madocks, one of the radicals, brought forward specific charges against Castlereagh and Perceval. The Whig leadership disliked these attacks and a majority in the Commons vindicated first the Duke of York (though the ministry felt it best that he resign) and then the two ministers. The calls for reform were strong however both outside and inside Parliament. A temporary union was forged between radicals like Burdett, Whigs like Whitbread and Sir Samuel Romilly, and William Wilberforce and others among the 'Saints'. Their prospects seemed bright when the moderate Whig, Curwen, brought in a bill to prevent the sale of seats by requiring an oath from members that no money had changed hands. During its passage through the Commons the bill was considerably amended; one of the first things to go was the oath itself. In effect it became a semi-official government bill and most of the Whigs and all of the radicals turned against it. Nevertheless the act which passed did legislate against the worst forms of corruption; parliamentary seats were no longer advertised in the papers, and if the Treasury still had an advantage in elections it only controlled three boroughs directly.[22]

Wardle's revelations not only sparked off demands for an end to corruption, they also revived agitation for parliamentary reform. The Commons' refusal to support the motion calling for the Duke of York's dismissal gave valuable ammunition to those who maintained that Parliament did not reflect the opinions of the country. The question was raised whether MPs were delegates or plenipotentiaries. The borough of Southwark called a public meeting to demand of its members first an account of their conduct and second assurances that they would support parliamentary reform. George Ponsonby, the titular leader of the Whigs in the Commons, and Lord Grey were left behind by the movement and viewed with some concern the manner in which it found its leaders among the radicals like Burdett, supported on occasions by men in their own party like Whitbread. Outside Parliament a new popular movement sprang up, centred on Westminster. On 15 June 1809 Burdett presented a motion for reform to the House; it bore a striking resemblance to the proposal put forward by Grey in 1797. It was defeated by 15 votes to 74, and at the end of the month Parliament went into recess until the following January. But this was only the first round in the revived campaign for reform which gathered momentum during the recess; and before the end of the year the Home Office was showing concern about an increase in the number of debating societies in the metropolis.[23]

While petitions for peace were signed and demands for reform grew, the flimsy machinery of local government plodded on with its wartime burdens. Out of the £20,000 paid out to the poor of Manchester in 1809 some £3600 went to the families of regular militiamen or of men originally balloted for the Army of Reserve who enjoyed the same privilege. Middlesex was so lax in paying militia family allowances to Warwickshire for the substitutes serving in its regiment's ranks that in 1809 the Midland county began court proceedings. After Windham's suspension of the militia ballot came Castlereagh's depletions of the militia by drafts of volunteers for the regular army and the reintroduction of the ballot to fill the gaps. In 1809 there was also the ballot to make up the quotas of the new local militia. The ballots, as ever, were a burden on both those required to organise them and those whose names appeared on the lists. The regular militia ballots brought the usual queries over exemptions, fines and substitutes. In Lanarkshire colliers, dissatisfied with the way militia lists were prepared, burned the haystack of a local magistrate who had been active in the balloting. George Stephenson, later to be a great railway engineer, but at this time only a colliery brakesman, was balloted for the Northumberland Militia; he borrowed money and spent his savings on a substitute. John Bradley was balloted for Bramfield in Hertfordshire; he was unable to find a substitute and paid the fine to avoid service. Bradley then went round the parish asking his neighbours to help him with the fine; John Carrington gave him four shillings. Apart from a heavy fine graduated according to income there was no way out of the Local Militia if a man was balloted, and James Asquith, a blacksmith of Mirfield, was heard to murmur 'Damn King George' as he was sworn in at Wakefield. Asquith was prosecuted at Knaresborough Quarter Sessions on two counts; first that his words were intended to stir up sedition, and second for the contempt and scandal directed at the King. Asquith actually admitted to 'a grumble'; his defence counsel made much of the enormous weight of two deputy lieutenants and two magistrates lined up against his poor client and he urged the jury that at the time of the 'grumble'

> there was a great ferment in the minds of the balloted men, and a great unwillingness to take the oaths required by the Local Militia Act, and it was very difficult to convince them, that if they did take the oaths,

they would not be liable to be transported from one part of the realm to the other.

The jury found him not guilty. William Brooke, one of the local officials involved, reported that they did so 'under the Idea that the words were spoken on the impulse of the moment, whilst he was vexed' at being balloted. However the prosecution was valuable since it quelled 'a spirit of opposition that had been excited to the Local Militia Act'.[24]

The first assemblies of the local militia were fraught with problems. There were strong-minded individuals who demonstrated their resentment when embodied. The Marquis of Tavistock had one such in his Bedfordshire regiment whose conduct 'from the first hour of his joining [was] . . . in the highest degree mutinous and disrespectful'. He explained to Whitbread that he expected a court martial to sentence the man to a flogging, in which case Tavistock intended a public pardon in front of the whole regiment. 'You will bear in mind that we have no-one in the Regt. capable of flogging a man'. Mr Ackerly, a shopkeeper of Liverpool, refused to join his regiment except by force; he was court-martialled and sentenced to be flogged, but after 'a most penitential letter' to his colonel he too was pardoned in a speech before the whole regiment. There was a confusion over the men's allowances, particularly the 'marching guinea' which they believed to be their due on marching off to training. There was a disorder in the Forbury, Reading, when the Marquis of Blandford's regiment began laying down their arms on parade in protest at not having received the money. A crowd, including volunteers who had not transferred to the local militia, encouraged the men and the riot act had to be read. One result of the disorder was the disbanding of the Reading Volunteers. A more serious disorder erupted in the Cambridgeshire Local Militia at Ely. A Lieutenant Black subsequently listed for the Home Office several of the regiment's complaints and problems. The NCOs were not efficient:

> The civil situations of most of the non-commissioned of the Local is a great impediment to their commanding their inferiors with sufficient firmness. For they are either publicans or little shopkeepers selected on account of their being able to read or write, or after their military duties are finished, become fellow labourers and perhaps inferior to those very men whom the day previous they were commanding.

The bread supplied to the local militia was the same 'contract bread' as was supplied to the regular army, and this was inferior to the bread which the locals had at their own, or their master's table. But the principle trouble in the Cambridgeshires, Black agreed, was money; by the time the men assembled for training they had spent their two guineas enrolment money and had to survive on their pay alone.

> From their age and former habits, mostly being farmers servants living at a plentiful table, or accustomed to the provision of parents, or from other circumstances not being in the habit of studying domestic economy, they were incapable of laying out this sum to the best advantage, and during the first week many men were literally without food for two days.

The men were not told about the appropriation of their marching guinea for various necessaries 'until their complaints assumed the complexion of absolute mutiny'. The mutiny was suppressed by four squadrons of cavalry from the King's German Legion and five mutineers were sentenced to be flogged. The floggings, and the use of German troops, provoked an outcry led by Cobbett in an article in the *Political Register* which earned him a heavy fine and a two-year prison sentence for seditious libel.[25]

The subsequent periods of annual training did not always go smoothly. In May 1810 local militiamen in St Albans rioted over their marching guinea and there was trouble in Worcester. Several of William Nicholson's Liverpool regiment used a march to Ormskirk for their training as an opportunity for a great drinking bout in every hostelry on their route. In 1811 the same regiment's complaints about the quality of their bread came close to mutiny.[26] During the distress of 1811 and 1812 a few local militiamen took part in provision riots, some may have been involved in Luddite attacks,[27] but the regiments were also used with effect against both kinds of disorder; their loyalty partly secured, perhaps, by the knowledge that while they were embodied their families were entitled to the usual militia allowance.

8. Victories Abroad, Crises at Home: 1810–15

I 'Welcome Ned Ludd, Thy Case Is Good': 1810–12

In September 1809 Portland's ministry collapsed about him; the old Duke resigned on 6 September and the country was virtually without a government for the next month. It was left to Perceval to try to save something from the wreck. Again there was an attempt to create a coalition, bringing in men from all the principal factions; again the attempt foundered. One contemporary described Perceval going out 'into the highways and hedges' to find ministers.[1] Perceval doubted whether Pitt's old friends would care to have Sidmouth with them in the Cabinet. His attempts to bring in the Whigs faltered because Grey and Grenville could not agree on a war policy, because they had not forgiven George III for their fall in 1807, and because they maintained a general fear of coalitions. The government which assembled under Perceval in October was consequently composed of largely the same personnel as Portland's ministry, but without the weight of Castlereagh and Canning. The general feeling among the press was that the Cabinet was made up of nonentities and incompetents; already there were demands for an enquiry into the Walcheren fiasco. The ministers themselves do not appear to have believed that they would last long. Yet this was the beginning of the ministry which was to see final victory over Napoleon, which survived a severe economic crisis, major popular disorder, a regency crisis, the assassination of its first leader, and which was to rule the country for over a decade.

Perceval's ministers were principally Pitt's men. They had a long experience of government. They were not, by and large, men whose political pedigree stretched back to the dim and distant past, but men

147

who owed their positions to the system. Perceval, though a son of an earl, was a lawyer who had risen by his own abilities and good luck; Lord Eldon, the Lord Chancellor, was also a lawyer, and the third son of a prosperous Newcastle business man; Lord Liverpool, the Secretary for War and Colonies was a second generation peer, whose political advancement had been boosted by his father's special relationship with George III as a political confidant. Such origins make more understandable their determination to maintain the *status quo* of a society which had given them everything; but they did not come together initially as a conservative government to oppose reform, though it is for such that they are principally remembered. The ministry was put together in a vacuum, and its intention was first and foremost to win the war. They stayed in power in the early years because there was no viable alternative. At the end of 1810 George III finally lost his reason; in February 1811 a regency was established under the Prince of Wales and it was generally expected that the Whigs, the Prince's friends, would now replace Perceval's Cabinet in the tradition of the eighteenth century. But the Prince was in a quandary; while recognising the tradition, he was reluctant to bring in friends who were against Perceval's energetic pursuit of the war, which the Prince himself favoured, and who threatened to cause problems by experimenting with the status of Roman Catholics. After a year of regency, when the limitations imposed on the Prince by the act of 1811 expired, the Regent wrote to Grey and Grenville asking them to join in a coalition, but in a letter which expressed support for Perceval's war policy and a reluctance to begin tampering with the Catholic question. Understandably the Whigs refused. At the same time Perceval was able to strengthen his ministry by bringing back Castlereagh as Foreign Secretary and Sidmouth as Lord President of the Council. Perceval's standing among the governing classes increased. In March 1812 Lord Sheffield recorded that 'Perceval rises daily in the opinion of the country and even the opposition, and some of the oldest members of parliament and best judges have told me that they think him in debate fully equal to Pitt . . .'; while 'the virulence of the Talent faction is perfectly disgusting'.[2] But within two months Perceval was dead, shot in the lobby of the Commons by a deranged bankrupt, and there was a ministerial crisis. Liverpool took over in Perceval's stead, and although the Cabinet was gloomy about its prospects it was prepared to continue. A majority in the Commons had doubts whether the ministry could survive without Perceval and on the 21 May a Commons address was presented to the Regent begging him to form an efficient administration; Liverpool and his colleagues resigned. During the next two and a half weeks there was no government as the different factions discussed plans for coalitions and the much desired broad-bottomed administration. Again the discussions foundered, and on the 8 June Liverpool and his ministers resumed as before. But their parliamentary backing was much greater since they appeared to be the only men prepared to put the national interest above particular projects. The national interest, for Liverpool and his ministers, as well as for the parliamentary majority, was the defeat of Napoleon; besides this all other questions, including those of reform and economic distress, were of secondary importance.

The ultimate success of Wellington in the Peninsula often conceals the tremendous effort that it was for Perceval to keep Wellington's army going in the first years of that war. When the new parliamentary session began in January 1810, the opposition had their knives well sharpened on what they considered to be Wellington's failure in Spain, which had resulted in his retreat back to Portugal, and on the disaster at Walcheren. The debate over Walcheren led, indirectly, to a major popular disturbance in London. The decision to clear the public gallery and an associated diatribe on democracy and the liberty of the press by Windham outraged one of the principal popular debating clubs in the metropolis, the British Forum. The club resolved to debate the matter; its Secretary, John Gale Jones, was brought before the bar of the House and committed to Newgate for contempt. Burdett took Jones's part but, unable to secure a motion for his release, he addressed his constituents in an open letter first published by Cobbett condemning Jones's imprisonment as a 'most enormous Abuse of Power and most dangerous of all encroachments upon the Rights and Liberties of Englishmen'. Perceval resolved to have Burdett sent to the Tower for a libel on the House; the problem however was to arrest him, for Burdett barricaded his house in Piccadilly, enormous crowds assembled in his support, and for the only time in the popular disorders which disturbed England in the eighteenth and early nineteenth centuries, barricades appeared on the streets of London. A dangerous farce continued from 6 to 9 April 1810, with troops and crowds skirmishing, the government unsure about whether their chosen officer legally could break down Burdett's door, Burdett himself preparing to call out the Middlesex *posse comitatus* in his own defence, while some of his supporters suggested serious armed resistance. On 9 April Burdett's house was forced, and he offered no resistance when committed to the Tower. The crowds left the streets; the trouble simmered for a few weeks when a Westminster coroner brought in a verdict of murder on a man shot by an unknown trooper of the Life Guards during the disorders, and the

Westminster electors sent a remonstrance to Parliament. There was also support for Burdett in the provinces, where petitions were signed and suspicious writings appeared on the walls; in North Shields, for example, Nelson's 'England expects every man to do his duty' appeared ominously beside pro-Burdett and revolutionary slogans. The deputies of the Post Office were consulted about the extent of the Burdett support in their neighbourhoods. There was concern about an attack on the Tower, where security was strengthened. But no disorder materialised, and on his release during the recess in June, Burdett avoided incitement and, to be on the safe side, Perceval made extensive military preparations to meet the trouble.[3]

In Parliament Perceval's government survived the attack on the Walcheren expedition by the skin of its teeth. The majority of independent members probably hoped that the government would take warning from the campaign, and considered that Perceval and his colleagues were preferable to the Whigs who had no policy, who were defeatists over events in the Peninsula, and undisciplined in their parliamentary behaviour. Some Whigs continued to carp about the war and to criticise first Wellington, and then, when Wellington's abilities became increasingly apparent in the campaign of 1812, they switched their attack to the government for not supporting him sufficiently. Such attacks, however, never won them support inside Westminster.[4]

Between 1809 and 1811 (when there was a reduction in the regular militia), numbers in the armed forces remained reasonably constant, despite the usual recruiting difficulties. There were, however, some improvements in supplying the army, and particularly in financing Wellington's Peninsular force. Equipping the army remained divided between several government departments, and the basic uniform of the soldier (excluding only shoes and greatcoats) continued to be the responsibility of the colonels. John Maberly, a London contractor, made an imaginative plea for rationalisation; he offered to take over all supply from the regimental colonels and do the task at a lower cost to the country and at a profit to himself. The government expressed some interest, but Maberly's proposals were never adopted. Corruption remained rife; some military contractors found ways of cheating the examinations of the new Storekeeper General. Then in 1811 Perceval appointed his former private secretary, John Herries, as Commissary in Chief and the tide turned against those whom Herries dubbed as 'the cursed contractors'.[5]

Keeping Wellington in the Peninsula obliged the Treasury to hunt for bullion. The Spaniards would only take dollars, and the private agents who remitted these from Latin America could amass considerable fortunes from peculation and fraud, as well as enormous profits. Dollars and credit were essential, too, for the Spanish and Portugese armies, but in 1811 Wellington persuaded the government that the best way to ensure that the three allied armies in the Peninsula acted in unison, was to pay the subsidies directly to him. As a consequence, for the first time since 1793, the government could be sure that all its subsidy money was being spent for military purposes only. Yet although from 1808 Britain's aid programme escalated as she became the armourer and financier of the national risings against Napoleon which began with that in Spain, for the first time her subsidy payments were less than the cost of keeping a British army in the field. Between 1808 and 1816 all the subsidy remittances put together amounted to only about one-half of the £80 million spent on Wellington's army.[6]

While British specie flowed abroad in torrents, shortages in Britain itself became alarming. Overseers of the poor in some districts experienced considerable difficulty in getting small change and began issuing their own tokens; in Birmingham the overseers issued notes for small amounts, some of which were marked 'For the convenience of paying the poor payable every Wednesday, when eight 2s 6d. notes or four 5s notes are brought together'. Some bankers also issued tokens. The paper money issued by the Bank of England and by other banks depreciated; it was exchanged for less than its face value in specie. In the second half of 1809 David Ricardo voiced the growing concern in letters to the *Morning Chronicle* and subsequently in his pamphlet *The High Price of Bullion*.

At the beginning of 1810 a Jewess named De Younge was charged by the solicitor of the Mint for selling paper guineas at 22s 6d. each. William Cobbett drew his conclusions from the career of the French *assignat*; 'Robespierre made it a capital offence to show this preference for metallic money; but Robespierre did not, by that means, prevent paper from depreciating, though he was quite successful in driving the very semblance of metallic money out of the country.'When De Younge was brought to trial the defence counsel argued that she had not sold gold at a premium, but had bought bank notes at a discount; the judges were forced to conclude that she had not in this case committed an offence. Other offenders were not as fortunate.[7]

The question of depreciation was raised in Parliament in February 1810 and a Commons committee was set up to investigate. Perceval took little notice of the members appointed to the committee and as a result it was strong in economists and Whigs sympathetic to the Riccardian point of view, while government supporters and spokesmen for the Bank of England were notably lacking. The committee completed its report in June, concluding that there had been an excessive issue of banknotes, which had led to high prices, the rise in the market value of gold and the fall in the pound's value on foreign exchanges. It recommended the resumption of cash payments within two years. Its conclusions, based on incomplete evidence, have since been proved erroneous; in particular there was very little correlation between the overall level of prices and the number of banknotes in circulation. The following May the question was debated in the Commons. Both sides, bullionists and ministerialists, produced minute and complex calculations to prove their points; increasingly the majority of the Commons appears to have become bored. John Fuller, member for Sussex, protested that the debates were all 'humbug' and suggested that if all Britain's gold went it would still be possible to use tallow, leather, oyster shells, or anything. On the final votes the committee's recommendations were defeated.

The verdict was significant for the war effort. The debate had created problems for Treasury agents negotiating in foreign money markets; had the bullionists won the day Britain would have been unable to support the peoples in arms against Napoleon. Yet the defeat in Parliament did not mean an end to the problem. In June 1811 Lord King, a relative of Grenville, informed his tenants that he would only receive his rents in gold or in paper money estimated by the price of gold. There was a possibility that other landlords would follow suit. The situation was saved by a private member's bill introduced to the Lords by Lord Stanhope, and piloted through the Commons by Perceval, which made banknotes legal tender.[8]

Demands for reforms ebbed and flowed. In May 1810 Thomas Brand, member for Hertfordshire and friend of Whitbread, moved for a committee to consider the case for parliamentary reform. His motion was defeated by 115 votes to 234, but this was the largest vote in favour of reform since the defeat of Pitt's plan in 1785. Two years later Brand introduced reform proposals again, and again they were defeated; this time he received only 88 votes, still more than twice as many as Grey's 1793 motion. Thereafter moderate reformers in Parliament lost their enthusiasm, but encouraged, rather than overawed, outside Parliament the cause of reform continued to spread, aided by the imprisonment of Burdett and the use of troops on the pro-Burdett crowd in London – 'Good God, are Britons to be treated in the East Indian method of government?!!!' – and by the long continuance and the high cost of the war. The American colonists' war cry of 'No taxation without representation' began to appear in a new context. Major Cartwright asked: 'Is this income tax, which must make itself felt like an earthquake in every house on this island, to be levied by REPRESENTATIVES OF THE PEOPLE; or by the ABSOLUTE POWER OF THE KING'S MINISTER?'[9] The question was taken up elsewhere, and could be linked with continuing demands for economical reform and an end to corruption which were heard from sources as far apart as 'Orator' Hunt and leading articles in *The Times*. But the most strident of the demands pressed on the government in 1811 and 1812 were for the repeal of the Orders in Council and for peace. These demands had their immediate impetus in a new economic crisis, which began towards the end of 1810.

Several different elements combined to bring an end to the boom of 1809 and the first part of 1810. During 1810 Napoleon tightened up his blockade against British merchandise, notably in North Germany. The produce bought in Latin America, in expectation that it could be re-exported to Europe, began to pile up in warehouses and lose its value; correspondingly speculation in Latin America was checked. The bubble was ready for bursting when, in the summer of 1810, twenty-six banks failed; twenty of these banks were in the provinces, the others were in the metropolis and included highly respected institutions of long standing. The failure of these banks was sufficient to put an end to speculation, ruin confidence and produce a chain reaction which spread throughout the economy. A poor harvest worsened the situation. Then on 2 November President Madison gave Britain three months to renounce the Orders in Council; when Britain refused Madison reintroduced the non-intercourse legislation and Britain's last major market was closed. There followed two years of industrial stagnation and general distress. Again the cotton industry was the hardest hit. 'Oh war what Havock as [sic] thou made' complained Rowbottom in October 1810, and three months later he feared that 'this distructive[sic] war will make thousands smart that are yet unborn'. Between 10,000 and 12,000 were reported to be out of work in Manchester in the summer of 1811; unemployment made it much cheaper to procure substitutes for the regular militia. The churchwardens of the parish of Manchester paid out some £25,300 in poor relief from Easter 1811 to Easter 1812, and £34,600 over the same period the following year.[10] Other textile industries suffered. There was a serious crisis in the West Riding wool trade; there is less evidence for what was happening in the West Country, but the picture here also appears to have been gloomy except for some manufacturers of fine cloth. The hosiery industry of Nottinghamshire and Leicestershire were hit; they had looked to America when the European market was closed to them, and suffered accordingly with the resumption of non-intercourse. The problems with the United States had repercussions for the metal industry. Iron itself was not badly affected, but America imported nails from south Staffordshire and the products of the metalworkers of Birmingham and Sheffield; in consequence there was short-time working in Staffordshire, and serious unemployment and distress in both Birmingham and Sheffield in 1811 and 1812.[11]

As large numbers of seamen were laid off in London, tempers became short and fights started. The worst trouble was among foreign seamen; Portuguese sailors were especially unpopular for undercutting the usual rates and allegedly drawing their knives in any disagreement. Native-born seamen do not appear to have been much involved, indeed native-born seamen working in the merchant service were now greatly diminished in numbers. At the end of 1811 William Fairbairn travelled from North Shields to London on a collier. In later life he recalled how the war had drained the coastal trade of able-bodied seamen.

> The collier ships from Shields and Sunderland were left almost destitute of men. The result of this reduction proved seriously injurious to the service, as every winter during the war increased the number of wrecks, and many lives were lost for want of hands to work the ship. In the ship which I had taken a passage (with my old friend and companion Hogg . . .), there were only three old men, with the captain, the mate, and three boys; altogether they numbered eight hands, whereas, in the midst of winter, twelve was the complement.

The impressment of men by the Royal Navy was one reason for this shortage, but there were enormous numbers of prisoners of war from the north-east ports in France, probably seized by French privateers, who continued to infest the North Sea. At the end of 1807 a collection was made in South Shields for British prisoners in France; the local rector estimated that from 140 to 150 men from South Shields were prisoners in France out of a total population of some 8500. In March 1812 the Prince Regent received a petition requesting an exchange of prisoners of war from 'the distressed wives, fatherless children, orphans, and aged weeping mothers of the towns of Sunderland, Bishopwear-mouth and Monkwearmouth'. The petition carried the names of 89 persons in Sunderland who claimed to have exactly 100 relatives prisoners in France; they estimated that there were about 700 prisoners of war from the three towns.[12] But this kind of distress was very different from that experienced in most areas during the economic crisis of 1811 and 1812.

The distress resulting from the slump was aggravated by poor harvests. Soup kitchens were established once again, and thousands sought parish relief. In the coalfields of the North-east coal-owners attempted to ease the distress by signing on supernumeraries, some of whom did work usually performed by horses. The lower orders of society reacted positively with petitions, and with the traditional forms of popular disorder such as provision riots and 'collective bargaining by riot', but it is difficult to deny that Luddism also had new political overtones. In the cotton districts where the slump hit hardest, petitions were drawn up by the workers early in 1811 requesting help first from their social superiors within the locality, and then help from Parliament. The Commons received a petition from Manchester, with 40,000 signatures, and others from 30,000 Scottish weavers and 7000 Bolton weavers. These sought relief from the distress created by the problems of the cotton industry. The organisers, at least, also showed a positive awareness that it was men from their social group who were physically fighting the war.

> Surely . . . the wisdom of the Legislature can devise some means to help us. We will do our duty, as Loyal, as peaceable subjects, but grant us existence otherwise who shall fight the Battles of our Country.

> Most of our youth are serving their country, but there are great numbers who are unfit for the army or navy, who yet have families to support; and Parochial aid, considering the numbers, is not adequate.

Some exchequer bills were released to enable manufacturers to keep their workmen employed, but the select committee appointed to consider the petitions came up with no answer to the weavers' distress other than perseverance, lower wages rates, or finding other employment. These recommendations infuriated the weavers. The committee in Manchester which had organised the town's petition issued an address to the signatories expressing their inability to understand why the Commons committee believed that any financial aid would endanger the balance of commerce, of manufacture and of agriculture, since the legislature had already involved itself 'in matters of apparently less moment' like the Corn Laws, wage rates for Spitalfields weavers and London tailors, the salaries of judges and clergyman, commercial regulations 'and a multitude of other things'. The address noted how previous governments abolished the slave trade, and helped 'the weak and defenceless' and 'the indigent'. 'We still see them able to provide the means for defending our common country against the attacks of Europe united against us.' The moral was clear; the Commons were now 'unfit to manage your affairs' and there had to be reform, extending 'the elective franchise as far as taxation'. 'Had you possessed 70,000 votes for the election of Members to sit in that House, would your application have been treated with such indifference, not to say inattention? We believe not.' Early in the following year the Commons received several petitions from the weaving districts demanding both peace and parliamentary reform.[13]

The framework-knitters of the Midlands also suffered from the slump. One of Whitbread's correspondents in Nottingham blamed 'that system of warfare and prodigality'.

> The manufactury of Nottm. and its neighbourhood depending very much on foreign demand, has never suffered so much as it now does, the Lace men and stocking making are now limited to make such a quantity of goods as will scarcely enable them to maintain their families; and there are numbers who are without any employ.

The framework-knitters of Leicester petitioned the Commons for the removal of the Orders in Council, which they saw as damaging their livelihood by causing trouble with the United States, and also for an end to the East India Company's monopoly of trade with the East which, they maintained, gave advantage only to the company and not to the country as a whole. A group of framework-knitters in Nottingham, led by Gravener Henson, looked beyond the immediate problem of the Orders in Council, and sought a long-term solution to the problems which beset their trade.

> 'Tis not the orders in Council, 'tis not the threats or power of BUONAPARTE, that have, or can ruin the Trade of these Counties. No! the evil arises from a far different source; 'tis in the manufactory itself; 'tis in speculating, unprincipled individuals that have made fraudulent goods, to cheat and rob the Public.

They considered profitable manufactures vital to any nation. They had enabled England 'to pay the continent, from the days of ELIZABETH, to fight her battles'. If France were to be given 'the almost despised Mechanics of these Counties . . . she would leave us SPAIN and PORTUGAL'. The Nottingham Knitters arranged for the preparation of a parliamentary bill 'For preventing Frauds and Abuses in the Frame-Work Knitting Manufacture, and in the payment of persons employed there in'. Henson and his committee sought the support of knitters across the length and breadth of the kingdom, and a petition supporting the bill collected 10,000 signatures – only men working in the trade were permitted to sign, not women. The correspondence of the committee reflects a confidence in themselves and in their endeavours; and if their main concern was with their trade, they were very conscious of the political situation within which they had to work and with which they had to contend. William Page joked with Henson about the Prince Regent's secretary, whose sinecure caused debate in Parliament and an outcry in the country. 'We [the committee] are up to the ears in business and papers like poor Col. McMahon only not paid quite so well, unless it is this we are paid in the good wishes of the people and he poor soul with the curses after taking their money!' Unfortunately for Henson and his committees, while sinecures might create an outcry they could still be granted, their bill on the other hand was thrown out by the Lords, and Sidmouth trusted that 'no such principle would be again attempted to be introduced in any Bill brought up to that House'.[14]

The government was forced to take more serious notice of violent protests by distressed workers. The year 1811 saw the first appearance of the followers of 'General' Ned Ludd. Luddism was centred in three principal areas: Nottinghamshire, the West Riding, and Lancashire. The movement began in Nottinghamshire at the beginning of 1811 when workmen smashed stocking frames as a protest against new pay rates, truck payments and other devices introduced by unscrupulous employers to defraud them of their pay. It reached its climax between November 1811 and February 1812 as groups of well-disciplined, masked or disguised men smashed the frames of those hosiers who failed to conform to Luddite demands. The attacks ceased early in February 1812, probably because they had been partially successful in forcing hosiers to comply with demands for better wages, and possibly also because some of the men had some faith in Henson's plan for a bill to regulate the trade, though most of the Nottinghamshire Luddites came from villages and the bulk of Henson's support was urban.[15] In addition another bill was making speedy progress through Parliament which made frame breaking a capital offence, and there were thousands of troops and special constables in the area. Troops and special constables however, did not deter the Yorkshire Luddites. In the West Riding new shearing frames and gig mills were attacked by the croppers, who believed that their livelihood was threatened. These disorders began in January, reaching their climax with the destruction of Forster's cloth mill near Wakefield, and with the unsuccessful assault on William Cartwright's mill at Rawfolds in the Spen valley in April 1812. In the West Riding papers and leaflets circulated, and threatening letters sent, possessed a more insurrectionary tone than anything in Nottinghamshire. There is also evidence to suggest that some of the West Riding Luddites were disappointed by the Prince Regent's decision to keep his father's ministers in power rather than permitting Grey and Grenville to form a ministry.

But it was in Lancashire where politics and Luddism were most closely fused. Early in 1811 there had been nocturnal mass meetings reminiscent of the unrest before the Peace of Amiens. Early in the following year there were major disorders throughout the North-west. There was a riot at the Manchester Exchange over an attempt to petition the Prince Regent on his decision to keep his father's ministers. There were serious provision riots, with Stockport rioters led by 'General Ludd's wives'. Cotton manufacturers employing cheap female labour were warned 'a Reform or Death', and there were attacks on mills operating new power looms, climaxing in the attack on a mill in Middleton and the death of at least seven of the assailants at the hands of the military. But the unsuccessful attacks at Rawfolds and at the Middleton mills did not mean the end of the disorder in the North. In the words of E. P. Thompson, 'sheer insurrectionary fury has rarely been more widespread in English history' than during the summer of 1812.[16] In Yorkshire and Lancashire arms were seized; if the Luddites themselves were losing members and going underground in con-spiritorial groups, areas that had been infected with Luddism rejoiced openly and cheerfully at the news of Perceval's assassination; threatening letters poured into the Prince Regent and his secretary, Colonel McMahon. In Yorkshire the threats assumed a positive form; William Horsfall of Ottiwells near Huddersfield, a manufacturer notorious for his opposition to the Luddites, was shot and killed; Joseph Radcliffe, a magistrate of nearby Milnsbridge who distinguished himself against the Luddites, had his house fired into, and was given a military guard for several months. Twelve thousand soldiers were deployed in the disordered counties during the summer and autumn of 1812 – more than had landed with Sir Arthur Wellesley in Portugal in 1808 – not until the winter of 1812–13 were they gradually withdrawn. Those Luddites who were arrested, brought to trial and found guilty were treated with the utmost severity.

Was Luddism a revolutionary threat? Before the 'Middleton fight' crowds besieged the armoury of the Bolton Local Militia; William Chippendale, a local magistrate and commandant of the local militia, barricaded himself in with his ten sergeants and defied the rioters' threats for two days. A provision riot in Sheffield became a raid on the local militia armoury; 198 muskets were destroyed (possibly so that they could not be used against rioters), but 78 others disappeared. Magistrates in Lancashire received information that a general rising was planned for the summer; but here the evidence runs out. There probably were former members of the United Englishmen in the Luddite districts, and men who hoped for some kind of insurrection. They had much hatred and anger to build on as the threatening letters, the jubilation at Perceval's death, and the sympathy for Bellingham, his assassin, testify. They probably did conspire and win some supporters, but no full-blooded insurrection materialised. Revolutions, moreover, require more than a lower-class uprising. Although Sir Richard Ryder, the Home Secretary, was indecisive – *The Times* believed that he allowed the Luddite disturbances to get so bad by not taking tough enough measures at the outset – the government never lost its nerve, even after Perceval's assassination. In the reshuffle following the assassination, Ryder was replaced by Sidmouth, altogether more capable and determined. During the attack on Cartwright's mill a soldier of the Cumberland Militia refused to fire on the attackers, but by and large the troops deployed against the Luddites remained loyal, despite attempts to subvert them, and although they probably disliked their task. Nor was there any mass flight of support from the government by the propertied classes. Luddism probably compounded the fears of some that law and order was breaking down. The savage murders of two families in east London in December 1811 encouraged such fears and led to the creation of a select committee to look into the policing of the metropolis. The fears generated by these murders spread far and wide across the country. Sir Henry Fitzherbert, whose Derbyshire seat was on the fringe of the Midland Luddite area, recorded Perceval's death sorrowfully in his almanac for 1812 and added (probably as an assumption rather than based on any statistical evidence): 'Within these 6 months there have been more murders, and attempts to murder than were ever known.' In this respect, the Luddite disorders probably served to unite the government and the propertied classes.[17]

Yet during the crises of 1811 and 1812 the propertied classes were not united behind government war policy. Coinciding with the union against working-class disorder came a serious division over the Orders in Council between what Professor Francois Crouzet has identified as the 'old' and the 'new' England. The orders were defended by eighteenth-century England – agricultural, mercantilist, and imperialist – which accepted that they were necessary for the country's prestige and honour, necessary for weakening France, and believed that a repeal would only weaken England's maritime rights. Furthermore the orders prevented neutrals from winning an unfair advantage; as a correspondent to the Leicester newspapers put it: 'Had it not been for these Orders, America would have run away with the trade of the world.' Yet for all that 'old England' was backward looking, it did recognise the new scale of warfare. A correspondent of *The Times*, supporting the orders, noted 'We are engaged in a war – a war of no common description – a war of system against system, in which no choice is left us, but victory or extirpation.' It was impossible to participate in such a struggle 'without sweat, and . . . without a wound'. Ranged against the orders were the new industrialists and merchants who were doing business on an unprecedented scale, who sought foreign markets for their products, and who looked particularly to the United States while Europe was closed; military, political and diplomatic arguments made no impression on these men, while maritime rights were, as one of them maintained, simply big words for an official toast. These were the heralds of nineteenth-century free trade, and in their quest for markets they also demanded an end to the monopoly which the East India Company had on eastern trade.[18]

Although there were petitions from Luddite areas against the orders, and against the East India Company's monopoly, signed by both manufacturers and workers, as well as from small-scale industries like the wool and linen trade of Shrewsbury and the wool trade of Kendal, both of which were suffering from the closure of the American market, the main thrust of the campaign came from elsewhere. In the manufacturing areas of the west Midlands the masters had not sought a way out of the economic slump by the introduction of machines or new practices as was often the case in those areas where Luddism was strong; here the masters and their workmen made common cause in opposing the orders. Especially significant was the campaign organised in Birmingham by a young country banker, Thomas Attwood, who in 1811 was chosen as the town's High Bailiff.

In Parliament the campaign against the orders was managed by Henry Brougham, a young and radical Whig. He brought forward scores of witnesses from the industrial areas to testify to the house of the distress attributable to the orders. In June 1812 the government gave way, revoking the orders in respect of American vessels; though endeavouring to find a face-saving formula. As Castlereagh confided to Wilberforce: 'One does not like to own that we are forced to give way to our manufacturers.' But within a year the government had given way to the provincial campaign's second demand by revising the East India Company's charter and abolishing its monopoly of trade with India (though not that with China). Brougham hoped that the new kind of mass agitation and petitioning could be used to secure other reforms, notably the reduction of war taxes. He also hoped that the provincial businessmen so prominent in the demand for the revocation of the orders would now see the need for their own representation in Parliament. In the short term this latter remained unfulfilled. However the entire movement against the Orders in Council and the East India

Company monopoly reflects a growing confidence among the expanding and, generally prospering, provincial middle classes, together with an antipathy from this group towards the old merchant classes of London who had long been a powerful lobby in Parliament. It is significant that the agitation for parliamentary reform in the late 1820s, which climaxed with the First Reform Act, closely resembled the campaign of 1812 – a union of the middle and working classes with a provincial power base in the Birmingham Political Union, organised again by Thomas Attwood.[19]

II   The End in Sight: 1813–14

There was concern about the 1812 harvest, especially in the West Country, where the population saw government contractors buying corn in great quantities, much of which went to the 11,000 prisoners of war kept on Dartmoor. A reply on Sidmouth's behalf to a concerned clergyman protested that the government never fixed on particular markets for public purchases, but only bought where grain was cheap; such a reply was not likely to assuage the fears of the Reverend John Jago's poor parishioners. Threatening letters appeared:

> Rouse Brittans and keep not silence but be possed [sic] with a spirit of desparation for a blody fray for it is high time to put a stop to this great opression and to rid these infernal thieves and robers of the face of the Earth for the[y] laugh at our calamity and we will mock when their fear cometh for the Crys of their poor is so great we are determing to put it into practice and these vipers shall fall victams to and inraged mob and their houses become dunghills.

A Devonshire gentleman warned that his county would soon be out of corn: 'This is an alarming consideration, arising from this long War and the dearth and scarcity will again produce riots and plunder and may eventually a revolution.' In the event, however, the price of bread fell slightly on average across the whole country in 1813 and popular disorder was muted.[20]

The euphoria at the revocation of the Orders in Council was short-lived, for Parliament's action, though giving a temporary relief to masters and men, and a temporary boost to the economy, was too late to prevent war with America. Reports from the industrial areas during the winter of 1812–13 were little brighter than those the year before. Thomas Babington, member for Leicester borough, sent Sidmouth gloomy descriptions of his constituency: 'On the revocation of the Orders in

Council the warehouses were relieved from their load of goods but they are filling up again.' The workmen, he reported, showed signs of poverty with their 'squalid looks and scanty cloaths and furniture'; their cry was for 'a good trade, and a big loaf and peace'. Whitbread was informed that in Hinckley 'even the middle class of people' were forced to practise rigid and self-denying economy so as to afford the taxes and poor rates, the latter having doubled within the preceding twelve months. Rowbottom noted the low ebb of weaving, with some people doing 'any kind of drugery'. 'A deal in this neighbourhood and about Chadderton, Middleton and other parts have been attacked with fevers and some have died. A large number of men have of late enlisted into the militias and different regements of the Line. Most of poor families are in a state of actual starvation.' But the news of Napoleon's disastrous Moscow campaign at the end of 1812 and the rising of the German peoples against him spelled an end to the blockade of Europe and promised relief through the reopening of European markets.[21]

Several of the organisers of the campaign against the Orders in Council and the East India Company's monopoly switched their campaign to demands for peace. A meeting was held in Loughborough in August 1812 with representatives from Derbyshire, Leicestershire and Nottinghamshire, which petitioned the Commons for peace and which resolved to urge petitions on 'Friends of Peace' in the United Kingdom. As a result the industrialist William Strutt, who chaired the meeting, sent copies of the resolutions and the petition to every county in the kingdom; he distributed about 2500 in all. In the general election at the end of 1812 about twenty-five candidates, including Brougham in Liverpool and Roscoe in Leicester, stood on a peace platform. They met with little success; another example, protested reformers, of the need to reform Parliament. 'The people have no constituted organ, by which their real opinions can be made known', wrote George Bown in his *Leicester Chronicle*; 'that organ is sought by the Friends of Peace, Reform and Religious Liberty, as the only means of rescuing the country from its perils'. The peace petitions, presented at the beginning of 1813, fared no better. In Birmingham some men were concerned that the government might retaliate against the petitioners by renewing the East India Company's monopoly. One of Strutt's associates suggested that the campaign had been sabotaged by a group in Hampshire who reprinted Strutt's material and despatched it themselves without paying the postage to annoy the recipients. But he also noted a general apathy; people, he believed, were largely insensible to the war because it had continued for so long: 'There are so many of our countrymen who have never known a state of peace except for one short interval, that they are led to regard it [war] as an evil inseparable from the very constitution of social life.'[22]

On the other hand the news from Russia did appear to bring the end of the war within sight. Merchants and manufacturers looked forward to unfettered trade with Europe. 'The success of the Russians', protested Whitbread's friend, Sir Peter Payne, 'has had the effect of wine on the brain of the country, and its views I dare say have as little wisdom in them as wine generally excites.' At the end of 1812 subscriptions were begun in the country to help the Russians. The *Independent Whig* was roused to fury, protesting that the editor of *The Times*, who had subscribed 100 guineas for 'our Russian Friends and Allies', had only recently had twenty of his journeyman printers gaoled for conspiracy to raise their wages; one of the men had died of 'extreme illness and want' leaving a wife and family. It went on to describe the plight of an unemployed coal-heaver of Spitalfields with a wife and twenty children whose goods had been distrained by the parish officers, and concluded urging advocates of war and Russian subscribers to remember that 'true charity begins at home'. But as 1813 progressed many of the depressed manufacturing industries began to revive with the reopened European markets, and distress in these areas declined. At the end of 1812 some 12,000 in Leeds had signed a petition for peace, but by June 1813 Rogerson recorded in his diary 'mill full of work: we were never paying so much wage in our Mill before'. Six months later he wrote:

> This year taking it altogether has been a very lucky one for us (tho' it has been in the midst of Wars) and I think I may say it has been a very good one for the country at large – thank God for it – I am sure we have great reason to be thankful in regard to the things of this world; our property keeps increasing more and more every year.

He had made a clear profit of about £17,000. Recovery on the other side of the Pennines appears to have taken slightly longer, but by the end of 1813 Rowbottom perceived an overall improvement in weaving and spinning 'for inconsequence of the repeated defeats of Bunoparte trade as taken a turn much for the better . . . [and] work of all denominations is quite plentiful'.[23]

The war continued to exact a heavy toll in lives and money. Its cost and the resulting inflation affected the pockets of all ranks. The rich could absorb the increases, and those who had invested in the annual loans which underwrote the war budgets were to see returns coming in long after the war. Some of those at the lower end of the social scale, especially with the reviving economy, were able to push up the price of their labour to meet the squeeze. Others, especially those on fixed incomes, had to tighten their belts. Perceval's last budget, introduced after his assassination by the new Chancellor, Nicholas Vansittart, was his least popular. It increased postal charges, the duty on glass and tobacco and the assessed taxes on male servants, horses, dogs, and game certificates; also there was to be an alteration in the tax on property sold by auction and a new tax on leather. It was the last tax which brought most hostility, principally because, it was maintained, it would hurt the poor. Lord Althorpe protested that 'the price of a labourer's shoes were from 12s. to 14s. and the tax would amount to 10 per cent on that sum, while it would not amount to 3 per cent on the shoes of the higher classes'. Brougham argued, by some tortuous logic, that the tax was tantamount to a new tax on everything. 'A tax on leather was a tax on machinery, on every implement used in husbandry, and on the shoes of all farmers' servants. *Pro tanto*, it went to raise the price of bread.' Furthermore as the 800,000 men serving in the army and navy wore out between two and six pairs of shoes each during a year the tax was 'taxing the government with one hand, to pay it with the other'. The leather tax passed through Parliament successfully, but an enquiry into its effects the following year concluded that tanning had declined by one-third and that shoemakers, as well as tanners, were suffering. Ralph Benson, member for Stafford, moved for its abolition, and his motion was only lost on its second reading by 120 votes to 125.[24]

Recruiting, troop movements and especially embarkation for overseas theatres of war continued to be a source of distress for families and for individuals. The Mayor of Huntingdon reported that his neighbourhood was infested with vagrants of all ages and both sexes, but admitted that his compassion was aroused by the large numbers of soldiers' wives travelling with their children either to their parishes, or to visit their husbands. Many of these families were distressed, and though it put an additional burden on the already heavy poor rate of the borough, he felt he had to assist them. The quarter sessions of the east division of Sussex acknowledged the problem, but suspected that large numbers of beggars and cheats sought relief 'under the pretence of being disabled seamen, soldiers' wives etc.'. There was still little that families could do to discover the fate of soldier fathers or sons, though an application to a magistrate might yield some results if the magistrate were sympathetic, like Samuel Whitbread, and prepared to write to the War Office. Innkeepers continued to suffer the burden of billeting troops; in July 1813 the Bristol Corporation supported the petition of their innkeepers for barracks or some other way of relieving 'the heavy burthens and inconveniences which they suffer from the number of soldiers quartered upon them'. Though ballots and recruiting parties had never been popular the possibility of final victory may well have made them that much more distasteful. An attempt to enrol local militia at Frome in January 1813 led to a riot of colliers. In October the rendezvous house in Liverpool was attacked by an angry crowd.[25]

Not every group of workers could keep abreast of rising prices during the upswing in the economy in 1813 and 1814. In July 1813 the lacemakers of Buckinghamshire, Bedfordshire and Northamptonshire held a meeting at the Swan Inn in Newport Pagnell to protest about French prisoners of war undercutting them. They protested that while their own lace sold at four shillings and six pence a yard, the prisoners, since they were provided with food, lodging and clothing by the government, were able to sell their product at three shillings a yard. They sought the advice and assistance of the Marquis of Buckingham and the members of Parliament for their counties. In the late summer the government prohibited the manufacture or sale of lace by prisoners of war. The work of the prisoners however does not appear to have been the only reason for the problems facing the lacemakers; already effective lace-making machinery had appeared in Leicestershire, Derbyshire and Nottinghamshire, and within twenty years machines were capable of performing every stage in the craft. If prisoners of war were considered a threat in some trades, elsewhere their help could be welcomed. Thomas Carter was a journeyman tailor in Colchester; his master was one of the men who had profited during the war years making officers' uniforms and contracting for entire regiments, and early in 1814 he was contracted to make uniforms for Italian prisoners of war who had volunteered to fight against Napoleon. To ease the pressure in the workshop half a dozen of the Italians, who were themselves tailors, were picked to work alongside the English journeyman. But the days of high profits for military contractors were numbered. Already during 1813 there was growing recognition in the iron industry that it possessed too much capacity for peacetime needs. South Wales iron-workers, who found their wages reduced, responded with anonymous letters, banded together and swore oaths to be true to each other.[26]

Farmers also saw wartime prosperity ebbing. The war years had seen vast acres of marginal land brought under the plough; cereal production had moved further up the hillsides and on to moorlands than at any time since the thirteenth century, the levels were not to be reached again until the Second World War. Between 1776 to 1790 twenty-five enclosure bills were, on average, passed by Parliament each year; the war had seen the number increase rapidly. An act of 1801 facilitated enclosure, and from 1802 to 1813 the average rose to 99. In addition there had been improvements in agriculture. All of these factors had contributed to the war effort by making Britain near self-sufficient. Although the population had increased by an enormous 14.3 per cent between 1801 and 1811, imports of wheat in 1812 were only 0.3 million quarters as opposed to 1.4 million in 1801. Though there was distress, there was no mass starvation on the scale that Napoleon had hoped for. Indeed he himself may have recognised the impossibility of starving Britain into submission when agreeing to allow corn exports to Britain in 1810 (he maintained that selling grain to Britain was draining her bullion, but he also had his own peasant farmers with an enormous surplus to appease). British farmers had certainly made profits during the war, though probably not greater than the returns enjoyed by industrialists; landlords, on average, probably made the most significant gains through their ability to increase rents without the investment outlay which farmers themselves needed to improve their production.[27] The bumper harvest of 1813 brought corn prices tumbling dramatically, and the farmers demanded protection. A Corn Committee was set up in the Commons; demands were made for foreign corn to pay tariffs until home-produced wheat had reached as much as 105s. a quarter. There was an immediate reaction from urban manufacturers and their workers, who petitioned against what they saw as an attempt at legislation to keep the price of bread artificially high. Farmers replied that the manufacturers were also protected; they could cite the Navigation Acts, the legislation which prevented the recruitment of English industrial workers and the export of machinery, and the duties on foreign iron, earthenware, cotton, cloth and glass. Early in 1815 Parliament passed the Corn Law, which prohibited the import of foreign corn while British corn was less than 80s. a quarter, and which was to provide the basis for enormous discontent over the next thirty years. The Corn Law is often described as 'class' legislation; yet this description conceals as much as it explains. It was another example of eighteenth-century Britain coming into conflict with nineteenth-century Britain, and cutting across the party lines which had evolved during the war. George Rose and Robert Peel, supporters of Liverpool's government, spoke against it; the Whig magnates, great landowners themselves, were in no way averse to it. Furthermore, considering the Corn Law in the light of Professor Andreski's military participation ratio, it could be argued that by the 1815 legislation the government was seeking to repay the agricultural interest which had been so vital in helping Britain through the war by improving its production to feed the population as well as in financing the war; the agricultural sector of the economy appears to have paid a disproportionately heavier share of the income tax than mercantile and manufacturing interests.[28]

III Postscript: Peace and the Waterloo War 1814–15

The war against the United States, which continued to the end of 1814, remained a side-show; the bulk of Britain's war effort in 1813 and in the early months of 1814 was directed against Napoleon. The Emperor's brilliant campaign of February 1814 temporarily checked the Allied armies pouring across France's northern and western frontiers, but there was no one of his capabilities to halt Wellington's advance across the Pyrenees and into southern France, and even Napoleon's genius and the bravery of his surviving veterans and raw conscripts could not long hold up his Austrian, German and Russian enemies. At the beginning of April 1814 he bowed to the inevitable and abdicated.

Peace brought great rejoicing in Britain; the festivities, according to the *Tyne Mercury*, revealed at last a truly '*united* kingdom'. Rogerson recorded: 'Bells Ringing Guns Firing and Tom Paines Quaking for very fear of the terrible day of the Louis's . . . like as if all was mad in Bramley'. Rowbottom described great celebrations in the North-west, where manufacturers gave dinners and ale to their workers and people of all ranks paraded the streets employing 'every degradation . . . to insult the memory of the fallen monarch whose tyrannical career was at an end'. Yet within weeks it became apparent that peace was not automatically going to produce plenty. At the beginning of June Rogerson complained: 'This peace makes all very slack – I think now as it is com'd nobody seems so very fond of it; there will be a deal of money lost in various ways.' Britain's European allies were not prepared to let their markets be flooded and their own industries destroyed by cheap British goods. There was the additional problem of an expanding labour market as soldiers and sailors began to be demobilised. Faced with a combination of framework-knitters in April 1814 the secret committee of master hosiers in Nottingham callously suggested that the men's union might be broken by disbanding the Derbyshire, Leicestershire and Nottinghamshire militias, thus increasing the number of men wanting work. In August the town clerk of Nottingham reported that the combination was destroyed as a result of depressed trade, the confusion and dismay caused by the seizure of the papers of the men's organisation, and 'an increasing supply of Labourers in the Manufactory from the Discharge of the Militia Regiments'.[29]

This dislocation was suddenly reversed in March 1815 with the news of Napoleon's return from Elba; within three weeks Louis XVIII had fled and Napoleon was back in Paris. John Hodgkinson, only just discharged from the navy after nearly eighteen years' service, wrote to his uncle in a tone of fatalism after the Admiralty Board had granted him an annual pension of £14 0s 8d. The pension depended on him serving again in case of a new war; 'I am afraid it will not be long before that will be the case as I understand our friend Bonaparte is come back to Paris, it was my intention if peace had been established to have come down to Lancashire and followed the weaving business.'

'Bonaparte in Paris and Emperor again!' an astounded Greathead wrote in his diary. 'These revolutions would be too incredible for romance.' A young Quaker woman reflected the horrified wonder of many when she wrote to her brother:

> In every action of his chequer'd life he seems to be invincible to fortune and is in reality the prov'd tho' blind instrument of Divine vengeance. This is evident to the most incredulous his escapes have been so miraculous that I almost tremble lest his work should not be finished. With such a mind, such soaring abilities, such grasping ambition and withal such a capacity for evil what a mass of heterogeneous must the heart of such a man display.

It looked like a repetition of the failure of the Peace of Amiens. George Cruikshank gave a visual representation to these fears with his cartoon of a tax-burdened British bull about to be sacrificed on an altar 'SACRED to the BOURBON cause' by the axe of 'NEW WAR TAXES'. Castlereagh, proud of his performance at the Allies' peace conference is unmoved by the bull's plea: 'Alas and must I come to this? Have I bled for so many years in your service and will you now take my life?' A few, grown fat on the profits of war, were relieved by the turn of events. John Carter recalled the tradesmen of Colchester and neighbouring farmers and market gardeners were soon busy supplying the town's garrison 'and were all sanguine in their hopes of another long-continued time of prosperity'.[30] But the battle of Waterloo, fought on 18 June 1815, and the resulting second abdication of Napoleon, extinguished both these fears and hopes. The wars were finally over.

9. Aftermath

The wars had lasted for a generation. Some of the men who fought at Waterloo were unborn when their fathers fought over the same territory in the first campaigns of the revolutionary war. Europe had changed enormously during the twenty-three years. Britain was the only major power which did not experience a major invasion or a significant change in its government structure during the period. Her institutions and her sovereignty had remained intact; but she was no longer the only country to boast a constitution and a constitutional monarchy.

The cost of the wars had been colossal for Britain. In a paper presented to the Royal Statistical Society during the Second World War it was estimated that loss of life among servicemen was proportionately higher between 1794 and 1815 than between 1914 and 1918. The effect on the population structure of the country does not seem to have been significant, but behind this frightening calculation is the untold human sorrow and suffering of families swept up in the war. In September 1795 Rowbottom noted as an example of 'British heroeism' the Buckly family of Beartrees: the father was in the army and bound for the West Indies, two of his sons were in the army also, a third was in the navy, the other three were, as yet, too young for the services. John Mayhall directed the readers of his *Annals of Yorkshire* to a monument in Leeds Parish Church, a memorial to three Neville brothers, all lieutenants in the army, the first killed in 1794, the others in 1799. Thirteen years after Waterloo a volume of memoirs of the Peninsular War was published in *Constable's Miscellany*; the preface commented: 'There are few families in the land who have not one or more relatives sleeping in a soldier's grave, among the Spanish *Sierras*; and there is certainly not one who had not, at some period or other, during the contest, a kinsman serving in the British ranks.'[1] The financial cost of the war was also high. Over £1500 million was raised during the war years in loans and taxes to pay for the war. Much of this was paid out to foreign powers as subsidies; in the last year of the struggle Britain paid £10 million to her allies; not until American involvement in the Second World War was there to be

169

any parallel to this aid programme. The most significant new tax, the income tax, raised only about 9 per cent of the total sum; the bulk of it came through increases in customs and excise, taxes which hit everyone regardless of their wealth. In spite of the sums raised during the war an enormous National Debt remained which, together with the repayments of the enormous loans and their interest, continued to provoke radicals as late as the time of the Chartists.

A few regretted the end of the war, like the small tradesmen of garrison towns and dockyards, and the farmers and market gardeners of the surrounding countryside who had profited from the influx of servicemen or government workers. James Ings, a butcher who owned some tenements in Portsmouth, dated his financial ruin from the post-war slump in the town; he sold his property, moved to London and plunged into extremist politics; in 1820 he was executed for his part in the Cato Street Conspiracy. The contractors who had supplied military equipment no longer had their enormous market; within two years of peace the profits of one Northamptonshire shoe firm fell from over £2300 a year to less than £400. After seeing the wretched state of troops returning from Corunna, Marc Brunel, father of the great engineer, produced a new scheme for manufacturing army shoes by machinery. The government, already in his debt for block-making machinery and other improvements in the naval dockyards, advised him to lay down a plant sufficient to supply the entire army. This Brunel did, manning his factory with disabled servicemen and producing four hundred shoes a day. But the government let him down over purchasing and when peace came he found himself landed with vast stocks of unwanted army shoes; the heavy financial loss contributed to his arrest for debt in 1821. Large numbers were laid off in the royal dockyards and arsenals; there were wage reductions for some of those who remained. A major slump hit the iron industry; works were shut down, many being sold off at a sixth or a seventh of their original cost. The *Annual Register* for 1816 reported that only ten of the thirty-four blast furnaces in Shropshire were still working; besides the iron-workers 8000 colliers had been thrown out of work. Some of the unemployed began to look for a solution to their problems in a new international war.[2] Riding through Hampshire in 1822 Cobbett 'Met with a farmer who said he must be ruined, unless another '*good war*' should come! This is no uncommon notion. They saw high prices *with* war, and they thought that the war was the *cause*.' The Corn Law of 1815 did not prevent a slump in agriculture. There were good harvests in 1815 and 1816 and the price of wheat fell to levels well below the wartime average. Much of the marginal land brought under the plough during the war now appeared uneconomic. Farmers had difficulty meeting the rent increases introduced during the war; some were granted abatements; others, especially those renting the smaller properties of about 250 acres and less, gave up their holdings.[3]

There were a few young men who, like Vigny, Musset and others in France, felt they had missed a great destiny. The Duke of Wellington was now hailed as the greatest soldier of the age; the success of his army in the Peninsula and at Waterloo allowed Britain to boast her military prowess as a great land power throughout the nineteenth century. It was something special to be a 'Waterloo man'. Thomas Morris described the eagerness with which his comrades accepted the Waterloo medal, and the feting of Waterloo regiments on the first anniversary of the battle. As a boy Alexander Somerville was brought up on stories of the heroism of the Scottish regiments especially at Waterloo. Almost thirty years after the battle the *United Service Gazette* could proclaim:

> Were you at Waterloo?
> I have been at Waterloo.
> 'Tis no matter what you do,
> If you've been at Waterloo.

The young Lord Brudenell dreamt of participating in such a battle; he placed bets at White's expressing his optimism about the possibility of a new international war; but it was not until nearly forty years after Waterloo that he was given the opportunity of leading his Light Cavalry to destruction at Balaclava.[4]

Given this thrilling memory of the war and the enthusiasm with which Waterloo Day was celebrated at least until Wellington's death in 1852, it is perhaps surprising that the wars do not fill a more prominent part in the canon of early nineteenth-century British literature. It is, of course, impossible to read Jane Austen without finding references to troop movements, militia camps, and naval prize money; it is significant that the new development at Sanditon has a Trafalgar House and a Waterloo Crescent. During the wars Jane Austen had two brothers serving as officers in the navy and a third as an officer in the Oxfordshire Militia, yet the war remained in the background of her works, as it was to do also with John Galt in *Annals of the Parish* and *The Provost*, Scott in *The Antiquary* and *St Ronan's Well* and Thackeray in *Vanity Fair*. Charlotte Brontë touched on the social effects of the war and the damaging effects of the Orders in Council in *Shirley*, but her hero Robert Moore is a mill-owner; indeed mill-owners and entrepreneurs are much more common heroes in early and mid-nineteenth-century British novels than the men who fought Napoleon. Byron's Childe

Harold surveyed the battlefields of Europe, Browning remembered the great naval victories in *Nationality in Drinks* and *Home Thoughts from the Sea*, but there was no great poetic celebration of the wars in their immediate aftermath. It was not until the last quarter of the nineteenth century that a significant creative author turned his attention to the war. In novels, short stories and finally in epic drama Thomas Hardy recorded the popular memory of the war on the embattled Wessex coast which veterans of the services, the volunteers, the 'Bang-up Locals', and their womenfolk had passed on to him as a boy.

It is arguable that there was no need for novelists and poets to turn their attention to describing the wars since the task was undertaken by veterans. Among the men who may be said to have profited from the war are the soldiers who learned how to read and write in regimental schools. Such schools, principally financed by the officers and established to provide regiments with literate NCOs, had been in existence at least from the second half of the eighteenth century. Their numbers increased during the revolutionary and Napoleonic wars and in 1808 the Duke of York suggested that any regiment which did not have a school for the children of its soldiers, its boy soldiers, young soldiers and NCOs, should open one. The schools were not compulsory; when the Colonel of the Bedfordshire Militia endeavoured to make his school compulsory, and to make a nominal charge on his NCOs, one of his sergeants took him to court. But men did attend, and at least one of those who learned to read and write at such a school, John Green, turned his new skill to recording *The Vicissitudes of a Soldier's Life*; Green's book was one of several appearing in the aftermath of the war. The campaign in the Peninsula is the first in British history to be written up by a score or so literate men from the other ranks; a fact not unnoticed by contemporaries. When he published *The Subaltern Officer* in 1825 George Wood informed his readers that he intended to give an accurate, plain and simple narrative, but he trusted that it would not be without novelty.

> The Journals and Memoirs of Private Soldiers have been frequently published; but not those of Subaltern Officers, on whom so much depends, and whose duties are of a different nature, and far more arduous than those imposed upon individuals in the ranks. Indeed one principal object which I have had in view, has been to correct the too general misapprehension, that the sufferings and hardships of war are almost exclusively the lot of the private soldier.[5]

Other memoirs were published by common soldiers and seamen who fought in different theatres. Some of these memoirs, like those of Nicol and Costello, were ghosted; nevertheless there is significance in the fact that they were considered to be worth ghosting and publishing. The common man's participation in war was recognised as important by him and by his readers; as such it presents another example of the developing consciousness among the lower classes of early nineteenth-century Britain.

But returning servicemen, even if they wrote and published their recollections, could not live on their memories. They may have broadened their horizons during the war, but in 1815 their future was bleak. They had to make the adjustment to civilian life, a difficult enough task for some men with money, connections and, consequently, some prospects. 'After fagging for near six years the prospect of half pay begins to stare me in the face', wrote William Freer to his brother at the close of the Peninsular War. 'What can I do who have from my infancy thought of nothing but soldiers? I could never exist idle and as for a profession I have none nor could I ever be brought to follow one.' Something was done for the officers; they, at least, retired on half pay. There was a noticeable increase in naval promotions at the end of the war, to ensure that men got better rates of half pay, which involved a large number of master's mates, midshipmen and cadets who were made up to lieutenant. But the bulk of the 200,000 common soldiers and sailors demobilised between 1814 and 1817 had no firm prospects on their return to civilian life, for the country's economy was contracting and readjusting after the boost of the war, and their pensions were meagre.

Jack Crawford, who had nailed his ship's colours to the mast to prevent them from being shot away again at Camperdown and who had received a medal for this from his native Sunderland, was lucky enough to find work on the keels of the Wear and he treated his mates on the days his pension was paid; eventually however he was forced to pawn his medal. Tom Plunket of the Rifle Brigade was invalided out after Waterloo; the commissioners at Chelsea Hospital awarded him sixpence a day, and when he protested they struck him off the pension list. On his colonel's intercession he was later awarded one shilling a day. An Irish seaman named Cashman was not as fortunate; he appears to have been owed several years' back-pay and prize-money, and his mother had not received the money which he had directed to be paid to her while he was serving. After a fruitless morning at the Admiralty in December 1816 he was persuaded to attend the radical reform meeting at Spa Fields; he was executed for his part in the ensuing riot. At his execution he protested to the sympathetic crowd about being exposed as a 'common robber'. 'I am not brought to this for any robbery. . . . If I was at my quarters, I would not be killed in the smoke: I'd be in the fire. I have nothing against my King and country; but fought for them.' Edward Costello could not maintain himself and his common-law French wife and child on his pension; he never saw them again after returning them to France, though he himself was fortunate in later life to become a Yeoman Warder of the Tower. John Green, returning to the carpet manufactories of Louth after nine years service, was sorry to find his old shopmates in the same state as when he had left, 'having little more than half employment . . . there was no hope whatever that I could meet with an engagement'. 'T. S.', a veteran of Corunna, Walcheren, the Peninsular War and Waterloo, could not get even labouring work in his native Edinburgh; not wishing to be a burden on his sister and her husband he wrote: 'I will go to South America. . . . Or, I will go to Spain. . . . If I succeed in the South, I will return and lay my bones beside my parents: if not, I will never come back.' Some veterans exchanged their pensions for a small lump sum and a land grant in Canada; Tom Plunket was one, but he could not settle down there.

There were former officers who took the situation of their men seriously; some fought for an improvement in the pensions of some individuals long after the war, others were in a position to take an interest in veterans as a group. The Duke of Wellington was sympathetic to his old soldiers, especially the NCOs, 'a very important Class of Men'. George Gleig, who fought in the Peninsular War as a junior officer and then took holy orders, took a particular interest in his old subordinates; he became chaplain to Chelsea Hospital in 1834 and subsequently Chaplain General of the Forces and inspector-general of military schools.[6]

The wartime belief that everything would be better when Napoleon was beaten began to be portrayed in folk song and popular poem as a deception carried out on the lower classes by their social superiors.

> You say that Bonyparty he's been the spoil of all,
> And that we have got reason to pay for his downfall;
> Well Bonyparty's dead and gone, and it is plainly shown
> That we have bigger tyrants in Boneys of our own.

Ebenezer Elliot savagely satirised post-war governing-class thinking in his *Corn Law Rhymes* of 1831:

> When Sabbath stills the dizzy mill,
> Shall Cutler Tom, or Grinder Bill,
> On footpaths wander where they will,
> Now Nap lies at Saint Helena?

> Dogs! would they toil and fatten too?
> They grumble still as dogs will do:
> We conquer'd *them* at Waterloo;
> And Nap lies at Saint Helena.

The begging ex-serviceman was a common figure in ballad literature, but these wars with the scale of participation and the wartime appeals to the lower classes gave the post-Napoleonic war ballads an additional edge. The ballad of *The British Tars* contained the stanza,

> When war at first assail'd us I quickly left my trade,
> Our country was in danger, I flew to lend my aid.
> And in my country's service, long, long fatigues I bore,
> But now I'm turned adrift to starve upon my native shore

The ballad of *The Labouring Man* made the same point, emphasising how 'every battle . . . was conquered by the labouring man' and underlining his indispensability in peace as well as war.

> Do what they will, do what they can,
> They can't do without the labouring man.

Possibly recalling the appeals of 1803 and 1805, some began to ask for what end they had fought, especially when the British army compared so unfavourably with that of Napoleon. Thomas Morris emphasised how good and courageous service under Napoleon could lead to the highest honours, while in Britain

> The chances of a man obtaining a commission are about one hundred thousand to one against him; and the only benefits he is likely to obtain, is an admittance to Chelsea Hospital, or a pension of one or two shillings a day, if disabled in the service: – to be taken from him, however, if he should exercise the rights of a citizen, and take part in any public ebullition of feeling against the ministry of the day.

The anonymous authors of *The British Tars* and *The Labouring Man* both signified that their subjects were ready to fight for their country again. Morris concurred, but hoped that there would be some democratisation of the army before that happened. Cobbett developed this line of thought to ask how a poor man could be expected to fight for his country while he was denied a share in government.[7]

Many of the ex-servicemen returned to their places of settlement and accepted the existing order of society. John Green and some comrades lodged with a shoemaker in Warrington after being demobilised. Their landlord was a Jacobin who railed 'in a most acrimonius manner against the King and government', which displeased the old soldiers who argued with him and finally forced him to be silent. Some veterans were soon involved in traditional forms of disorder. On Tyneside the shipowners proposed to keep the low manning levels of wartime and reduce pay; the seamen responded with a strike paralysing the north-east coast trade for many weeks during the summer and autumn of 1815. The seamen's recent service was emphasised by where they looked for assistance; they petitioned the Admiralty for support and used Captain Caulfield, the local Impress Officer, as their go-between with the employers and the local authorities. Caulfield was sympathetic to the seamen's cause, like his predecessor Rothe, but the service which he represented had lost none of its unpopularity and in October 1815 the seamen turned to settling scores with their neighbours who had acted as informers for the press-gangs during the war.[8]

Other veterans became involved in radical politics. Soldiers and sailors returning to the industrial districts of the North found their families and friends more used to petitioning and acting on their own behalf; the veterans, faced with the squalor and unemployment of the post-war depression, could contemplate the same kind of demand which Cobbett articulated: if a poor man was expected to fight for his country, he should have a voice in its government. An anonymous pamphlet published in Manchester in 1817, *Petitioning Weavers Defended*, argued that the war and the blockade, which were simply to restore the Bourbons against the wishes of the French people and which had given 'the entire supply of the continental market to the continental manufacturer', would never have occurred had there been a truly representative parliament. Old soldiers drilled their friends and neighbours to ensure orderly behaviour at 'Peterloo'; one of the eleven persons killed there was a Waterloo veteran. When arms were taken up by radical groups veterans were also present. William Turner, the stonemason of South Wingfield, executed with Brandreth for his part in the Pentrich rising, had transferred from the Derbyshire Militia to the regulars and had fought in Egypt; John Mackesswick, a stockinger transported after the rising, showed 'a complete knowledge of managing a Vessell', which suggests naval service. Old soldiers were prominent among radicals in Barnsley and the Grange Moor rebels were led by two veterans. Andrew Hardie and Robert Baird, who commanded the tiny rebel force of Scottish weavers at the battle of Bonnymuir, were both veterans. Arthur Thistlewood had been a militia officer, at least two of his fellow conspirators in Cato Street had served in the army, and a third, Thomas Brunt, had been a shoemaker with the army.[9]

The middle classes had not gone off to war in the same proportion as the lower classes, but the war had profoundly affected them. The war had given British industry a head start over its Continental rivals. Britain's mastery of the seas during the war had given her a monopoly of overseas markets which had been a powerful stimulus to industrial growth. The ideology of free trade, to which the provincial middle classes were soon firmly wedded, evolved during the war and as a result of this industrial superiority. The war had also given them a growing awareness of, and confidence in, their communal strength, manifested particularly in the campaign against the Orders in Council and the London-based East India Company monopoly in 1812, and again in their unsuccessful opposition to the 1815 Corn Law. The demand for a reform of Parliament was not yet central to their platform – they remained concerned about the unruly behaviour associated with urban elections which wartime and immediate post-war disorders only served to aggravate – but the precedents for union with the working classes and massive campaigning to force Parliament's hand had been created in wartime.

The kind of men who had administered Britain at national and local level before the war remained in control. The war had, perhaps, made them more insular. Except for those in the services or engaged on diplomatic missions, and apart from the short respite of Amiens, Europe had been closed to them for twenty years. The Grand Tour, perforce, became a thing of the past. In 1814 Castlereagh founded the Travellers' Club to encourage the exchange of ideas between British and foreign gentlemen. The Travellers', together with the United Service Club (founded in 1815 by Lord Lynedoch, one of Wellington's most capable subordinates) inaugurated the era of the great nineteenth-century gentleman's club. In some ways the war may have strengthened the traditional paternalism of the governing class. It was not only former officers who were conscious of the debt owed to veterans from the other ranks. During the seamen's strike of 1815 Sidmouth urged that 'Consideration and Liberality' be shown to British seamen as their 'due'.[10] But paternalism, and even giving veterans 'their due', were, at the same time, under attack from the inexorable laws of economics which the war had brought forth from Malthus and Ricardo, while the growing self-confidence and self-awareness of middle and lower classes, again fostered by the war, was soon to force changes in the old system.

The religious divisions in Great Britain had been highlighted by the war. It was not that men were discriminated against for their religion when they were in the army, though a Catholic gentlemen might be rejected for a commission if the King was aware of his religion. 'Any man may go to mass who chooses and nobody makes any inquiry about it', wrote Wellington in September 1809. 'The consequence is that nobody goes to mass.' Local militia units were different; the orderly book of the Leyland and Ormskirk regiment records the large numbers of Catholics in the corps being paraded and marched to their own church separately on Sunday mornings. The question now raised was why should a Catholic fight for a country which denied him rights simply because of his religion and irrespective of his class. The union with Ireland in 1801 emphasised the problem by bringing so many more Catholics directly under the control of the Westminster Parliament. In the aftermath of the 'No Popery' election of 1807 the Reverend Sidney Smith published his letters of Peter Plymley.

> It is, indeed, a most silly and affecting spectacle to rage at such a moment against our own kindred and our own blood; to tell them they cannot be honourable in war, because they are conscientious in religion; to stipulate (at the very moment when we should buy their hearts and swords at any price) that they must hold up the right hand in prayer, and not the left; and adore one common God, by turning to the east rather than to the west.

At the end of 1810 one of the popular debating clubs in the metropolis discussed the question; one speaker deplored the condition of Catholics 'at this time when they were fighting for us and spilling their blood in our defence'; a Welsh Catholic asked: 'how could it be supposed that a soldier who was a Catholic could wield a sword in defence of those who denied him the free toleration of his religion?' A third speaker however railed against Irish 'ignorance' and argued that relief would lead to the ascendancy of Irish Catholics in England. The union with Ireland, itself prompted by the war, and the rehearsal of the arguments for Catholic relief to win the Irish away from potential support for France made the question central in British politics; but it was not until fourteen years after Waterloo that emancipation was won.[11]

The union with Ireland was the most significant institutional change in the government of Britain during the war. In general the governing institutions of the kingdom stood up to the stress and strain of war. The peak of the pressure on local government had been reached during the invasion scares of 1803 and 1805; with the end of the war the nagging demands for militiamen and militia allowances also ceased and local government administration could slip back into its easy-going eighteenth-century pattern once again. The post-war slump and unemployment however meant that overall poor rates continued to rise. The war left local administration unchanged, but the professionalisation of central government had gathered momentum. Most government departments remained tiny, and the administration of many was still chaotic, but there was increasingly less room for ministers and civil servants who sought only comfortable sinecures. The increased business of government meant that the men of Lord Liverpool's administration were civil servants and politicians who maintained a front as landed gentlemen rather than the opposite tradition of the eighteenth century. While the war had not been the sole cause of this change the increases of business resulting directly and indirectly from the war had accelerated it. The development of the board of trade offers a striking example. The pressure of wartime shortages and the blockade necessitated regular meetings of the board which busy members of the Cabinet could not attend; often the president of the board was the only member present at these nominal meetings and was required to take executive action. The collective activities of the board never recovered and recognition of the new system came in 1817 with the granting of a salary to the vice-president, and ten years later to the president himself.[12] The most significant changes in administration were to be found in the Treasury as a result of the complete reorganisation carried out during the war. When Parliament voted the abolition of the income tax in 1816 there was some run-down of the Treasury staff, but no one attempted to restore the old system or oust the new financial experts.

The war also led to some change in the ideas of a government's responsibility. War had aggravated both food shortages and the fluctuations of the economy; in turn this had highlighted the problems of the poor and of businessmen. The government was forced to involve itself in the supply of necessary foodstuffs, though it still lacked the machinery or the sophistication to introduce rationing or to institute a country-wide campaign to bring about a general change from eating the less economical and less nutritious white bread to eating brown bread. Parliament had denied positive help to petitioning weavers in the last decade of the war on the grounds that it was no business of Parliament to involve itself in such matters. But in 1793 and 1811 the government released exchequer bills to support credit and increase liquidity throughout the country; it had acted similarly in the specific cases of West Indies merchants and planters in 1795 and Liverpool and Lancaster merchants in 1799. During the war also the government had invested in public works like the Isle of Dogs canal, which, it was believed, would make imports cheaper and easier and thus justify the expenditure in spite of the increasing financial demands of war. The

Poor Employment Act of 1817 initiated government loans for public works on a regular basis; this act also made some acknowledgement of a government's obligation to combat unemployment. In the following year, in spite of the cries for economy and tax reductions now that the war was over, Parliament voted £1 million for the building of 600 new churches in the industrial towns; the measure was designed as a bulwark for the established order of society, but there was also a sincere belief that the churches could help to improve the situation of the urban poor. In general however, a *laissez-faire* attitude predominated, though less because of ministerial acceptance of the dogma and more because it was expedient and the traditional policy of governments who viewed the distress of the poor principally from the threat this posed to public order and who had no machinery for alleviating distress. In an emergency, like the distress of 1817, the government did exert itself to push through the Poor Employment Act; but when the immediate crisis was over it did not consider that it had any duty to push through other alleviating legislation for the poor's benefit. The post-war Parliament initiated enquiries into factory conditions and the workings of the Poor Law; it showed itself sympathetic to the plight of the poor, but no legislation was passed.

Parliament itself had changed through the introduction of the Irish members in 1801, but in other respects it remained the same. It was not a representative body; it still divided roughly along the lines indicated by Namier. However, wartime cries against corruption and the passage of Curwen's bill had contributed to the weakening of the government's patronage in Parliament; also the war had given the factions a severe hammering. The great coalition established in the second year of the war had crumbled in 1801; the ministers in 1815 were still Pitt's men, but lacking the most brilliant, Canning, and the aristocratic Grenville. The Whigs remained in the political wilderness; in the war against rev-olutionary France the small band which followed Fox appeared unpatriotic to the majority in Parliament, and to a majority of established political society. After their brief and uninspiring period in power during 1806 to 1807, they again seemed unpatriotic in the way in which they appeared to put party before country, and in their reluctance to support the vigorous conduct of the war pursued by Perceval and Liverpool. The Whigs were also compelled to change their criticism of royal intervention in politics; George III was a force to be reckoned with, as his stand over Catholic emancipation revealed, but his recurrent illness and then the regency of his son meant that the old charge that the Crown's influence was increasing could no longer be substantiated. More important however were the new methods, adopted by young Whigs like Brougham, to influence Parliament which worked so successfully against the Orders in Council in 1812 and the maintenance of the income tax in 1816. Indeed the impression given by the agitation of the post-war years is that the country was solidly Whig and radical, though probably this is largely a testimony to the lack of Tory organisation in the country. Liverpool's government was not prepared to embark on counter-agitation, even though, as in the case of the income tax abolition, they might have won considerable support. During the debates on the income tax in 1816 George Rose remarked:

> If people were told that by petitioning they would get relief, they would naturally take the advice given to them. He recollected a meeting which he attended when it was proposed to petition against the tax. Every hand was held up in favour of the proposition, which was seconded by a friend of his who paid nearly £3,000 per annum property tax. If any person had then stated that, if the tax were removed, the sum would probably then fall on individuals not so wealthy as he was, he had no doubt that some difference of opinion would have been excited.[13]

The men who governed Britain in 1815, and for the next fourteen years, had inherited the watchwords 'Church and King' together with a great fear of popular disorder and revolution which had arisen with the French Revolution. They had persevered at enormous cost and against enormous odds to combat 'Jacobinism' in both its Republican and its Bonapartist forms. Their desire for government efficiency to win the war led them to support, and often institute administrative reform; such reform was rarely apparent to the public at large. Their fear of organic change in the Constitution, to which they were indebted for their position and their power, led them to set their face against all popular demands for major reform.

Societies are never static and it is fruitless to speculate how British society would have developed and how its institutions would have changed had there been no wars against revolutionary and Napoleonic France. If in the long term the changes may be considered as beneficial and important in the development of British government and society, this is not to deny the material distress caused by the war's economic effects or the sorrow and anguish resulting from a husband, father, son or brother departing for war often never to be heard of again. The scarlet squares at Waterloo, swimming in the sea of French cavalry, look heroic and glorious in picture and on film; it is unlikely that the men whose bodies comprised those squares viewed them in this light at the time. 'They are shapes that bleed, mere mannikins or no,' comments

Thomas Hardy's Spirit of the Years early on in *The Dynasts*. The characters in Hardy's epic are powerless before the Immanent Will; the same spirit tells the defeated Napoleon:

> Such men as thou, who wade across the world
> To make an epoch, bless, confuse, appal,
> Are in the elemental ages' chart
> Like meanest insects on obscurest leaves
> But incidents and grooves of Earth's unfolding;
> Or as the brazen rod that stirs the fire
> Because it must.

Few would take quite so deterministic a view of history today, but the long duration of the wars and the changes in attitudes and institutions demonstrate that if men do make their own history, they do not necessarily make it in the way that they had intended.

Select Bibliography

Where, in the course of this book, quotations, interpretations or statistics have been used or alluded to, references can be found in the appropriate note. The following bibliography is for those readers who want to follow up particular aspects of British history during the wars, and perhaps take issue with some of my generalisations. (Unless otherwise stated, the place of publication is London.)

List of Abbreviations

Adm.	Admiralty
Assi.	Assizes
BL	British Library
CL	Central Library (e.g. Manchester)
CRO	County Record Office
CUL	Cambridge University Library
HM	Historical Manuscripts Commission
HO	Home Office papers
PC	Privy Council
Pol. Reg.	[Cobbetts] Political Register
PRO	Public Record Office
QS	Quarter Sessions
SRO	Scottish Record Office
TS	Treasury Solicitor's Papers
VCH	Victoria County History
WO	War Office

General Surveys

Arthur Bryant, *The Years of Endurance, 1793–1802* (1942).
——*Years of Victory, 1802–1812* (1944).
——*The Age of Elegance 1812–1822* (1950).

Carola Oman, *Britain against Napoleon* (1943).

H. F. B. Wheeler and A. M. Broadley, *Napoleon and the Invasion of England: The Story of the Great Terror* (2 vols, 1908).

Biographies

Denis Gray, *Spencer Perceval, 1762–1812: The Evangelical Prime Minister* (Manchester, 1963). [A mine of information on the wartime government.]

J. Holland Rose, *William Pitt and the Great War* (1911). [As much a general survey of the first half of the war as a biography.]

Philip Ziegler, *Addington: A Life of Henry Addington, First Viscount Sidmouth* (1965).

Economic History

François Crouzet, *L'Economie britannique et le blocus continental, 1806–1813* (2 vols, Paris, 1958). [Indispensable.]

A large number of articles have been published in recent years relating to economic aspects of the war. The following cover the war as a whole:

Phyllis Deane, 'War and Industrialisation' in *War and Economic Development* ed. J. M. Winter (Cambridge, 1975).

A. H. John, 'Farming in Wartime' in *Land, Labour and the Industrial Revolution*, ed. E. L. Jones and G. E. Mingay (1967).

Glenn Hueckel, 'War and the British Economy, 1793–1815: A General Equilibrium Analysis', *Explorations in Economic History*, x (1973).

——, 'English Farming Profits during the Napoleonic Wars, 1793–1815', *Explorations in Economic History*, xiii (1976).

Military Organisation

C. Emsley, *North Riding Naval Recruits: the Quota Acts and the Quota Men 1795–97* (North Yorks. CRO Publications no. 18, 1978). [The introduction analyses the men enlisted for six counties in addition to the North Riding.]

J. W. Fortescue, *The County Lieutenancies and the Army 1803–1814* (1909).

Richard Glover, *Peninsular Preparation: The Reform of the British Army 1795–1809* (Cambridge, 1963).

——, *Britain at Bay: Defence against Bonaparte 1803–14* (1973).

Michael Lewis, *A Social History of the Navy, 1793–1815* (1960).

J. R. Weston, *The English Militia in the Eighteenth Century* (1965).

Regional Surveys

M. Y. Ashcroft, *To Escape the Monster's Clutches: Notes and Documents Illustrating the Preparations in North Yorkshire to Repel the Invasion Threatened by the French from 1793* (North Yorks. CRO Publications no. 15, 1977).

J. A. Huitson, 'Defence and Public Order in Northumberland 1793–1815' (M. Litt. thesis, Durham, 1966).

R. G. E. Wood, *Essex and the French wars* (SEAX Teaching Portfolio: Essex CRO Publications no. 70, 1977).

Social History

The best social history books covering the period 1793 to 1815 only touch on the war tangentially, but see:

J. L. and Barbara Hammond, *The Skilled Labourer 1760–1832* (1919).

M. I. Thomis, *The Luddites* (Newton Abbot, 1970).

E. P. Thompson, *The Making of the English Working Class* (2nd ed. 1968). [Monumental and controversial.]

The controversy over Thompson's work continues, particularly in the pages of *Past and Present* and *Social History*.

References

(Unless otherwise stated London is the place of publication. In some cases where the author has been unable to verify publication and other details, a question mark has been inserted.)

Introduction

1. J. W. Fortescue, *British Statesmen of the Great War 1893–1914* (Oxford, 1911) p. 12.
2. Arthur Bryant, *The Years of Endurance 1793–1802* (1942) p. xi.
3. C. Northcote Parkinson (ed.), *The Trade Winds* (1948) p. 17.
4. J. L. and B. Hammond, *The Skilled Labourer 1760–1832* (1919) p. 8.
5. Quoted respectively in G. Lefebvre, *The French Revolution*, 2 vols (1962–4) ι 217; and Paul H. Beik (ed.), *The French Revolution* (New York, 1970) p. 252.
6. The decree is quoted in virtually every history of the Revolution; the original, including the report on requisitioning citizens for the defence of France, may be found in *Le Moniteur*, 25 Aug 1793.
7. D. B. Horn, *Great Britain and Europe in the Eighteenth Century* (Oxford, 1967) p. 22.
8. W. Markov and A. Soboul (eds), *Die Sansculotten von Paris* (East Berlin, 1957) p. 248.

1 Britain in 1792

1. E. J. Hobsbawm, 'The Machine Breakers', *Past and Present*, 1 (1952).
2. J. Stevenson, 'Food Riots in England, 1792–1818' in *Popular Protest and Public Order*, ed. J. Stevenson and R. Quinault (1974) p. 34.

3. L. B. Namier, 'Monarchy and the Party System', in L. B. Namier, *Crossroads of Power* (1962) especially p. 229.
4. *Leeds Intelligencer*, 1 Oct 1792.
5. M. Lewis, *Napoleon and his British Captives* (1962) pp. 28–9.
6. J. R. Western, *The English Militia in the Eighteenth Century* (1965) p. 246.
7. G. S. Veitch, *The Genesis of Parliamentary Reform* (1913) chs 6, 7.
8. *London Chronicle*, 12 Nov 1792.
9. PRO, TS 11.952.3496, John Frost and Joel Barlow to SCI, 29 Nov 1792.
10. *Annual Register 1792*, State Papers, pp. 355–6.
11. Ibid.
12. C. Emsley, 'The London "Insurrection" of December 1792: Fact, Fiction or Fantasy', *Journal of British Studies*, xvii (1978).
13. PRO, HO 42.22, Petition of Norwich Corporation, 24 Oct 1792.
14. D. E. Ginter, 'The Loyalist Association Movement of 1792–93', *Historical Journal*, ix (1966) 187.
15. HMC *Dropmore Papers*, ii 359.
16. *The Times*, 15 and 18 Dec 1792; Countess of Minto (ed.), *Life and Letters of Sir Gilbert Elliot, First Earl of Minto*, 3 vols (1874) ii 110; Buckinghamshire RO Hawtrey Family Papers D. 65.2/1/2, Rev. John Hawtrey to Rev. Edward Hawtrey, 25 Jan 1793.
17. *Northampton Mercury*, 2 Feb 1793; Manchester CL (Reference), Broadsides F. 1793/3.
18. F. Knight, *University Rebel: The Life of William Frend* (1971) p. 121; *Morning Chronicle*, 30 and 31 January 1793; TS 11.953.3497, Resolution of division 12, 5 Dec 1793.
19. Bucks. RO Hawtrey Papers D. 65.2/1/2, Rev. John Hawtrey to Rev. Edward Hawtrey, 15 Feb 1793. For the origins of the war see especially J. T. Murley, 'The Origin and Outbreak of the Anglo-French War of 1793' (D. Phil., Oxford, 1959).

2 The Initial Impact: 1793–4

1. W. Fox, *The Interests of Great Britain respecting the French War* 5th ed. (1793) pp. 6–7, 10–13; (D. I. Eaton[?]), *Extermination, or an Appeal to the People of England on the Present War with France* (1793 [?]) p. 7 note; *Objections to the War examined and refuted by a Friend to Peace* (1793) pp. 3–4; J. Bowles, *The Real Grounds for the Present War with France* (1793) p. 11.

2. *Oracle*, 6 February 1793; *Times*, 15 and 21 February 1793; HO 42.27, Parker to Nepean, 31 December 1792.

3. *Parliamentary History*, xxx 585, 593 and 642.

4. *Parl. Hist.*, xxx 587; W. Pitt, *Orations on the French War* (1906) p. 20.

5. N. Hampson, *The Life and Opinions of Maximilien Robespierre* (1974) pp. 212–15.

6. Sir Charles Webster, *The Foreign Policy of Castlereagh: 1812–15* (1931) p. 7; Bishop of Bath and Wells (ed.), *Journals and Correspondence of William, Lord Auckland*, 4 vols (1861–2) iii 168; HO 42.26.113, Richmond to Dundas, 13 Oct 1793; Duke of Buckingham and Chandos (ed.), *Memoirs of the Court and Cabinet of George III*, 4 vols (1853–7) ii 245; HMC *Dropmore Papers* ii 454–5.

7. *Parl. Hist.*, xxx, debates of 21 Jan and 3 Feb 1794; *Parl. Hist.*, xxi, debates of 10 and 30 May 1794; Pitt, *Orations*, p. 44.

8. Quoted in F. O'Gorman, *The Whig Party and the French Revolution* (1967) p. 196.

9. Lord John Russell (ed.), *Memorials and Correspondence of Charles James Fox*, 4 vols (1854) iii 78; HO 42.28, Lord Mount Edgecombe to Dundas, 28 Jan 1794 (see also J. M. Bingham to Dundas, 24 Feb and HO 42.29, Andrew Hill to Dundas, 9 Apr 1794); Cambridge-shire RO Correspondence of the Huddlestons of Sawston 488/C3/B57, John Bullock *O. P.* to Richard Huddleston, 4 Feb 1794; Oldham Local Interest Centre, Diaries of William Rowbottom, 5 Feb 1793.

10. HO 42.31, L. Wickham to William Wickham [?], 28 June 1794.

11. HO 42.30, Dundas to Nepean, recd 12 May 1794; HO 42.29, *passim*.

12. HO 42.31, Paul Le Mesurier to Nepean, 12 June 1794.

13. J. Stevenson, 'The London "Crimp" Riots of 1794', *International Review of Social History*, xvi (1971); J. R. Hutchinson, *The Press Gang: Afloat and Ashore* (1913) pp. 221–2; HO 42.27, Captain Smith Child to the Admiralty, 27 Oct 1793.

14. *Newcastle Chronicle*, 20 Apr 1793; PRO ASSI 35/234; HO 42.29, Elston to Ives 31 March 1794 and White to Nepean (?), 8 Apr 1794.

15. A. Redford, *Manchester Merchants and Foreign Trade 1794–1858* (Manchester, 1934) p. 27.

16. T. S. Ashton, *An Economic History of England: The Eighteenth Century* (1955) p. 254, gives bankruptcy figures as 609 for 1792 and 1256 for 1793. Leone Levi, *The History of British Commerce* 2nd ed. (1880) p. 69 note 3, noted 934 commissions of bankruptcy in 1792 and 1956 (including 26 against bankers) in 1793. *London Chronicle*,

1 March 1794, lists seventy-one country banks which stopped payment in 1793, twelve of them in Yorkshire.

17. Judith Blow Williams, *British Commercial Policy and Trade Expansion 1750–1850* (Oxford, 1972) p. 191 note 3. 396.

18. D. J. Rowe, *Cornwall in the Age of the Industrial Revolution* (Liverpool, 1953) p. 174. *London Chronicle*, 6 March and 20 Apr 1793.

19. Birmingham Reference Library, Garbett – Lansdowne Correspondence (510640, Photostats), Garbett to Lansdowne 19 Oct 1793 (see also letters of 27 Nov 1793, 18 March and 24 Oct 1794); *Second Report of the Committee of Secrecy of the House of Commons* (1794) appendix E, Birmingham to SCI, 6 Nov 1793; VCH *Warwickshire* VII 116–17; S[cottish] R[ecord] O[ffice] Melville [Castle Muniments] G.D. 51.1.374 William Smith to Dundas, 29 Jan 1795.

20. For wool purchase at fairs see *London Chronicle*, 20 June, 1, 11, and 31 July and 9 Aug 1793; Knight, *University Rebel*, pp. 122–23; HO 42.25.65 Robert Harvey jr to Nepean, 12 March 1793.

21. *Times*, 28 Jan 1794; *Morning Chronicle*, 14 Dec 1793.

22. *Thoughts on the Causes of the Present Failures* (1793), quoted in Blow Williams, *British Commercial Policy* pp. 393–94.

23. M. I. Thomis, *Politics and Society in Nottingham 1785–1835* (Oxford, 1969) p. 173; ASSI 35/234.

24. J. Donaldson, *General View of the Agriculture of Northamptonshire* (1794) p. 10; Rowe, *Cornwall*, ch. 3, R. Glover, *Peninsular Preparation: The Reform of the British Army 1795–1809* (Cambridge, 1963) pp. 48–52 and 64.

25. *Times*, 3, 5 and 6 Dec 1793; *London Chronicle*, 3, 5 and 7 Dec 1793.

26. Ashton, *Economic History*, p. 226. H. G. Macnab, *A Letter Addressed to John Whitemore MP Member of the Committee of the House of Commons on the Coal Trade* (1801) p. 48, gives slightly different figures, but they still indicate a substantial increase during the war.

27. I have estimated the number of men of military age in the United Kingdom from the calculations made by W. A. Armstrong on the age structure of the male population of England and Wales during this period. W. A. Armstrong, 'La Population de l'Angleterre et du Pays de Galles (1789–1815)', *Annales de démographie historique*, II (1965).

28. Bryant, *Years of Endurance*, p. 82; *London Chronicle*, 29 Feb 1793.

29. HO 42.24.149, Petition of 11 Feb 1793; HO 42.23, James Rudman to Dundas, 7 and 9 Feb 1793; *London Chronicle*, 6 Feb 1793; *London Chronicle*, 6 Feb 1793; East Sussex RO Hoper MSS D435.

30. N. McCord and D. E. Brewster, 'Some Labour Troubles of the

1790s in North-East England', *International Review of Social History* XIII (1968); *Newcastle Courant*, 23 Feb 1793.

31. PRO Adm 1.1618, Smith Child to Admiralty, 6 Oct 1794; M. Lewis, *A Social History of the Navy* (1960) pp. 90–2; HO 42.27, Smith Child to Admiralty, 27 Oct 1793.

32. J. Howell (ed.), *The Life and Adventures of John Nicol, Mariner* (1937 ed.) pp. 179–80.

33. Rowbottom, 8 and 18 March 1793.

34. J. W. Fortescue, *A History of the British Army*, 13 vols (1899–1930) IV part I, 212 note 3.

35. PRO, WO 1.1081.87–9 and 187–90, W. Wickham to M. Lewis, 29 Jan and 2 May 1794; West Riding RO Q[uarter] S[essions] Indictment Books, Bradford Sessions 16 July 1795, Rotherham Sessions 29 July 1795.

36. West Riding RO QS Indictment Books, Sheffield Sessions 15 Oct 1794, Pontefract Sessions 13 Apr 1795; Warwickshire RO QS 39/10 Michaelmas 1797 and 1799; Rowbottom, 8 March and 26 June 1793.

37. Fortescue, *British Army*, IV part 1, 314 and part 2, 298–9 899–902; A. Forbes, *A Short History of the Army Ordnance Services*, 3 vols, (1921) I 156; WO 3.12.175, General Orders, 12 Oct 1794; HO 42.28, Lodge to Nepean, 19 Jan 1794.

38. *London Chronicle*, 21 Feb 1793; HO 51.147.30, Dundas to Amherst, 25 Feb 1793.

39. J. R. Western, 'The Volunteer Movement as an anti-Revolutionary Force', *English Historical Review* LXXI (1956).

40. Western, *The English Militia*, p. 279.

41. HO 42.27, Capt. J. Bainbrigge to Dundas (?), 28 Nov 1793 and draft from Dundas, 19 Nov 1793.

42. Western, *English Militia*, p. 289.

43. SRO Melville G.D.51.1.367. 1–2, R. Burdon to Dundas, 17 Sept 1793 enclosing Overseers' letter; W. Marshall, *The Review and Abstract of the County Reports to the Board of Agriculture*, 5 vols (York, 1818) I 31; Tyne and Wear RO All Saints Parish Records, Rate Books 183.1.57–95. During 1793 the rate fluctuated between 4*d* and 6*d.*; in January 1797 it reached 1*s.*

44. *Parl. Hist.*, xxx, 1353–62.

3　Crisis upon Crisis: 1795–97

1. *Parliamentary Register* XL, contains peace petitions from Carlisle, City of London, Southampton, Norwich, York, Southwark, Man-

chester, New Sarum, Durham and Liverpool, and counter petitions from Carlisle, Liverymen of London, Southwark, Manchester, Durham' and Liverpool.

2. HO 42.34.99, W. Elford to Portland 6 Apr; HO 42.35, W. Symons to Portland (?), 21 July 1795; Stevenson, 'Food Riots' p. 47.

3. *London Chronicle*, 7 Apr 1795; HO 42.34, Rev. J. Turner to Portland 28 Apr and 6 May 1795; WO 40.17, six letters r.e. 114th Foot, 8–13 Apr 1795; F. Willan, *History of the Oxfordshire Regiment of Militia* (Oxford, 1900) pp. 26–30; HO 42.35 Mr Shelley to Portland, 19 July, and Mr Langridge to Portland, 20 July 1795.

4. WO 1.1092.139–45, Richmond to Windham, 13 Apr; WO 1.1092.149, Memorandum, 14 Apr 1795; Stevenson, 'Food Riots', p. 48.

5. HO 42.34.119 J. Carne to Portland, 19 Apr 1795.

6. W. M. Stern, 'The Bread Crisis in Britain, 1795–96', *Economica*, XXXI (1964).

7. Quoted in M. Olson, *The Economics of the Wartime Shortage* (Durham, North Carolina, 1963) p. 34.

8. W. E. Minchinton, 'Agricultural Returns and the Government during the Napoleonic Wars', *Agricultural History Review*, I (1953).

9. SRO Melville G.D.51.1.381, Muncaster to Dundas, 11 Sept 1795; Northumberland R. O. Swinburne MSS 2 SW 613/1–9, Northumberland to Sir John E. Swinburne, 22 July 1795.

10. HO 42.35.197, S. Garnett to Portland, 18 July 1795; HO 42.36, Rev. H. W. Coulthurst to Portland, 16 Nov 1795.

11. R. Lee (?) *The Rights of Swine. An Address to the Poor* (1795 ?); *A Picture of the Times, in a Letter addressed to the People of England by a Lover of Peace*, 2nd. ed. (1795) pp. 12, 16.

12. HO 42.36.235, R. Fellowes to Portland (?) 19 Oct 1795; HO 42.37.129, Report on Thelwall's lectures, 25 Oct 1795.

13. *The Correspondence of the London Corresponding Society, revised and corrected . . . published for the use of Members* (1795).

14. R. I. and S. Wilberforce, *Life of Wilberforce* 2 vols (1838) II, 114.

15. Place MSS BL Add MSS 27808 fo. 52. *London Chronicle*, 23 Nov 1795.

16. Chatham MSS PRO 30.8.104 George III to Pitt 13 Nov; Portland MSS [University of Nottingham] PwF. 4104, George III to Portland, 13 November 1795.

17. WO 30.64.1.
18. *Correspondence of London Corresponding Society* p. 66.
19. G. Wallas, *Life of Francis Place* (1898) p. 25 note 1.
20. *The Times*, 7 January 1795; see also 10 August 1795.
21. Rowe, *Cornwall*, p. 281; *The Times* 15 May 1801.
22. *Parl Hist.* xxxii, 1035.
23. *Parl Hist.* xxxii, 1256–1273; J. Holland Rose, *William Pitt and the Great War*, (1911) pp. 305–06.
24. D. Gray, *Spencer Perceval: The Evangelical Prime Minister* (Manchester, 1963) p. 308.
25. Fortescue, *British Army*, iv part 1, p. 496; Bedfordshire RO Whitbread MSS, W1/861 Lt. Gen. Sir Charles Grey to Whitbread, 9 September 1794; *The Times*, 11 March 1795.
26. SRO Melville, G. D. 51.1.236 Colquhoun to Dundas, 7 January 1794.
27. WO 4.157.54–56. Circular, 11 March 1795.
28. C. Emsley, *North Riding Naval Recruits: the Quota Acts and the Quota Men 1795–97* (North Yorks CRO Publications No. 18, 1978).
29. Pitt Correspondence C[ambridge] U[niversity] L[ibrary] (copies) Add 6958.2002 Buckingham to Pitt, 24 October 1796, and Add 6958.2003 J. Mitford to Pitt, 26 October 1796; *Northampton Mercury*, 10 December 1796; *London Chronicle*, 17 November, 8 and 10 December 1796; D. Neave, 'Anti-Militia Riots in Lincolnshire, 1757 and 1796', *Lincolnshire History and Archaeology* xi (1976).
30. Rowbottom, 3 March 1797; Sheffield C. L. Spencer Stanhope Muniments 60564/453 B. W. Cooke (?) to Walter Spencer Stanhope, 15 Feb 1797.
31. Cambridgeshire RO, Quarter Sessions Orders 1796–1802, 12 June 1798; Newcastle C. L. Northumberland Lieutenancy Papers vol. I, E. Codd to J. Davidson, 22 Nov 1796.
32. WO 4.157.214 Circular, 27 March 1795; *London Chronicle*, 9, 14, 16 July 1795; *The Times*, 9, 13 and 14 July 1795.
33. E. H. Stuart Jones, *The Last Invasion of Britian* (Cardiff, 1950) pp. 6–7.
34. Stuart Jones, *Last Invasion*, pp. 101, 148–60 and 262; A. K. Hamilton Jenkin (ed.) *News from Cornwall* (1951) p. 45; A. J. Eagleston, 'Wordsworth, Coleridge and the Spy', E. Blunden and E. L. Griggs (eds) *Coleridge: Studies by Several Hands on the Hundredth Anniversary of his Death*, (1934); HO 42.40 G. Dunbar to

Portland, 18 and 17 February and 4 March, Gen. John Morrison to Portland, 15 March 1797.

35. Holland Rose, *Pitt and the Great War*, p. 308.

36. HO 42.40 Earl of Berkeley to Portland, 3 March 1797; Hamilton Jenkin, *News from Cornwall*, p. 45; *Annual Register 1797*, Appendix to Chronicle, pp. 83 and 86–87; E. Cannan, *The Paper Pound of 1797–1821* (1929) pp. XIV–XVII.

37. Quoted in Bryant, *Years of Endurance*, p. 193.

38. *Annual Register 1797*, Appendix to Chronicle, p. 89.

39. Emsley, *North Riding Naval Recruits*, pp. 11–13.

40. J. A. Huitson, 'Defence and Public Order in Northumberland, 1793–1815' unpublished M. Litt. (Durham, 1966) p. 250; HO 42.40 G. Dunbar to Portland, 16 May 1797; HO 42.47.24 Mr Parker to W. Wickham, 14 May 1799; H. F. B. Wheeler and A. M. Broadley, *Napoleon and the Invasion of England*, (2 Vols, 1907) I, 203–06; ASSI 35/288 Part 1.

41. HO 42.212.

42. Manchester C. L. (Reference), F1797/7; PRO PC 1.38.A123 circular from Portland, 21 July 1797; Thomis, *Nottingham*, p. 181.

43. Holland Rose, *Pitt and the Great War*, pp. 300–03 and 322–23; Fortescue, *British Statesmen*, pp. 124–26; Pitt, *Orations*, p. 252.

44. T. S. Ashton, *Iron and Steel in the Industrial Revolution* 2nd ed. (Manchester, 1951) p. 175; E. P. Thompson, 'Time Work Discipline and Industrial Capitalism', ed. M. W. Flinn and T. C. Smout in *Essays in Social History*, (Oxford, 1974) pp. 47, 48.

45. Beds. RO Whitbread MSS W1/866 and 867, Grey to Whitbread, 16 Oct and 5 Nov 1797.

4   *From Rebellion to Respite: 1798–1801*

1. *The Anti-Jacobin, or Weekly Examiner*, 4th ed., 2 vols (1799) I 25 and 104; Wendy Hinde, *George Canning* (1973) pp. 58–65; Draper Hill, *Mr. Gillray: The Caricaturist* (1965) p. 65.

2. Wheeler and Broadley, *Napoleon and the Invasion*, I 223 and ch. 7; Hill, *Mr. Gillray*, pp. 68–81.

3. Lord Rosebery, *Pitt*, (1908) p. 208; *Sheffield Iris*, 20 Apr 1798; Holland Rose, *Pitt and the Great War*, p. 338 (for Mallet du Pan's comments on the Jacobin dictatorship see J. Godechot, *The Counter Revolution* (1972) p. 79).

4. Rosebery, *Pitt*, p. 205; Lord Stanhope, *Life of Pitt*, 4 vols (1862) III 127–8; *Anti-Jacobin* II 295–6.

5. T. Pakenham, *The Year of Liberty* (1969) pp. 147–9; *Memorials of Fox*, III 146.

6. Huitson, 'Defence in Northumberland', pp. 85–9; North Riding RO Wyvill Papers ZFW 7/2/120/1–10; *Sheffield Iris*, 20 Apr 1798; *Cambridge Intelligencer*, 14 July 1798; HO 42.45, Galloway to Portland, 11 Oct 1798.

7. G. Wakefield, *A Reply to some Parts of the Bishop of Llandaff's Address to the People of Great Britain* (1798); F. K. Prochaska, 'English State Trials in the 1790s: A Case Study', *Journal of British Studies*, XIII (1973).

8. Northumberland RO Delaval MSS 2/DE.4.57/93; Devon RO Sidmouth MSS c1798/OZ 29; Leicestershire RO Turville Constable – Maxwell MSS DG/39/1431.

9. P. Ziegler, *Addington* (1975) p. 79; D. G. Vaisey, 'The Pledge of Patriotism; Staffordshire and the Voluntary Contribution of 1798', in *Essays in Staffordshire History Presented to S. A. H. Burne*, ed. M. W. Greenslade (Stafford, 1970).

10. Stanhope, *Pitt*, III 94; J. Steven Watson, *The Reign of George III* (Oxford, 1960) p. 375 and note.

11. J. R. Western, 'The Formation of the Scottish Militia in 1797', *Scottish Historical Review*, XXXIV (1955).

12. *A View of the Moral and Political Epidemic . . . by a Friend to the King and Country* (1798) p. 41; Wheeler and Broadley, *Napoleon and the Invasion*, I 27–9, 107–9.

13. R. G. E. Wood (ed.), *Essex and the French Wars 1793–1815* (Chelmsford, 1977) document 26; *York Chronicle*, 17 May 1798; *York Courant*, 7 May 1798; Cambs RO Huddleston MSS 488/C2/HD19; North Riding RO Wyvill Papers ZFW 7/2/120/5 and Chayter MSS ZQH (uncatalogued); M. Y. Ashcroft, *To Escape the Monster's Clutches: Notes and Documents Illustrating the Preparations in North Yorkshire to Repel Invasion . . .* (North Yorks CRO Publications no. 15, 1977) pp. 27–60; Lancashire RO L.C. 16/1–5.

14. Manchester CL (Archives) Misc/49, Thomas Kershaw to Major William Lee, 8 Apr 1797; Notts. RO Seymour of Thrumpton MSS DDSY 169 XXII; Beds. RO BS 2094; SRO Melville G.D.51.1.409, W. Devaynes to Dundas, 17 June 1798; Hardwicke MSS BL Add. MSS 35670, ff. 214, 252; HO 42.47, J. Singleton to J. King, 27 May 1799.

15. *York Courant*, 16 July 1798; *Cambridge Intelligencer*, 7 July 1798.

16. HO 42.45 J. Cartwright to Portland, 2 Nov 1798; WO 40.17 Lt Col. Napier to Maj.- Gen. Murray, 17 May 1800 and Lt Col. Grey to Maj.- Gen. Horneck, 18 May 1800.

17. Bucks. RO Hawtrey MSS 2/1/4, John Hawtrey to Edward Hawtrey, 12 Nov 1798.

18. *Parl. Hist.*, xxxiv 1–26, 73–109 and 131–48; *Memorials of Fox*, iii 282; Gray, *Perceval*, pp. 41–2.

19. Cumbria RO (Carlisle) Senhouse MSS, Mrs Michelson to Catherine Senhouse, 9 May 1798.

20. *Memorials of Fox*, iii, 149; SRO Melville G.D.51.1.415 J. Park to Dundas, 25 Dec 1798; Beds. RO Longuet – Higgins MSS H.G.12/3/13–14 and H.G.12/4/62; B. E. V. Sabine, *A History of Income Tax* (1966) p. 31; Manchester CL (Archives) BR ff 942.72 L15 No. 2; Cambs RO Huddleston MSS 488/C2/HD20; Somerset RO QS Minute Book CQ2 2/4(3).

21. *Parl. Hist.*, xxxv, 329–39.

22. *Parl. Hist.*, xxxiv, 33–73; Devon RO Sidmouth MSS c 1799/OM8.

23. Fortescue, *British Army*, iv, part 2 appendix D; P. Makesy, *The Strategy of Overthrow 1798–99* (1974) p. 93.

24. Gover, *Peninsular Preparation*, p. 225 note 1; Cambs. RO Huddleston MSS 488/C2/HD204.

25. Western, *English Militia*, pp. 228–33 and 264–71.

26. Forbes, *Army Ordnance Services*, i, 177–80; Hardwicke MSS BL Add. MSS 35670, ff. 94, 111, 310–13, 321; Sheffield CL Spencer Stanhope Muniments, 60565/24, Samuel and Nathaniel Wathen to Walter Spencer Stanhope, 19 May 1798; B. Pool, *Navy Board Contracts 1660–1832* (1966) pp. 120–6 and 130–1; *Parl. Hist.*, xxxv 699–700.

27. Ashton, *Economic History*, p. 226; Hardwicke MSS BL Add. MSS 35670, ff. 319–20; A. Aspinall, *The Early English Trade Unions* (1949) pp. 35–6; D. Wilson, 'Government Dockyard Workers in Portsmouth 1793–1815' (Ph.D., Warwick, 1975) especially ch. 3; A. Geddes, *Portsmouth During the Great French Wars 1770–1800* (Portsmouth, 1970) pp. 20–1; Devon RO Sidmouth MSS c1801/OZ.73; R. A. Morris, 'Labour Relations in the Royal Dockyards, 1801–05', *Mariner's Mirror*, lxii (1976).

28. Aspinall, *Trade Unions*, pp. xi, 23–32, 92; *Parl. Hist.*, xxxiv 1429–30.

29. Cambridge U.L. Pitt Correspondence Add. 6958 Wickham to Pitt, 19 January 1799.

30. R. A. E. Wells, *Dearth and Distress in Yorkshire 1793–1802* (Borthwick Papers, no. 52, York, 1977) pp. 10–12; A. Booth, 'Food

Riots in North-West England 1790–1801' *Past and Present*, 77 (1978); Rowbottom, 3 May 1801.

31. HO 42.50, W. Packes to Portland, 16 May, Wrottesley to Portland, 1 May, and Mr Legge to King [?], 13 May 1800; Bucks. RO Hawtrey MSS 2/1/4, John Hawtrey to Edward Hawtrey, 16 Sept 1800; Notts. RO Seymour of Thrumpton MSS 284/6; HO 42.55.89, Bancroft to King, 15 Dec 1800; HO 42.49, Rev. Dr Breton and R. Marshall to Portland, 1 Jan 1801 (the letter is wrongly dated as 1800); Kent RO Q/SMa E9.

32. W. F. Galpin, *The Grain Supply of England during the Napoleonic Period* (New York, 1925) p. 19; E. P. Thompson, 'The Crime of Anonymity'; D. Hay *et al.*, *Albion's Fatal Tree* (1975) pp. 338 and 340; HO 42.49, P. George to Master of the Rolls, 13 and 16 Nov 1800; HO 42.50, Rev. Mr Meyrick to Portland, 12 June 1800; HO 42.49, R. Jesson to Lord Gower, 11 Apr 1800.

33. Sheffield CL Wentworth Woodhouse Muniments F. 44/62, Deposition of W. Warris, 2 Dec 1800; J. R. Dinwiddy, 'The "Black Lamp" in Yorkshire 1800–01', J. L. Baxter and F. K. Donnelly, 'The Revolutionary "Underground" in the West Riding: Myth or Reality?' *Past and Present*, 64 and 75 (1974). M. Elliot, 'The "Despard Conspiracy" Reconsidered' *Past and Present*, 75 (1977).

34. HO 42.55, A. Graham to King, 26 Dec 1800; R. Wells, 'The Revolt of the South-West, 1800–01. A Study in English Popular Protest", *Social History*, 6 (1977); Hammonds, *Skilled Labourer*, p. 66; Devon RO Sidmouth MSS c 1801/OZ 73, Bastard to Addington 'After March 1801'; Thompson, 'Crime of Anonymity', p. 333.

35. O. D. Rudkin, *Thomas Spence and his Connections* (1927) pp. 102–8.

36. *Parl. Hist.*, xxxiv, 1205–6; *Memorials of Fox*, iii 174; Leics. RO Turville Constable – Maxwell MS DG/39/1478.

37. Berkshire RO D/EZ 6, vol. 2, Braybrooke to Glastonbury, 16 Oct 1801.

38. F. Bickley (ed.), *Diary of Sylvester Douglas*, 2 vols (1928) i 266–7; Berks. RO D/EZ 6, vol. 2, Braybrooke to Glastonbury; Hamilton Jenkin, *News from Cornwall*, p. 91; *Newcastle Chronicle*, 17 Oct 1801; *Newcastle Courant*, 17 Oct 1801; HO 42.67, Fenwick to Pelham [?] 11 Apr 1803; Rowbottom, 14 Oct 1801.

5 The Amiens Interlude

1. J. Stevenson, *A Soldier in Time of War* (1841) pp. 29–30; Hardwicke MSS BL Add. MSS 35671, ff. 160–1; Worcestershire RO QS Order Book, vol. 7, ff. 152–3; Durham RO QS Order Book (1798–1810) ff. 163–5.
2. Zeigler, *Addington*, pp. 148–50.
3. Notts. RO Seymour of Thrumpton MSS DD.SY 284/9; Elliot, 'The "Despard Conspiracy" '; Zeigler, *Addington*, p. 153.
4. *The Times*, 28 Oct 1801; Aspinall, *Trade Unions*, pp. 38–9, 47–8, 54, 66.
5. S. Bamford, *Early Days* (1967 3rd ed.) p. 175; Rowbottom, Aug 1802; Aspinall, *Trade Unions*, p. 58; Hammonds, *Skilled Labourer*, pp. 172–3.
6. Place MSS BL Add. MSS 27818, fol. 34; Derbyshire RO Register of the Parish Church of Morley 1742 to 1800; J. Bowles, *Reflections at the Conclusion of the War* (1801).
7. Zeigler, *Addington*, p. 165; O. Browning (ed.) *England and Napoleon in 1803* (1887) pp. 52–3.
8. Berks. RO D/EZ 6, vol. 2, Braybrooke to Glastonbury, 16–17, Sept 1802.

6 Wooden Walls and Volunteers: 1803–5

1. Albert Sorel, *Europe and the French Revolution* (1969 ed.) p. 367.
2. Zeigler, *Addington*, pp. 189, 198.
3. HO 43.14. 88–9, 104–5; HO 42.71, Draft to *Custodes Rotolorum* of Maritime Counties, 30 June 1803; for Chester riot see HO 42.78, *passim*; N. McCord, 'The Impress Service in North-east England during the Napoleonic War', *Mariner's Mirror*, LIV (1968).
4. HO 42.71, J. Fleming to Pelham, 28 July 1803; HO 42.72, same to same, 4 Aug 1803; HO 43.14. 73–5; Nicol, *Life and Adventures*, pp. 206–9.
5. J. W. Fortescue, *The County Lieutenancies and the Army 1803–1814* (1909) pp. 73–4; Glover, *Peninsular Preparation*, p. 233. Glover takes a far more favourable line to Addington's military preparations than Fortescue.
6. Fortescue, *County Lieutenancies*, pp. 57, 71–2; Ashcroft, *To Escape the Monster's Clutches*, pp. 70–1; Bucks. RO L/V 6/4.
7. Diary of William Upcott, BL Add. MSS 32558, ff. 40–1; [*Cobbett's*]

Pol. Reg. IV 214; HO 42.72, Harriot and Bragge to Pole Carew, 30 Aug 1803.

8. Bucks RO Howard–Vyse MSS D/H.V 17 no. 17 and 21 no. 46; HO 43.14. 299–301; E. Phipps (ed.), *Memorials of the Political and Literary Life of Robert Plumer Ward*, 2 vols, (1850) I 142–3.

9. Gover, *Peninsular Preparation*, pp. 238–9.

10. Fortescue, *County Lieutenancies*, pp. 35–7, 99; Oxfordshire RO L/M I/vii/1; Berks. RO D/EZ 6, vol. 2, Braybrooke to Glastonbury, 5 Dec 1803; Berks. RO D/ERa 08/2; Leics. RO Turville Constable–Maxwell MSS DG 39/1604 and 1621; W. Branch Johnson (ed.), *Memorandums for . . . the diary between 1798 and 1810 of John Carrington* (Chichester, 1973) pp. 88–9.

11. *Parl. Hist.*, XXXVI 1486; Sabine, *Income Tax*, ch. 2; A. Hope Jones, *Income Tax in the Napoleonic Wars* (Cambridge, 1939) p. 110.

12. Gray, *Perceval*, pp. 310–14.

13. Glover, *Peninsular Preparation*, pp. 61–3.

14. R. G. Albion, *Forests and Sea Power: The Timber Problem of the Royal Navy 1652–1862* (Hamden, Connecticut, 1965) pp. 317–24 and ch. 10.

15. K. R. Gilbert, *The Portsmouth Blockmaking Machinery*, (1965) pp. 1–7.

16. Quoted in S. Giedion, *Mechanization Takes Command: A Contribution to Anonymous History* (New York, 1948) pp. 87–8.

17. Leics. RO Turville Constable-Maxwell MSS DG 39/1612; HO 42.79, C. Goring to King (?), 18 Apr 1804, and 'Information sent to Sir Richard Ford', 22 Apr 1804; Ashton, *Iron and Steel*, pp. 146–7.

18. HO 42.83, 'Abstract of Answers to Lord Hawkesbury's circular', 28 Nov 1805; B. Trinder, *The Industrial Revolution in Shropshire* (Chichester, 1973) pp. 361–2; Wilson, 'Government Dockyard Workers in Portsmouth', pp. 227–8, 294; Morris, 'Labour Relations in the Royal Dockyards'.

19. HO 42.83, 'Abstract of Answers . . .', 28 Nov 1805; O. Wood, 'A Cumberland Colliery during the Napoleonic War', *Economica*, LXXXI (1954); O. Wood, 'The Collieries of J. C. Curwen', *Transactions of the Cumberland and Westmoreland Archaelogical Society*, LXXI (1971); W. Pole (ed.), *The Life of Sir William Fairbairn, Bt.* (1877) pp. 69–70; A. H. John, 'Farming in Wartime 1793–1815', in *Land, Labour and Population in the Industrial Revoluton*, ed. E. L. Jones and G. E. Mingay (1967) p. 33; Northumb. RO Delaval MSS 2 DE 4/27/30; P. Grey, 'The Pauper Problem in Bedfordshire from 1795 to 1834' (M.Phil. Leicester, 1975) p. 55; Sussex RO Shiffner MSS 3113–4.

20. *The Times*, 2 March 1804; *Newcastle Chronicle*, 9 July 1803; Rowbottom, 21 June, 27–29 Aug 1803.

21. Cambs. RO Huddleston MSS 488/C3/179; Wheeler and Broadley, *Napoleon and the Invasion*, II 43, 73, 136; Bucks. RO Howard–Vyse MSS D/HV 21 no. 44.

22. Wheeler and Broadley, *Napoleon and the Invasion*, II 40–41; *Pol. Reg.*, IV 24–7; HO 42.68, Clanricarde to Yorke, 26 Aug 1803; HO 42.75, *passim*.

23. *Sheffield Iris*, 28 July 1803; S. Morley, *Memoirs of a Serjeant*, (Ashford, 1818) p. 17; Lancs. RO Hodgkinson MSS DDX/211/3 1 and 5; J. Wheeler, *Manchester: Its Political, Social and Commercial History*, (1836) p. 100 note; Zeigler, *Addington*, pp. 200–201; Humberside RO Grimston MSS DDGR 43/23, Charles Grimston to Thomas Grimston, 6 Oct 1803.

24. Stanhope, *Pitt*, III 116.

25. Wheeler and Broadley, *Napoleon and the Invasion*, II 39, 250, 253–5; Branch Johnson, *Memorandums for . . .*, p. 89. J. Ashton, *English Caricature and Satire on Napoleon I* (1888), p. 240; J. Ginger, *Alfred's Address to the Ladies of England* (1803); F. J. Klingberg and S. B. Hustvedt (eds), *The Warning Drum: The British Home Front Faces Napoleon* (Berkeley and Los Angeles, 1944) pp. 76–9.

26. *An Address to the People of the United Kingdom of Great Britain and Ireland on the Threatened Invasion* (Edinburgh, 1803) pp. 7, 14–15; Manchester CL (Reference) F 1803/2/D; W. Burdon, *Advice Addressed to the Lower Ranks of Society*, (Newcastle upon Tyne, 1803) pp. 21–2; Wheeler and Broadley, *Napoleon and the Invasion*, II 291–2, 301–3; Klingberg and Hustvedt, *Warning Drum*, pp. 163–4.

27. C. Hall, *The Effects of Civilization on the People in European States* (1805, reprinted 1850) pp. 130–31; HO 42.73, Reports of Sgt Bourke 11 and 12 Sept 1803 with Aaron Graham's comments; HO 42.78, Draft to R. Fletcher, 26 March 1804, and Notary's report, 18 Jan 1804.

28. *Memorials of Fox*, III 231; Cumbria RO (Carlisle) Curwen MSS D/Cu/3/69; HO 42.68, Braybrooke to Hobart, 9 Aug 1803; HO 42.81 Fletcher to Hawkesbury, 10 Aug 1805; Klingberg and Hustvedt, *Warning Drum*, pp. 155–6.

29. HO 42.69, J. Browne to King, 13 Oct 1803; HO 42.73, Draft to Attorney and Solicitor Generals 'Most Secret', 3 Oct 1803; HO 42.78, Draft to same, 1 March 1804; Wheeler and Broadley, *Napoleon and the Invasion*, II 134; HO 42.73, H. Clark to King (?) 21 Oct 1803.

30. HO 42.77, Haden to Hawkesbury, 6 Nov 1804; HO 42.79, same to

same, 9 Dec 1804; HO 43.15. 95–6 and 124–6; HO 42.82, F. Cartwright to Hawkesbury, 7 Feb 1805, and Vernon to King, enclosing Attorney General's opinion, 21 Apr 1805.
31. D. G. Barnes, *A History of the English Corn Laws 1660–1846* (1930) pp. 88–90; HO 42.80, Fletcher to King, 16 Feb 1805.
32. Lincolnshire RO Hill MSS 22/2/3/14; *York Herald*, 4 Jan 1806; Lincs. RO Letters of Sir Gilbert Heathcoat 3 Anc 9/7/28.
33. War. RO Journals of Bertie Greathead, 23 Jan 1806.

7 Blockade: 1806–9

1. HO 42.87, Chippendale to Fletcher, 29 Jan 1806; *Leeds Intelligencer*, 3 Feb 1806.
2. *The Times*, 3, 5 and 7 March 1806.
3. A. D. Harvey, 'The Ministry of All the Talents: The Whigs in Office, February 1806 to March 1807', *Historical Journal*, xv (1972).
4. *The Times*, 25 Feb 1806; *Pol. Reg.*, ix 483; Ashton, *Iron and Steel*, pp. 176–7; *The Times*, 8 and 9 May 1806.
5. Quoted in R. Glover, *Britain at Bay* (1973) p. 224.
6. Glover, *Peninsular Preparation*, pp. 242–5; HO 42.91, B. Frank to King [?] 8 March 1807.
7. *York Herald*, 2 July 1808; Gray, *Perceval*, pp. 321, 355–8.
8. Quoted in Gray, *Perceval*, p. 170.
9. E. Costello, *Adventures of a Soldier; Written by Himself* (1967 ed.) pp. 3–4; Bamford, *Early Days*, pp. 245, 248–52, 258–60; Glover, *Britain at Bay*, pp. 66–72, 200–204.
10. R. Glover, 'The French Fleet, 1807–1814: Britain's Problem and Madison's Opportunity', *Journal of Modern History*, xxxix (1967).
11. *The Times*, 4 and 5 Dec 1807; Liverpool MSS BL Add. MSS 38242, fo. 180; War. RO Journals of Greathead, loose, undated letter (probably early summer 1806) from Parr.
12. L. M. Marshall, *The Rural Population of Bedfordshire 1671–1921* (Bedfordshire Historical Records Society, 1934) pp. 14–15; Grey, 'The Pauper Problem', pp. 67–9; HO 42.87 and HO 4291, letters from Samuel Dight, Apr–Nov 1806 and June 1807; HO 43.17. 55–6; HO 42.127, J. Drummond to Transport Office, 1 Sept 1812.
13. Cumbria RO (Carlisle) Senhouse MSS, Wood to Catherine Senhouse, 12 Oct 1806.
14. F. Crouzet, *L'Economie britannique et le blocus continental 1806–1813*, 2 vols (Paris, 1958) i 334–6, 340, ii 503–10; W. B. Crump (ed.), *The Leeds Woollen Industry 1780–1820* (Leeds, 1931) pp. 77–91;

Beds. RO Whitbread MSS W1/4206 and W1/3786; Rowbottom, 1806, 1808, *passim*; *Manchester Mercury*, 25 July 1809.

15. Beds. RO Whitbread MSS W1/4190 and W1/4199; *Manchester Chronicle*, 14 and 21 Nov 1807; *The Times*, 11 and 14 Nov 1807; *Manchester Gazette*, 5 Dec 1807; *Leeds Mercury*, 24 March 1808.

16. *Leeds Mercury*, 24 March 1808; Beds. RO Whitbread MSS W1/4193 and W1/4196.

17. HO 42.91, Fletcher to Hawkesbury, 27 Dec 1807; Beds. RO Whitbread MSS W1/4201; HO 42.95, Cookson to Hawkesbury, 2 June 1808.

18. Gray, *Perceval*, pp. 176–7; *The Times*, 17 Nov 1807; *York Chronicle*, 19 May 1808; *Leeds Intelligencer*, 6 June 1808; Beds. RO Whitbread MSS W1/2448 and W1/4203; War. RO Journals of Greathead, loose, undated letter from Parr.

19. *Independent Whig*, 10 July and 4 Sept 1808; Hammonds, *Skilled Labourer*, pp. 72–80; Gray, *Perceval*, pp. 174–5.

20. HO 42.95 Rev. Dr Drake to Hawkesbury, 4 June 1808; Aspinhall, *Trade Unions*, pp. 98–101; *Manchester Gazette*, 21 Nov 1807; Wheeler, *Manchester*, p. 104; Crump, *Leeds Woollen Industry*, p. 230; Rowbottom, 7 Sept 1811.

21. *The Times*, 4 July 1807.

22. *Independent Whig*, 30 Oct 1808; M. Roberts, *The Whig Party 1807–1812* (1939) pp. 197–216; Gray, *Perceval*, pp. 194–212.

23. HO 42.99, Draft to Attorney and Solicitor Generals, 24 Nov 1809.

24. Manchester CL (Archives) M 3/3/6A; P. Styles, *The Development of County Administration in the Late XVIII and Early XIX Centuries illustrated by the Records of the Warwickshire Court of Quarter Sessions 1773–1837* (Dugdale Society Occasional Papers, no. 4, Oxford, 1934) p. 19; HO 42.95, A. Colquhoun to Hawkesbury, 22 March 1808 and enclosure; Hunter Davies, *George Stephenson* (1975) p. 12; Branch Johnson, *Memorandums for . . .,* p. 150; *Leeds Intelligencer*, 9 Oct 1809; HO 42.99, Brooke to Liverpool, 15 July, 14 and 21 Oct 1809.

25. Beds. RO Whitbread MSS W1/456: Manchester CL (Archives) C 17/3/46/5–6; Berks. RO D/ERa 025; HO 42.106, Black to Ryder, 4 Apr 1810; *Pol. Reg.*, xv, 993–4.

26. *The Times*, 30 May and 1 June 1810; Manchester CL (Archives) C 17/3/46/4, 8–9.

27. According to the guards outside William Cartwright's mill during the attack in April 1812, some of the attackers wore 'military uniforms'; Cartwright, however, discounted much of their story. *See* Hammonds, *Skilled Labourer*, p. 305.

8   Victories Abroad, Crises at Home: 1810–15

1. Beds. RO Whitbread Papers W1/2488.
2. Sussex RO Sheffield MSS Add. MSS 5440/424.
3. *Pol. Reg.*, xvii 425; Gray, *Perceval*, pp. 289–98; HO 42.106, *passim;* HO 42.107, R. Laing to Ryder, 12 May 1810.
4. Roberts, *Whig Party*, pp. 147, 158–9.
5. HO 42.99, Maberly to Cecil Jenkinson, 19 Apr 1809; Liverpool MSS BL Add. MSS 38251, ff. 208, 248, 260; Gray, *Perceval*, pp. 325–30.
6. Gray, *Perceval*, ch. 8; J. M. Sherwig, *Guineas and Gunpowder: British Foreign Aid in the Wars with France 1793–1815* (Cambridge, Massachusetts, 1969) pp. 351, 354–5.
7. Maberly Phillips Tracts in Newcastle City Library (LO42/0742), no. 13, 'Emergency Issues of Notes and Tokens consequent upon the passing of the Bank Restriction Act of 1797', p. 13; no. 1, 'Portugal Gold circulating in England', pp. 3–4; *Pol. Reg.*, xvii 34; *The Times*, 24 and 27 Apr and 23 Sept 1811.
8. Gray, *Perceval*, pp. 372, 384–5.
9. Beds. RO Whitbread MSS W1/2512; J. Cartwright, *Reasons for Reformation* (1809) pp. 22–3.
10. Crouzet, *L'Economie britannique*, ii 632–3 and 638; Rowbottom, 17 Oct 1810 and 1 Jan 1811; Beds. RO Whitbread MSS W1/3665; Manchester CL (archives) M3/3/6A.
11. Crouzet, *L'Economie britannique*, ii 729–31 and 740–41; Ashton, *Iron and Steel*, pp. 150–1.
12. HO 42.117, *passim*; Pole, *Life of Fairbairn*, p. 85; Maberly Phillips Tracts no. 10, 'The Escape of Two French Prisoners of War from Jedburgh in 1813', p. 168; HO 42.121, Petition, 4 March 1812.
13. *Newcastle Courant*, 12 May 1812; Beds. RO Whitbread MSS W1/3663; Hammonds, *Skilled Labourer*, pp. 83–5.
14. Beds. RO Whitbread MSS W1/2535; *Parl. Debates*, xxii 2; Notts. RO DD. TS addit. 16/8/5 and CA 3984/I; Hammonds, *Skilled Labourer*, p. 229.
15. R. A. Church and S. D. Chapman, 'Gravener Henson and the Making of the English Working Class', Jones and Mingay, *Land, Labour and Population*, p. 141; for the Luddites in general see E. P. Thompson, *The Making of the English Working Class* (1968 ed.) pp. 604 ff.; and the critical view of Thompson in M. I. Thomis, *The Luddites* (Newton Abbott, 1970).
16. Thompson *English Working Class*, p. 624.

17. HO 42/122, William Chippendale to Joseph Chippendale, 21 Apr 1812, and Stuart Wortley to Ryder, 15 Apr 1812; *The Times*, 29 June 1812; Hammonds, *Skilled Labourer*, pp. 305–06; T. A. Critchley and P. D. James, *The Maul and the Pear Tree: The Ratcliffe Highway Murders 1811*, (1971) pp. 79, 96–7; Derby. RO 239M/F1011.

18. Crouzet, *L'Economie britannique*, II 827–9; *Leicester Journal*, 6 March 1812; *Leicester Chronicle*, 7 March 1812; *The Times*, 15 Feb 1812.

19. D. Read, *The English Provinces c. 1760–1960: A Study in Influence*, (1964) pp. 57–61.

20. Devon RO Sidmouth MSS c. 1812/OG; HO 42. 129, R. Palk to Sidmouth, 14 Nov 1812; Essex RO D/DSe 11.

21. Devon RO Sidmouth MSS c. 1812/QH; Beds. RO Whitbread MSS W1/4246; Rowbottom, Nov 1812.

22. *Leicester Chronicle*, 31 Oct 1812; Beds. RO Whitbread MSS W1/4218, 4242 and 4257.

23. Beds. RO Whitbread MSS W1/4241; *Independent Whig*, 27 Dec 1812; Crump, *Leeds Woollen Industry*, pp. 152, 159–60; Rowbottom, 20 Nov 1813.

24. *Parl. Debates*, XXIII 785, 875, XXVI 267–70.

25. HO 42. 132, W. Margett to Sidmouth, 10 March 1813; HO 42. 134, W. Balcombe Langridge to Sidmouth, 19 July 1813; A. F. Cirkett (ed.), *Samuel Whitbread's Notebooks*, 1810–11, 1813–14 (Bedfordshire Historical Records Society, 1971) nos. 557–8; HO 42.134, E. Prothero to Sidmouth, 7 July 1813; HO 42.132, Messrs Jolliffe, Horner Knatchbull and Ireland to Sidmouth, 26 Jan 1813; HO 42.135, S. Staniforth to Sidmouth, 6 Oct 1813.

26. HO 42. 135, *passim*; Thomas (or John) Carter, *Memoirs of a Working Man* (1845) pp. 171–2 (Carter's home town is identified as Colchester in A. F. J. Brown (ed.), *Essex People 1750–1900* (Chelmsford, 1972) p. 104); HO 42. 133, Messrs Forman, Fothergill and Monkhouse to Sidmouth, 15 Apr 1813.

27. G. Hueckel, 'English Farming Profits during the Napoleonic Wars, 1793–1815', *Explorations in Economic History*, XIII (1976).

28. P. Deane, 'War and Industrialisation', J. M. Winter, *War and Economic Development* (Cambridge, 1975) p. 97, For the military participation ratio see S. Andreski, *Military Organisation and Society* (1954) pp. 33–8.

29. *Tyne Mercury*, 19 Apr 1814; Crump, *Leeds Woollen Industry*, pp. 163–4, 166; Rowbottom, 25 Apr 1814; Hammonds, *Skilled Labourer*, pp. 233–4.

30. Lancs. RO Hodgkinson MSS DDX/211/3/12; Warwicks RO Journals of Greathead, 18 March 1815; Oxfordshire RO Marshall XVII/i/1, fo. 162.

9   Aftermath

1. M. Greenwood, 'British Loss of Life in the Wars of 1793–1815 and 1914–1918', *Journal of the Royal Statistical Society*, cv (1942); Rowbottom, 21 Sept 1795; J. Mayhall, *The Annals of Yorkshire from the Earliest Period to the Present Times* (1878) p. 193; *Memorials of the Late War*, (Edinburgh, 1828) pp. xi–xii.
2. R. A. Church, 'Messrs. Gotch and Son, and the Rise of the Kettering Footwear Industry', *Business History*, viii (1966); L. T. C. Rolt, *Isambard Kingdom Brunel* (1957) pp. 14–15; Ashton, *Iron and Steel*, p. 154; Hammonds, *Skilled Labourer*, p. 188.
3. W. Cobbett, *Rural Rides* (1967 ed.) p. 59; Marshall, *Rural Population of Beds.*, p. 37; J. R. Wordie, 'Social Change on the Leveson-Gower Estates 1714–1832', *Economic History Review*, xxvii (1974) 599.
4. J. Selby (ed.) *Military Memoirs: Thomas Morris: The Napoleonic Wars* (1967) pp. 104–5; A. Somerville, *The Autobiography of a Working Man* (1967 ed.) p. 125; D. Thomas, *Charge! Hurrah! Hurrah! A Life of Cardigan of Balaclava* (1974) pp. 5, 18.
5. Col. A. T. C. White V. C., *The Story of Army Education* (1963) pp. 19–22; G. Wood, *The Subaltern Officer* (1825) pp. vi–vii.
6. Leics. RO Freer MSS 16 D. 52/54; M. Lewis, *The Navy in Transition 1814–64* (1965) pp. 67–8; W. Crockie, *Sunderland Notables* (1894) pp. 83–9; Costello, *Adventures of a Soldier*, p. xiii and ch. 3; Thompson, *English Working Class*, pp. 663–4; J. Green, *The Vicissitudes of a Soldier's Life* (Louth, 1827) p. 222; 'Journal of a Soldier of the 71st Regiment from 1806–15' in *Memorials of the Late War*, p. 139: E. Longford, *Wellington: Pillar of the State* (1975 ed.) pp. 31, 307; White, *Army Education*, pp. 31 ff.
7. *Thomas Morris*, p. 51; W. Cobbett, *Advice to Young Men* (1829) para. 338.
8. Green, *Vicissitudes of a Soldier's Life*, p. 221; N. McCord, 'The Seamen's Strike of 1815 in North East England', *Economic History Review*, xxi (1968).
9. Huitson, 'Defence and Public Order', p. 530; 'Operator', *Petitioning Weavers Defended in Remarks on the Manchester Police Meeting of January 13 1817* (Manchester, 1817) p. 4. S. Bamford, *Passages in*

the Life of a Radical, 2 vols (1844) I 177–9; J. Stevens, *England's Last Revolution* (Buxton, 1977) pp. 101, 112; F. J. Kaijage, 'Working-Class Radicalism in Barnsley, 1816–1820', in *Essays in the Economic and Social History of South Yorkshire* ed. S. Pollard and C. Holmes (Sheffield, 1976) pp. 128–9; M. I. Thomis and P. Holt, *Threats of Revolution in Britain 1789–1848* (1977) pp. 77–9; C. Emsley, 'The Cato Street Conspiracy', in *Popular Politics 1750–1870* (Open University Course A401, Block II, Milton Keynes, 1974) p. 27.

10. McCord, 'The Seamen's Strike of 1815' pp. 139–40.
11. J. R. Western, 'Roman Catholics Holding Military Commissions in 1798', *English Historical Review*, LXX (1950); Roberts, *Whig Party*, p. 32 note 1; Lancs. RO D. P. 375, Orderly Book of Leyland and Ormskirk Local Militia; *The Works of the Rev. Sydney Smith*, 3 vols (1848 ed.) I 79; HO 42. 109, Report on the Debate at the British Forum, 14 Dec 1810.
12. Sir Hubert Llewellyn Smith, *The Board of Trade* (1928) pp. 50–1.
13. Quoted in W. R. Brock, *Lord Liverpool and Liberal Toryism*, (1967 2nd. ed.) pp. 110–11.

Index